CONSTITUTIONAL CHALLENGERS

Praise for *Constitutional Challengers*

Constitutional Challengers devotes a full section on Indigenous Rights to shed light on five intrepid persons who chose to challenge the government, regardless of the risk.... Adam is a master storyteller.

— DOM BAUTISTA, executive director of the Amici Curiae Friendship Society

For decades, courts have protected some rights and weakened others. Behind every judicial decision, there's a person who endured the stress, expense, and, often, notoriety of being a litigant fighting for change. They could have just walked away. Adam Dodek, one of the country's great legal scholars, tells the stories of these determined people with clarity, empathy, and skill.

— MARK BOURRIE, PH.D., J.D., lawyer and award-winning author

Constitutional Challengers is a compelling read. The book is thought-provoking, educational, and insightful and needs to be a required text for all law schools, nationally and internationally. Adam Dodek's inclusion of a section on Indigenous rights strongly speaks that Indigenous people matter. Law students, lawyers, governments, and educators need to read and learn from the fundamental historical knowledge well-articulated by Adam Dodek. Let's all be constitutional challengers.

— CLAUDETTE COMMANDA, L.L.B., Algonquin Anishinabeg First Nation, chancellor of University of Ottawa

Just as every superhero has an origin story, so does every landmark decision from the Supreme Court of Canada. This book shares some of the most compelling tales behind Canada's most celebrated and notorious legal victories. And if you've ever wondered what happened to Oakes, Sparrow, Vriend, or Multani, start reading!

— ALISON CRAWFORD, founder of Good Yarn Communications and host of *Verdict and Voices*

Adam Dodek has the unique ability of taking profoundly complex topics and not just simplifying them but humanizing them. Reading the personal journey of individuals through the Canadian legal system was like stepping back into his classroom: I was both educated and entertained!

— DEIDRA DIONNE, lawyer and Olympic bronze medallist

A great contribution to Canadian legal history, written for regular folks in an engaging, plain-language narrative style that brings to life the people and cases that have shaped our rights.

— SEAN FINE, former justice reporter, *The Globe and Mail*

These carefully curated stories, related vividly and with sensitivity, illustrate the impact on our constitution of personal sacrifice and persistence in the defence of our constitutional rights and freedoms. An informative and rewarding read!

— THE HONOURABLE MORRIS J. FISH, retired justice of the Supreme Court of Canada

Constitutional Challengers is an important contribution to Canadian legal literature. A must-read for anyone interested in the human stories behind some of the most important cases in Canadian constitutional history.

— THE HONOURABLE MARC GOLD, P.C., former senator of Canada

Canada is defined by its people. *Constitutional Challengers* demonstrates that our constitution is a reflection of Canadians. It walks through the journey of everyday people who fought for principles that have inevitably shaped a nation. A must-read to understand the human side of Canada's constitution.

— THE HONOURABLE YASIR NAQVI, E.C.O., M.P., former attorney general of Ontario

Always an engaging lecturer, it is no surprise that Dodek's writing is equally compelling. This book is more than an opportunity to revisit some of the seminal decisions that we learn as law students from a fresh perspective — Dodek's accounts of the heroes, villains, crusaders, and passengers that have shaped Canadian constitutional law remind us that our laws are never made nor applied in a vacuum.

— CRISTY NURSE, lawyer and Olympian

Behind every landmark legal decision shaping Canadian society stands a person. Their names endure, but their stories fade from view. Adam Dodek changes that. With meticulous research, deep insight, and captivating storytelling, he illuminates the human beings at the heart of cases that have transformed Canadian law. These pages reveal the complex journeys of individuals who — often by accident — became catalysts for change. Dodek's retelling reminds us that the law is not abstract —it is a profoundly human endeavour.

— JOSH PATTERSON, K.C., executive director of the Law Foundation of BC and former executive director of the BC Civil Liberties Association

In the midst of these times, *Constitutional Challengers* is essential and required reading for Canadians of all ages. In it, Dodek and contributors explore many of the unlikely heroes' journeys that set the foundation for how we arrived at this moment. Throughout, I found myself newly inspired by the folks who had the bravery to take on their own proverbial Goliaths. This text is a reminder that courage is wielded one small step at a time and an offer to find it when it calls.

— KENYA-JADE PINTO, filmmaker and photographer

The law of Aboriginal rights and title can be hard to understand, but *Constitutional Challengers* brings to life the Aboriginal litigants and their stories, explaining in easy-to-read prose the importance of these decisions to Canada's legal landscape.

— DOUGLAS SANDERSON (AMO BINASHII), professor and bestselling co-author of *Valley of the Birdtail*

In his trademark style, Adam Dodek distills complex legal cases and theories into digestible chapters that humanize the most important events in Canadian legal history. The book tells the story of individuals, some of whom are willing heroes, some of whom are vile antiheroes. All of them have had a profound impact on the way Canadian society is organized and governed. It is a perfect mix of legal summary, history, and Canadian pop culture wrapped in easy-to-read pages.

— MATTHEW SHOEMAKER, mayor of Sault Ste. Marie

We live in an age of great cynicism where many think they can't make a difference or question the utility of the Charter. Dodek confronts the doubters head on. In *Constitutional Challengers*, he shows how ordinary Canadians took on the status quo and, using the constitution, were able to make a difference. For them and for all Canadians.

— THE HONOURABLE ARIF VIRANI, P.C., K.C., former minister of justice and attorney general of Canada

ADAM DODEK

CONSTITUTIONAL CHALLENGERS

The Heroes, Villains, and Crusaders Behind Canada's Biggest Cases

DUNDURN PRESS

Publisher: Meghan Macdonald | Acquiring editor: Kathryn Lane | Editor: Carrie Gleason
Cover designer: Laura Boyle
Cover image: shutterstock.com/AndryDj

Library and Archives Canada Cataloguing in Publication

Title: Constitutional challengers : the heroes, villains, and crusaders behind Canada's biggest cases / Adam Dodek.
Names: Dodek, Adam, author
Description: Includes bibliographical references and index.
Identifiers: Canadiana (print) 20250281139 | Canadiana (ebook) 20250281309 | ISBN 9781459755222 (softcover) | ISBN 9781459755239 (PDF) | ISBN 9781459755246 (EPUB)
Subjects: LCSH: Canada. Supreme Court—Cases. | LCSH: Constitutional law—Canada—Cases.
Classification: LCC KE8244 .D63 2026 | LCC KF8764.ZA2 D63 2026 kfmod | DDC 347.71/035—dc23

We acknowledge the support of the Canada Council for the Arts and the Ontario Arts Council for our publishing program. We also acknowledge the financial support of the Government of Ontario, through the Ontario Book Publishing Tax Credit and Ontario Creates, and the Government of Canada.

Printed and bound in Canada.

Dundurn Press
1382 Queen Street East
Toronto, Ontario, Canada M4L 1C9
dundurn.com, @dundurnpress

To Chris Manfredi
For igniting my interest in constitutional law ... and in teaching.

Contributors

Yasmeen Atassi
Jamie Bell
Dominique Charland
Bionca Chu
Sean Cousins
Sébastien Cyr
Asha Sahota
Marna Swart

Contents

Part III: Indigenous Rights

Introduction

People Matter

The Supreme Court decides cases on big constitutional issues that directly impact the lives of Canadians: Do Canadians have the right to assisted suicide? What rights does a person have when they are arrested on criminal charges? Do women have the right to an abortion? Can the government outlaw hate speech or child pornography? It also decides issues of broader principle that indirectly affect Canadians: Are government officials — including premiers and the prime minister — subject to the law? How far does freedom of religion or the freedom to protest go?

Some of these landmark decisions are well known to some Canadians, but most are not. Even less known are the people behind these historic cases that changed the lives of Canadians. Lawsuits are brought by people, by groups, and sometimes by governments. In criminal prosecutions, the state marshals its significant resources against individuals. Some of the people involved in these monumental decisions are heroes, others are villains, a determined few are crusaders, and many are unlikely passengers.

Heroes, Villains, Crusaders (and Passengers)

Most of us have heroes — people we admire for something they did or stood for. We need heroes in our lives and in our society: people to admire, venerate, and celebrate. They make us feel good, and they give us faith that we and our society can do better, and that we can do good. Canada has national heroes like Terry Fox, Rocket Richard, Viola Desmond, David Suzuki, Tommy Douglas, and Rick Hansen, among others. Our heroes can change over time or with the times. Sometimes they fade into history because we forget about them or because we learn things about their past that tarnish our views of them. But we often forget that our heroes are human, not saints. We shouldn't judge them by a standard of perfection.

We live in a deeply flawed world, in which horrible people have done horrible things over the course of history. Although I have never seen a Canadian on a list of global villains, we have certainly had our share of bad characters. I grew up in Vancouver in the 1980s, when mass murderer Clifford Robert Olson was abducting and killing children. I was a student at McGill University when Marc Lépine murdered fourteen women across town at the École Polytechnique. These killers were the evilest of villains. The villains featured in *Constitutional Challengers* are people who did things or stood for things most of us find abhorrent, that strike at the core of our values. They aren't simply distasteful; they are repulsive.

Of course, whether someone is a hero or a villain is a matter of perspective. Prime ministers are often embraced as heroes by some and disdained as villains by others. The labels also change with time and historical perspective. The same applies to groups. In the 1930s and 1940s, a small group of Jehovah's Witnesses were seen as villains by many in Quebec. Others saw them as an unpopular religious minority that was being unfairly targeted. Today, many see them as heroes for championing civil liberties and freedom of religion against an authoritarian state.

Some heroes or villains are crusaders: people who campaign for a cause and set out to change other people's views and make broader social change. Dr. Henry Morgentaler was a crusader for abortion rights. James Keegstra was on a crusade to impart his antisemitic views to his students. Terri-Jean Bedford was a crusader for the rights of sex workers, and Harry Daniels was a crusader for Métis rights. These people devoted significant portions of their time or their lives to a cause bigger than themselves.

But most of the people behind landmark legal decisions are not crusaders. I call them passengers because they were carried along by our legal system, often all the way to the Supreme Court. They weren't championing a cause; they were just trying to achieve a result for themselves that ended up being much bigger than themselves. They were along for the ride — often a long and convoluted one — in the Canadian justice system.

There are different types of passengers. Some people get caught up in the criminal justice system, having been arrested on a criminal charge, and all they want to do is stop the car and get out, however they can. They aren't trying to change the world, just to get out of trouble. Many of the biggest criminal decisions featured passengers as protagonists. Other passengers were using the justice system as a way to get what they needed or wanted: to become a lawyer as a non-citizen in Canada (Mark David Andrews); to wear a kirpan to school (Gurbaj Singh Multani); or to get married to a same-sex partner (Michael Leshner and Michael Stark).

All of these people are part of the Canadian constitutional story. Readers will reach their own conclusions whether these constitutional challengers are heroes or villains.

An Extremely Brief Constitutional History of Canada

Many stories can be told about Canada's constitutional history, and they can differ depending on who is telling them, and from what perspective. There are English stories of Canada, and there are French stories, Indigenous stories, immigrant Chinese stories, and so on.

One story from 1867 is the development of Canada's constitutional independence. Unlike the United States and other countries, Canada was not created through a revolution. Instead, it evolved as an independent country over two centuries. And unlike many other countries, there is no single document in Canada called "the Constitution." Instead, our Constitution is made up of more than twenty documents, including British and Canadian statutes and orders in council passed by the British Cabinet. One of the most important Canadian constitutional documents is the British North America

Act (often simply called the BNA Act), which created the Dominion of Canada in 1867. Canada was no longer a colony, but it was not quite a fully independent country. The BNA Act, a law made by the British Parliament, was concerned mostly with the structure of government: the Crown, the division of powers between the federal and provincial governments, the House of Commons, the Senate, and the courts. It left a lot unwritten. We continued to rely on British constitutional principles, British courts, and the British Parliament for a long time.

The Supreme Court of Canada was created in 1875, but it did not become truly supreme until 1949. Until then, Canadians could appeal decisions of the Supreme Court to the Judicial Committee of the Privy Council in London. That body, the highest court of law in the British Empire, was largely composed of "Law Lords" from the House of Lords who had never set foot in Canada. Civil liberties, like freedom of expression or freedom of assembly, were not protected under the BNA Act.

In 1960, Prime Minister John Diefenbaker enacted the Canadian Bill of Rights, but it was just an ordinary statute that did not stand above other federal laws. And it did not apply to any provincial laws. In cases like *Bliss* (chapter 4), the Supreme Court gave the Canadian Bill of Rights a narrow and technical interpretation. This fuelled the movement for a constitutionally entrenched bill of rights that would be superior to all laws, federal and provincial — a goal that was achieved in 1982 with the patriation of the Canadian Constitution, the enactment of the Canadian Charter of Rights and Freedoms, and the recognition of certain Indigenous rights (known in the Constitution as "Aboriginal rights").

Overview of This Book

Constitutional Challengers is divided into three parts. Part I tells the stories of several cases that contributed to the making of our Constitution. Some, like *Roncarelli v. Duplessis* (1959), are celebrated as great wins for big constitutional principles like the rule of law. But as you will read in chapter 3, the person at the centre of this case — Montreal restaurateur Frank Roncarelli — lost a lot along the way. Other cases, like *Bliss*, are considered losses and are not widely known, even in legal circles. But the determination of Stella Bliss in bringing her case all the way to the Supreme Court paved the way for the constitutional protection of equality rights in the Canadian Charter of Rights and Freedoms in 1982.

Part II includes cases under the Canadian Charter of Rights and Freedoms. Some of these featured high-profile personalities like abortion crusader Henry Morgentaler, child pornographer Robin Sharpe, and Canada's most famous dominatrix, sex worker Terri-Jean Bedford. Others, high-profile as they were, had protagonists who were not well known, though their last names may be: David Oakes, the most famous name in Canadian constitutional law, and Elijah Askov, whose name became synonymous with delays in our criminal justice system. Other protagonists achieved brief notoriety during their cases but returned to lives of relative obscurity: Chantale Daigle captured the interest of the media when she fought an injunction obtained by her ex-boyfriend to prevent her from having an abortion; Delwin Vriend became a lightning rod for social debate over gay rights when he was fired from his job in Alberta for being gay and the Supreme Court ruled in his favour. In almost all of these cases, the legal rule established by the Supreme Court lives on, but knowledge of the people involved has faded.

Part III tells the stories of people and nations who fought for constitutional recognition of Indigenous rights. There was little mention of Indigenous Peoples in our Constitution before 1982. In the British North America Act, 1867 (now the Constitution Act, 1867), the federal Parliament was given the power to make laws for "Indians and lands reserved for Indians." Until 1982, therefore, Indigenous persons, nations, and communities were constitutional objects, treated as persons or groups to be regulated. With the enactment of the Constitution Act, 1982, they became constitutional actors. The new Constitution recognized "Aboriginal Rights" in section 35, and it allowed the participation of Indigenous leaders in certain discussions on amending the Constitution. This part tells the stories of Indigenous activists, like Donald Marshall Jr. and Harry Daniels, who fought for the rights of their communities, the Mi'kmaq and Métis. It includes the story of the Tŝilhqot'in, who never relinquished their claim to their land and who succeeded in obtaining the first declaration of Aboriginal title under section 35 of the Constitution Act, 1982.

Each of the people profiled in this book mattered. Each of them had an impact on the legal system and on Canadian society. I hope you enjoy their stories.

PART I

1

Janey Canuck, Personhood, and the Famous Five: Emily Murphy

Emily Murphy wanted to be a senator. But she could not even be considered for appointment to the upper house in Parliament because women were not considered "persons" under the Constitution. For two decades, Emily led a campaign to have women recognized as persons, ultimately culminating in a 1929 decision by the Judicial Committee of the Privy Council in her favour. The *Persons Case* did more than just establish the principle that women were considered persons under the Constitution. It immediately became a symbol and a lightning rod in the fight for women's equality in Canada. At the centre of the case were the Famous Five — five audacious women who were leaders of first-wave feminism in Canada. Emily Murphy was the leader of the Famous Five.

The Making of Janey Canuck

Emily Ferguson was born in Cookstown, Ontario, in 1868 to Irish Canadian parents. Unlike many other girls who grew up during the late nineteenth century, Emily received a formal education at the Bishop Strachan School, a private all-girls school that was one of the first to provide an adequate higher-level education for women in Canada. It still operates in midtown Toronto.

At Bishop Strachan, Emily met her future husband, Arthur Murphy, who was an Anglican minister at the school. The couple married when Emily was nineteen, and the first of their four daughters was born the next year. Arthur travelled extensively throughout southwestern Ontario for their first eleven years of marriage, and Emily often accompanied him. Arthur's work would later take him abroad. The Murphys set sail for Europe in 1898, where they spent several years.

The travel bug had a big impact on Emily's career. The family's trip to England and Western Europe inspired Emily to create "Janey Canuck," a fictitious character she used to document her journeys and reflections on life both in Canada and abroad. Emily's first book, *The Impressions of Janey Canuck Abroad*, was published in 1902.

When the family returned to Toronto in 1899, Emily began writing for the *National Monthly of Canada* magazine. This work allowed her to earn a living at a crucial time, as Arthur fell ill and was unable to provide for the family. Emily became responsible for the house finances until he recovered. Shortly after their return, the couple's six-year-old daughter died of diphtheria. A second daughter had died before her first birthday. Those years were hard, and the family needed a new start.

Westward Bound

In 1903, the family moved westward, settling first in Swan River, Manitoba. Emily continued writing in her new community. From 1904 to 1912, she served as literary editor for the *Winnipeg Telegram* newspaper.

But Manitoba was a temporary sojourn in the Murphys' journey westward. Their final destination was Edmonton, Alberta. Emily continued writing as Janey Canuck throughout all these life transitions, documenting their move to Manitoba in *Janey Canuck in the West* (1910) and to Alberta in *Our Little Canadian Cousin of the Great Northwest* (1923). Emily's affinity for writing led her to her lifelong friend Henrietta Muir Edwards, a fellow women's activist, through the Canadian Women's Press Club. The club remained an essential part of Emily's life, and she led it from 1913 to 1920.

Appointment as a Police Magistrate

At the time, courtrooms were seen as unfit places for women and children during trials for serious crimes. Emily advocated for the establishment of women's courts where women could participate in the justice system. The attorney general of Alberta agreed and appointed Emily to preside over the new court. In 1916, Emily was appointed as a police magistrate — or lay judge — in Alberta. She became the first female magistrate not only in Canada, but in the entire British Empire.

Emily's experience as a police magistrate also bolstered her dedication to issues of temperance — the restriction and prohibition of alcohol — and drug use. In her courtroom, she had frequent exposure to crimes committed while the accused were under the influence of drugs such as cocaine, opium, and marijuana. She published her opinions and calls to action in her book *The Black Candle* (1922), presenting expert evidence on the state of opioid addiction in Canada and her analysis of the epidemic. But her writing was infected with racist attitudes about the role of Chinese immigrants in the spread of drug use in Canada. These perceptions had a lasting impact on the way the drug epidemic was handled, indirectly leading to the creation of the Chinese Immigration Act of 1923, which severely restricted Chinese immigration.

First-Wave Feminism and the Making of the Famous Five

Emily was part of a group of women who advocated for greater recognition of women's rights under law, focusing especially on the right to vote (known as suffrage) and the appointment and election of women to public office. These first-wave feminists also worked on social issues such as property reforms for married women and temperance. Through this work, Emily met the other activists who would become members of the Famous Five.

Henrietta Muir Edwards was one of Canada's leading temperance and suffrage activists, and an advocate for women's property rights. Her work contributed to legislative reform in Alberta.

Louise McKinney was a teacher who served as president of the Alberta Women's Christian Temperance Union and, from 1908 to 1930, as the vice-president of the Dominion Women's Christian Temperance Union. In 1917, she was elected to the Legislative Assembly of Alberta, the first woman elected to a legislature in the British Empire. She served only one term because her strong stance on prohibition impacted her re-election bid.

Irene Parlby was an activist with the United Farmers of Alberta, becoming the president of its first women's auxiliary, which she helped transform into the United Farm Women of Alberta. She was elected to the Alberta Legislature in 1921 — the second woman in the British Empire to be elected to a legislative assembly. Serving as minister without portfolio, Irene worked mostly on issues of health care, social services, and an improved standard of living for women and rural families. She was re-elected for two more terms, in 1926 and 1930. Irene became known as the Women's Minister because of her steadfast advocacy for women's equality.

Nellie McClung was the most famous member of the Five. Like other members of the group, she hailed from Ontario but had moved west. She was active in the women's suffrage movement, and after women were granted the right to vote in Manitoba in 1916, Nellie was elected to the Legislative Assembly of Manitoba in 1921. A powerful orator, she was labelled the "Canadian Joan of Arc," travelling across the country speaking on prohibition, women's suffrage, Canadian economic development, and women's wartime efforts.

Maternal Feminism

The Famous Five were products of their social class and reflected the societal norms and beliefs of their time. Women's activism was largely rooted in first-wave feminism, a movement that championed women's equality and inclusion on the basis of gender roles tied to maternalism and the division of labour. The focus was on equality for women through the lens of their role as caretakers in raising the next generation. In that role, women could ensure that "desirable traits" were nurtured and passed on to their offspring. Unfortunately, these traits devolved to mean race, ethnicity, and mental capacity. First-wave feminism contributed to the birth of the eugenics movement in North America, which promoted the idea that certain "undesirable" people should be prohibited from having children.

The Campaign for Appointment to the Senate

Emily Murphy launched the campaign for women to be appointed to the Senate soon after she was appointed a magistrate in 1916. She herself wanted to be appointed to the Red Chamber, as the Senate is colloquially known due to its red carpeting. The campaign sent petitions imploring the prime minister to appoint a woman to the Senate. Newspaper editorials supported the campaign. Emily had strong political connections and personally corresponded with Prime Minister William Lyon Mackenzie King. The government resisted her entreaties and others, relying on a legal opinion that said women could not be considered persons under the Constitution and therefore did not qualify for appointment to the Senate.

Emily convinced the government to obtain the Supreme Court's opinion on this issue through a procedure known as a "reference." She invited the other four members of the Famous Five to Edmonton in August 1927 to sign a petition publicly requesting that the government initiate the reference. Through this means, the Famous Five would be able to participate in the case.

From Ottawa to London

The Supreme Court of Canada heard the reference in March 1928 and disposed of the Famous Five's petition quickly, releasing its decision a month later. In a decision written by the chief justice, the court held that the meaning of the word "persons" in the Constitution was to be interpreted as it was understood at the time of Confederation in 1867 — that is, "male persons."

This was not the end of the road for the Famous Five, however. Until 1949, decisions from the Supreme Court of Canada could be appealed to the Judicial Committee of the Privy Council in England. The Judicial Committee agreed to hear the appeal in the summer of 1929, and the Lords delivered their decision on October 18, 1929, declaring that women were indeed considered "persons" under section 24 of the British North America Act, making them eligible for appointment to the Senate. It is a paradox that one of the greatest rulings in the history of Canadian constitutional law, and in the struggle for women's equality, was produced by a court outside of Canada after the case was so soundly rejected by Canada's Supreme Court.

A Canada Post stamp commemorating Emily Murphy and the *Persons Case*.

In the decision, Lord Sankey stated: "[t]he exclusion of women from all public offices is a relic of days more barbarous than ours ..." He went on to assert that the British North America Act planted in Canada "a living tree capable of growth and expansion within its natural limits." This ruling, which would become known as "the living tree doctrine," meant that the language of the Constitution was not frozen in time at the moment of its creation but could grow and adapt to new circumstances.

National and International Reaction

The decisions of both the Supreme Court of Canada and the Judicial Committee of the Privy Council attracted media attention throughout Canada and the British Empire. Although most of the coverage was neutral, focusing on explaining the legal issue and the impact of the Privy Council's decision, some articles were not supportive of women's equality and increased representation in public and political life. An Australian magazine article from January 29, 1930, congratulated the Famous Five extensively on their accomplishment, but interspersed their praise with warnings about the trouble the decision might create for the Senate if women became members of that body. The same sentiments were espoused in the *Montreal Gazette*'s coverage. Some people saw the increased opportunity for women in politics as a threat to gender roles in the home. But public sentiments on the issue were multifaceted, and many were eager for women's position in society to advance.

Senate Dreams Dashed

Many people expected that Emily Murphy, as the leader of the Famous Five, would be appointed to the Senate. Women across Canada, most notably her four colleagues, petitioned the governor general and the prime minister to appoint Emily as Canada's first female senator. But it was not to be. When the first Senate vacancy came about, in 1930, the Constitution required that the senator be appointed from Ontario, so Emily was ruled out. In any case, since Emily was seen as a Conservative, it seemed unlikely that Liberal Prime Minister Mackenzie King would appoint her. Indeed, the first woman appointed to the Senate was the Liberal Cairine Wilson, in 1930. A Senate vacancy did arise for an Albertan seat in 1931, but once again Emily was passed over for it, even though her political ally and friend Conservative R.B. Bennett was now prime minister. The vacancy was slated for a Catholic, and Emily was Anglican. Emily's fight for a place in the Senate ended with her death in 1933 at the age of sixty-five.

The Famous Five

Henrietta Edwards and Louise McKinney died before Murphy, shortly after Lord Sankey's decision. The remaining two members of the Famous Five, Irene Parlby and Nellie McClung, had long careers, though neither had any interest in a Senate appointment.

Prime Minister Mackenzie King appointed Nellie as a governor of the new Canadian Broadcasting Corporation (CBC) when it was formed in 1935. She also participated in international politics as part of the League of Nations delegation in Geneva in 1938. As she reached her seventies, Nellie was content with ending her political career and retiring to Victoria, British Columbia. She passed away in Victoria in 1951 at the age of seventy-seven.

Irene Parlby continued as a member of the United Farmers of Alberta for a few more years. She also served as a delegate at the League of Nations in

Geneva in 1930. She retired from public activism in 1934 and passed away in 1965, at the age of ninety-seven, in Red Deer, Alberta.

The Legacy of the *Persons Case*

In 1979, on the fiftieth anniversary of the Privy Council's decision, the Government of Canada designated October 18 as Persons Day to commemorate the ruling. It also created an award to recognize outstanding contributions to advancing equality for women in Canada. The Famous 5 Foundation was established in 1996 to support girls and women as they "courageously lead change that contributes to a society without boundaries for women." In 2000, a monument to the Famous Five and the *Persons Case* was unveiled on Parliament Hill. A similar statue sits at the Olympic Plaza in Calgary, commemorating the origin of the case and the movement. From 2004 to 2012, the $50 bill contained an image of the statue, making the Famous Five the first women aside from Queen Elizabeth II to appear on Canadian currency.

The living tree doctrine now serves as the bedrock of Canadian constitutional law, but for decades after the *Persons Case*, it was largely ignored by Canadian lawyers and judges. It was revived by the Supreme Court of Canada more than fifty years later, after the enactment of the Canadian Charter of Rights and Freedoms in 1982. Every first-year law student in Canada learns about the living tree doctrine and the *Persons Case*, but few know of Emily Murphy and her colleagues in the Famous Five.

2

Fighting Racism in Western Canada: Quong Wing

Quong Wing was a prominent member of an emerging Chinese business class in Moose Jaw, Saskatchewan, in the 1910s. He was one of many young Chinese men who had immigrated to Canada on their own to seek a better life for themselves, and sometimes for their families left behind in China. But in Canada, they frequently faced racism and discrimination. Much of the discrimination was embedded in social practices, but some was enacted into law. Few challenged these attitudes or laws. Quong Wing did. He lost his court battle but succeeded in exposing the racism within Canadian society and law.

From China to Moose Jaw

Quong Wing was born in China and moved to Moose Jaw sometime around 1902. He was part of a wave of immigration from China that was almost exclusively male. Few of these men brought their wives or children with them. We don't know who Quong Wing may have left behind back home.

Although the vast majority of Chinese immigrants settled in British Columbia, some pursued a better life by venturing farther east, to the Prairies.

Moose Jaw had been chosen as a local operations centre for the Canadian Pacific Railway in 1882, and by 1906 — the year after Saskatchewan became a province — it was a bustling railway town with a population of over six thousand people. Quong Wing was one of the early members of a small but growing Chinese community in Moose Jaw. Between 1910 and 1913, the Chinese population in Moose Jaw tripled from 150 to 452.

At some point after arriving in Moose Jaw, Quong Wing started going by the name Charlie. It was common for immigrants from China — and other countries outside the British Empire — to adopt English names when they arrived in Canada to appear more "Canadian." He became a naturalized British subject in 1905. (Canadian citizenship would not be created until 1947.) The naturalization process gave Quong Wing the same status as a natural-born British subject. His decision to become a naturalized citizen was one that was uncommon for Chinese immigrants at the time — only 5 percent of the Chinese population in Moose

Main Street from the Canadian Pacific Railway station in Moose Jaw, Saskatchewan. The C.E.R. Restaurant is located on the right-hand side below the billboard that reads "STAG."

Jaw were naturalized citizens. Most Chinese immigrants in the early twentieth century sought to one day return to China, after they had earned enough money in Canada. That never seemed to be part of Quong Wing's plans.

Quong Wing was a prominent member of Moose Jaw's Chinese business community. He ran the C.E.R. Restaurant at the corner of Main and Manitoba streets. He lived and worked at the restaurant. Given its location, one block from the Canadian Pacific Railway station and across the street from the three-storey Maple Leaf Hotel, Quong Wing's restaurant was probably quite busy. Anyone coming into town from the train station would have passed by the restaurant. The intersection was also the site of large gatherings such as the Spring Carnival Day and the Labour Day Parade.

As a manager, Quong Wing seems to have been well liked by his employees. Nellie Lane, a server at the C.E.R. Restaurant, said that he always paid her on time and that she had "never worked for a better master."

Racial Dynamics in the Service Industry

It is unlikely that Quong Wing's decision to open a restaurant was inspired by a love of cooking. Rather, his choice was likely determined by economic and social factors. Asian workers were largely excluded from the higher-paying jobs in the labour market due to hostility from white employers and trade unions. There were, however, many opportunities in domestic service businesses such as restaurants and laundries. These businesses were traditionally considered "women's work," and frontier towns like Moose Jaw were skewed heavily male. Chinese restauranteurs like Quong Wing were typically able to squeeze out modest profits by working long hours and offering simple meals at a low price.

In the early 1900s, it was typical for Chinese-run restaurants to employ white women as servers. Many white patrons would only dine at restaurants with white servers, and restaurants would advertise with signs such as "None but white help employed." White women, rather than men, were more often employed in these positions because their wages were significantly lower — white women were paid about half as much as white men at the time. Quong Wing employed two white women: Mabel Hopman and Nellie

Lane. Without the help of white female servers, a business like Quong Wing's would have had a hard time making a financial go of it.

A Law "For the Protection of White Women"

On March 4, 1912, without any debate, the Saskatchewan Legislature passed An Act to Prevent the Employment of Female Labour in Certain Capacities (Female Labour Act). This new law made it illegal for "any Japanese, Chinaman or other Oriental person" to employ a "white woman or girl." Offenders could be fined up to $100 and jailed for up to two months if they didn't pay the fine. It was the first labour law of its kind in Canada. It was not the first time, however, that legislatures had enacted racist legislation targeting Chinese immigrants. In 1908, just three years after Quong Wing became a naturalized British subject, the Saskatchewan Legislature followed the lead of British Columbia and passed a law to deny Chinese persons the right to vote.

The new Female Labour Act was motivated by two overarching forces: the economic interests of white businesses and labour groups, and the "moral interests" of social reformers. White business owners from across Saskatchewan were unhappy with the growing number of Asian-owned businesses in the province. The law was also justified on "moral" considerations. Asian men were stereotyped as opium addicts and gamblers, and the prevailing belief among white Canadians was that Asian societies were "backward" and "primitive." White women were seen as susceptible to, and in need of protection from the influences of Asian men. This view was pushed forward not just by white men but also by white women's groups, including the National Council of Women of Canada.

Quong Wing and Quong Sing: Test Cases for the Chinese Community

The Female Labour Act became law on May 1, 1912. The Chinese community of Moose Jaw held a mass meeting to discuss the law, and they decided they would continue employing white women and fight a test case challenging it. It was uncommon for immigrants and racial minorities to challenge governments in the courts in Canada at this time. The Chinese community of Moose Jaw was ahead of its time in seeking to protect their rights through the courts. Their faith — or rather their hope — would turn out to be misplaced.

On May 20, three weeks after the law came into force, Quong Wing was charged with violating the labour law by employing the two white women as servers at the C.E.R. Restaurant. Another Chinese restauranteur in Moose Jaw, Quong Sing, was charged on the same day for employing a white woman as a housekeeper at a different restaurant.

Quong Wing's trial was held on May 27, 1912, just one week after charges were laid against him. His lawyer was Netson R. Craig, a well-respected litigator who had moved from Nova Scotia to Moose Jaw in 1907. Prior to Quong Wing's trial, Craig had represented many members of the Chinese community on charges of illegal gambling.

Craig's defence strategy was to challenge the Crown's ability to prove Quong Wing's racial identity. While the witnesses all claimed that Quong Wing was Chinese, Craig challenged them to actually define what they meant by "Chinese." His cross-examination uncovered that none of them could definitively swear that Quong Wing had been born in China, that his parents were Chinese, that his allegiances were to China, or that he had ever even set foot in China.

Although Craig's strategy of questioning the very idea of race could be seen as ahead of its time, it was ultimately unsuccessful. The magistrate made a finding of fact that Quong Wing was Chinese, and he was found guilty.

Quong Sing was also represented by Netson Craig, and his trial unfolded in much the same way. He was also found guilty.

Due to the test nature of these two cases, the magistrate fined Quong Wing and Quong Sing only $5 each, significantly below the maximum of $100.

Appeal to the Saskatchewan Supreme Court

Both men appealed their cases to the Saskatchewan Supreme Court — the highest court in the province. They hired Wellington B. Willoughby to represent them on appeal. Willoughby was Netson Craig's senior partner, as well as the leader of the Conservative Opposition in the Saskatchewan

Legislature. The case became a constitutional tussle over the division of powers between the federal and provincial governments over who had the power to enact a law like the Female Labour Act.

The court rejected the appeals 3–1. The majority of the judges concluded that the law was valid provincial legislation. They characterized the purpose of the law as "the protection of white women, and not the exclusion of the Chinese." Based on this characterization, Quong Wing's and Quong Sing's convictions were affirmed, and the appeal was dismissed.

The chief justice of Saskatchewan wrote a notable dissent, in which he said the true aim of the law was to "deprive the Chinese, whether naturalized or not, of the ordinary rights of the inhabitants of Saskatchewan." On this basis, the chief justice concluded that Saskatchewan's law interfered with Parliament's exclusive jurisdiction over naturalization, which he determined should include all matters relating to the rights and privileges of naturalized citizens.

Fighting On

Quong Wing immediately announced that he would appeal the decision to the Supreme Court of Canada. He was alone in doing so, as Quong Sing dropped out — presumably, he paid his $5 fine and continued on with his life. The Chinese community of Moose Jaw continued to support Quong Wing's case, both morally and financially. They contributed funds to the $500 bond Quong Wing had to post to appeal his case to the Supreme Court. The case was obviously important to members of the Chinese community outside Saskatchewan too, as Quong Wing later received a donation of $1,175 from the Chinese Benevolent Association headquartered in Victoria.

In 1914, there were only six judges on the Supreme Court of Canada (there are nine today). Like most cases of this era, Quong Wing's case was heard by five judges. The judges took just eleven days to release their decision after the appeal was argued — this was faster than usual for the time and did not bode well for Quong Wing. He lost his appeal 4–1.

As at the Saskatchewan high court, the case at the Supreme Court of Canada focused on the division of powers between the provinces and the federal government. Quong Wing's lawyer argued that the federal power over "naturalization and aliens" in section 91(25) of the British North America Act, 1867, prevented provinces like Saskatchewan from restricting the rights of naturalized citizens like Quong Wing. The court did not accept this argument. By upholding the Female Labour Act, the Supreme Court validated the legality of racial discrimination in Canada.

It was probably only of small comfort to Quong Wing and Chinese Canadians that one judge sided with them. Justice John Idington served a mostly undistinguished twenty-two years on the Supreme Court of Canada; his dissent in *Quong Wing* is probably his most notable decision. He wrote that because the Naturalization Act granted naturalized citizens all the same rights and privileges as natural-born British subjects, the Female Labour Act must be interpreted as applying only to Chinese who had not become naturalized British subjects. Because Quong Wing was a naturalized British subject, Idington did not need to go further in his judgment. He did not say whether he would have upheld the law as applying to alien Chinese.

In 1914, Quong Wing attempted an appeal to the Judicial Committee of the Privy Council in England, but his application was rejected. His legal saga had come to an end. There are no records indicating that he ever paid his $5 fine, but he likely did.

Quong Wing continued running the C.E.R. Restaurant for a few years, but by 1918 he was no longer listed in the Moose Jaw directory. His fate after 1918 is not known.

Darker Times Ahead for the Chinese Community in Canada

Saskatchewan's Female Labour Act was one of many anti-Chinese labour laws passed in Canada. Other provinces followed Saskatchewan in prohibiting Chinese business owners and managers from employing white women. In February 1913, prior to Quong Wing's appeal at the Saskatchewan Supreme Court, Manitoba enacted a copy of Saskatchewan's Female Labour Act. In May 1914, just a few months after the Supreme Court of Canada's ruling, Ontario passed a similar law, as did British Columbia in 1919. Although Saskatchewan amended its law in 1919 to remove explicit reference to Chinese employers, its law remained in force until it was repealed in 1969.

In the decade following Quong Wing's battle at the Supreme Court, anti-Chinese racism continued to rise in Canada, leading Parliament to pass the Chinese Immigration Act of 1923 (colloquially known as the "Chinese Exclusion Act"). The new act repealed the Chinese head tax but created an almost complete ban on Chinese immigration to Canada, with only a few exceptions for students, merchants, and farmers. Over the next twenty-three years, just fifteen Chinese immigrants were admitted into Canada. The Chinese Immigration Act was repealed in 1946.

Quong Wing's Legacy

As a legal precedent, *Quong Wing* is not discussed for its relationship to racial discrimination. In subsequent Canadian case law, the *Quong Wing* decision has been cited primarily for what it says about division of powers. The type of analysis found in *Quong Wing* was a common feature of division of powers cases before the advent of the Charter. Where a discriminatory law was challenged under the division of powers, courts would generally focus on the purpose of the law rather than on its discriminatory effects. In *Quong Wing*, this meant upholding a discriminatory law because the "protection of white women" was taken to be a valid purpose.

Cases like *Quong Wing* helped spur the movement for the enactment of the Canadian Bill of Rights in 1960 and for a constitutionally entrenched bill of rights that explicitly protected against discrimination based on characteristics like race or national origin. This culminated in the enactment of the Canadian Charter of Rights and Freedoms in 1982, nearly seventy years after Quong Wing began his ill-fated legal challenge.

3

Unlikely Champion of the Rule of Law: Frank Roncarelli

Frank Roncarelli was an immigrant to Canada who took on the most powerful man in Quebec in the first half of the twentieth century — Premier Maurice Duplessis. His fifteen-year legal battle culminated in a landmark victory at the Supreme Court of Canada, which recognized the foundational principle of the rule of law under the Canadian Constitution. The name Roncarelli has become synonymous with the idea that everyone — even the premier or the prime minister — is subject to the law. However, few Canadians know the name, let alone anything about Frank Roncarelli himself.

An Immigrant Story

Francesco ("Franco" or "Frank") Roncarelli was born in Bologna, Italy, in 1904 and immigrated to Canada with his parents at a young age. Frank grew up in Montreal and, like many Canadians, learned to play hockey. He studied engineering at McGill University and played on the McGill hockey team.

Frank's parents were successful small businesspeople. His mother, Argentina, was a dress designer who owned the Madame Roncarelli dress shop. In 1912, Frank's father, Ettore, opened a restaurant on Crescent Street, a popular area in downtown Montreal. The restaurant was known by various names, including Café Roncarelli. It was also known as Quaff, which means to drink something heartily, especially an alcoholic drink. "Quaff" can also simply refer to an alcoholic drink. Much quaff was quaffed at Quaff, as Ettore Roncarelli successfully secured a liquor licence, a critical ingredient for commercial success in the restaurant business in Montreal.

Returning to Italy and Exposure to Fascism

After graduating from McGill, Frank returned to his native Italy, where he worked in engineering and played hockey for the top club in the country, HC Milano. He played for the Italian national team at the 1929 European Championships and at the World Championships between 1930 and 1934. The years that Frank spent in Italy — 1926–1936 — coincided with the rise of fascism under the dictatorship of Benito Mussolini, known as Il Duce ("the leader"). Frank married a Milanese woman named Mimi, and the couple had two sons, Ettore and Robi.

In 1934, Frank faced criticism from the fascist Italian media when he was awarded one of Mussolini's new national medals of athletic merit as an outstanding player in the Italian national hockey championships. Il Duce himself awarded the medals, and Frank appeared to be the only dual citizen among the winners. The fascist press criticized him because he was a Canadian citizen and had "foisted" his citizenship on his young Milanese wife and their child. In fact, Canadian citizenship did not exist until 1947, although Frank and his family could have been considered British subjects. In any event, the Associated Press reported on the controversy and North American newspapers carried the wire story.

Not much more is known about Frank's activities in Italy, but the political climate impacted him. He saw the close cooperation between the Catholic Church and the fascist authorities in Italy, and that led him to turn away from Catholicism and become a Jehovah's Witness around 1935.

The Jehovah's Witnesses are a religious group that emerged in the United States in the 1870s. They are a Christian denomination whose interpretation of the Bible differs dramatically from established Christian doctrine. They believe that Armageddon — the destruction of the current world — is imminent and that God's kingdom will replace it and bring solutions to all of humanity's problems. The Jehovah's Witnesses are known for their fervent commitment to their beliefs, such as their refusal to salute a flag because they believe that constitutes idolatry in violation of the Second Commandment ("Thou shalt not make unto thee any graven image"). Jehovah's Witnesses are also known for their proselytizing — actively working to convert others to their faith through face-to-face discussions, giving out pamphlets, publishing magazines, and holding meetings.

Returning to Canada: A Religious Awakening

Frank returned to Canada in the late 1930s with his young family, working in construction and eventually taking over the successful Quaff Café from his father.

In Quebec, the Jehovah's Witnesses actively sought converts among Catholic Quebeckers by handing out pamphlets in the streets, giving public lectures, and holding meetings in supporters' homes. They were a small group — estimated at no more than several thousand adherents in the province in the 1940s — but they aroused the ire of the Catholic Church and the regime of Premier Maurice Duplessis.

In 1945, provincial authorities launched a harsh crackdown on the Jehovah's Witnesses. The police arrested over a thousand young men and women under local bylaws that required a licence for public gatherings. Most of the arrests took place in Montreal, and the penalty under the bylaw was a fine of $40, a not insignificant sum that is roughly equivalent to $700 in 2025 dollars. The same year, Frank was reportedly part of a group of Jehovah's Witnesses who escaped an angry mob outside Montreal.

Frank acted as a surety — a person who promises to pay bail for an accused person if they do not appear for their scheduled court date — for about 380 cases in Montreal. The court in Montreal recognized Frank as a man of means due to the commercial success of Quaff and other investments, so his signature was accepted as a guarantee in such cases. This was his sole connection to the controversial action of the Jehovah's Witnesses. He was an adherent of the group, but he never took part in the distribution of religious materials, and he certainly was never arrested.

Frank's liquor licence was set to expire in December 1946. The month before, the head of the Liquor Commission spoke with the chief prosecutor in Montreal about their belief that Frank's acts were enabling a large number of Jehovah's Witnesses to be "at large" (i.e., out of jail) and to continue to carry out their campaign, which they viewed as disturbing settled Catholic beliefs and generally arousing community dissatisfaction. They called Premier Duplessis. He told them that the matter was serious; they needed to determine without a doubt that the person furnishing bail and the person holding the liquor licence for Quaff were one and the same. A private investigator was sent to confirm Frank's identity. The head of the Liquor Commission

Frank Roncarelli, circa 1946.

again spoke with Premier Duplessis, who instructed him to revoke Frank's liquor licence.

On Wednesday, December 4, 1946, police stormed into Quaff Café without warning during the lunch hour and seized all the liquor, to the astonishment of both Frank and the assembled diners. The event immediately became a cause célèbre. In Quebec City, Premier Duplessis held a press conference proudly announcing that he had ordered the cancellation of Frank's licence because of the restauranteur's support of the Jehovah's Witnesses. Others rallied to Frank's defence with petitions and editorials in the press.

Taking on Le Chef

Within six months, Frank was forced to close Quaff. Without a liquor licence, the restaurant just wasn't commercially viable. Duplessis had put him out of business. Unlike the many of his co-religionists who had been arrested for proselytizing the Jehovah's Witness faith, Frank faced no charges. He decided to take the highly unusual step of commencing a legal proceeding against the premier himself, on the grounds that the premier's unlawful actions had put him out of business and caused him damages.

Frank hired A.L. Stein, a Jewish lawyer concerned with civil liberties who had represented the Jehovah's Witnesses in other cases. Stein tried without success to find a French-Canadian lawyer to serve as co-counsel, but none seemed eager to take on Le Chef ("the boss"), the nickname by which Duplessis was widely known. Instead, Stein turned to noted McGill law professor, civil libertarian, and poet Frank Scott as co-counsel. Scott was a socialist who had been one of the founders of the Co-operative Commonwealth Federation, the forerunner to today's New Democratic Party. He was considered one of the brightest legal minds of his generation, especially in his field of constitutional law. There was only one problem: Scott had never before set foot in a courtroom as a lawyer. In this, he was totally unexperienced. But no one had ever successfully sued the premier of Quebec before, so it was all uncharted territory.

To the surprise of many, Frank won at trial in a decision rendered in 1950, but he was awarded only $8,123.53 in damages against Duplessis. That victory would be short-lived, however. The Quebec Court of Appeal reversed the judgment. The next step was the Supreme Court of Canada. Throughout this time, Duplessis remained premier while Frank, unemployed, got by through taking odd jobs.

A Quartet of Jehovah's Witnesses Cases

Roncarelli v. Duplessis was part of a quartet of cases involving Jehovah's Witnesses in Quebec decided by the Supreme Court in the 1950s. In 1951, it had overturned a conviction for seditious libel against a Jehovah's Witness who had distributed pamphlets entitled "Quebec's Burning Hate for God and Christ and Freedom Is the Shame of All Canada," which criticized the government of Quebec's suppression and persecution of Jehovah's Witnesses in the province (*Boucher v. The King*). A year later, the Supreme Court struck down a Quebec City bylaw that prohibited the distribution of pamphlets in the streets without permission from the chief of police (*Saumur v. The City of Quebec*). And in 1955, the high court allowed a homeowner who had hosted a Jehovah's Witnesses meeting that was broken up by police to sue the police for damages caused by them to his property in the raid (*Chaput v. Romain*).

Victory for the Rule of Law

Frank's case was heard at the Supreme Court over five days in the first week of June 1958, more than a decade after he had first lost his liquor licence. All of the high court's nine judges sat on the case, which was not the usual practice at the time. At the end of January 1959, the court ruled 6–3 in Frank's favour, with two of the three Quebec judges siding with Duplessis. Each judge wrote separate opinions, as was the practice at the time.

In the most famous opinion, Justice Ivan Rand held that Premier Duplessis had acted wholly without legal authority. He warned that when "an administration according to the law is ... superseded by action dictated by and according to the arbitrary likes, dislikes and irrelevant purposes of public officers acting beyond their duty," it would signal "the beginning of disintegration of the rule of law as a fundamental postulate of our constitutional structure."

The court awarded Frank $33,123.53 in damages. It was a relatively modest sum, even in 1959, and it would not replace Frank's beloved Quaff Café, the livelihood he lost as a result of the premier's arbitrary actions. But it was a moral victory. And not just for Frank. A.L. Stein's son was in Professor Scott's law class at McGill the day the decision was released. In those pre-Internet days, lawyers were advised of the decision by telephone. Scott was pulled out of class to take the call. He returned triumphantly, and the entire law school celebrated the momentous victory: classes were cancelled, and students and professors joined together at a general assembly to toast the victory with champagne. Frank himself joined the celebrations later that evening at Scott's home.

Final victory was not certain, however. Duplessis had one more card to play, if he chose. Although appeals to the Judicial Committee of the Privy Council in London had been abolished in Canada in 1949, cases that were already in the system at that time still could be appealed to the Privy Council. (The last Canadian appeal was not decided until 1959, the same year the Supreme Court decided *Roncarelli*.) Duplessis weighed his options for over a month while Frank, his lawyers, and their supporters waited. Groups urged Duplessis to appeal to London. A branch of the nationalist Saint-Jean-Baptiste Society outside Quebec City adopted a resolution asking the premier to appeal, stating that he had acted in the best interests of the Roman Catholic and French population of the province in cancelling Frank's liquor permit. They included a $25 cheque to the premier, along with a copy of the resolution, presumably to help cover the costs of the appeal.

On March 11, nearly six weeks after the Supreme Court handed down its decision, Duplessis announced that he would not appeal to London. He said he was leaving his decision to cancel Frank's permit "to the grand tribunal of public opinion in the province of Quebec."

After the Supreme Court Decision

Duplessis died six months later, on September 7, 1959. He had been premier since 1944, and in total he led Quebec for eighteen years, making him the province's longest-serving premier. His tenure is generally not remembered well. The period was dubbed *le noirceur* ("the darkness"), reflecting the dominance of the state and the Catholic Church over the lives of Quebeckers. The death of Duplessis was followed by the election of Liberal leader Jean Lesage and the ushering in of the Quiet Revolution, a period of economic growth and social liberalization that included the abandonment of persecution of Jehovah's Witnesses.

Frank watched the Quiet Revolution from outside the country. After his landmark legal victory, he had moved to the United States. For a few years, he operated a restaurant in Watertown, New York, near the Canadian border. He then moved to Connecticut, where he returned to his original profession as an engineer. In 1965, he made a five-minute appearance on the top-rated CBC game show *Front Page Challenge*. Frank claimed he held no ill will toward Duplessis — that the two had met socially and Duplessis had been quite convivial.

The Legacy of *Roncarelli v. Duplessis*

Justice Morris Fish — a Montrealer and a justice of the Supreme Court — called *Roncarelli v. Duplessis* "Canada's most important decision on the rule of law." It was the last in a series of cases between 1930 and 1959 known as the "implied bill of rights" cases, in which the Supreme Court found "implied" civil rights to be constitutionally protected in the absence of written protections. These decisions provided important safeguards for civil liberties until the enactment of the Canadian Charter of Rights and Freedoms in 1982. Canadian law students still study *Roncarelli v. Duplessis* today. Sadly, the case is largely ignored outside of legal circles.

An Unacknowledged Hero

After Frank was forced to close Quaff, other restaurants and businesses came and went over the years at 1429 Crescent, including the popular Café République. Today, the notorious American chain Hooters is located next to the space where Quaff once was.

Frank died in Connecticut of an aneurysm in 1981 at the age of seventy-seven. His passing was noted in modest obituaries across the country. The *Montreal Gazette* said the debt Canada owed Frank was incalculable. The champion of civil liberties, whose name became synonymous with the rule of law in Canada, did not receive the Order of Canada or any public recognition. There is no street, no school or public building named after Frank Roncarelli, let alone a statue in his honour.

4

Ahead of Her Time: Stella Bliss

In 1978, Stella Bliss exposed the Supreme Court of Canada as a dated institution that was not ready to come to grips with the new reality of women's equality. Stella would not have considered herself an activist, but she galvanized an entire generation of women and their allies to advocate for the constitutional protection of women's equality. Their efforts would eventually lead to the entrenchment of strong equality protections in the Canadian Charter of Rights and Freedoms.

From Across the Pond to Vancouver

Stella Bliss was born and raised in England. She moved to Vancouver in 1965, but she did not stay long and returned to England four years later. Stella dreamed of opening an antique store and planned to return to Vancouver to launch her business. She had a job offer from the Vancouver company she had previously worked for, but that fell through.

In August 1975, Stella married her American common-law spouse, not knowing that she was two months pregnant. The couple arrived in Vancouver during a recession. Neither of them had a job. It was a bad time to start a business, so Bliss put her dreams of opening an antique store on hold. She found a job with Brown Bros Ford in Kerrisdale as a leasing secretary and started work the third week of September. Soon after, she discovered she was pregnant. She did not tell her employer. Events would quickly reveal the likely reason Stella was hesitant to reveal her pregnancy to those at work.

Pregnant? You're Fired!

In January 1976, Stella was fired when her employer found out she was pregnant. She complained to the BC Human Rights Commission, which ordered Brown Bros to reinstate Stella; it was illegal to fire someone because they were pregnant — although, as her case illustrated, it was not an uncommon experience for women in the 1970s. Stella returned to the car dealership and continued working until March 12, when she was fired again. She gave birth to a baby boy on March 16 and reapplied for regular unemployment benefits on March 22.

Stella was caught between two provisions of the Unemployment Insurance Act. In order to qualify for regular unemployment benefits, an

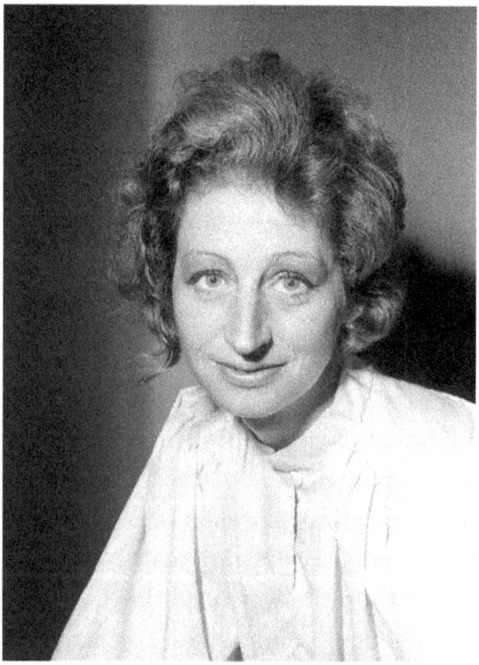

Stella Bliss, circa 1976–77.

employee had to work at least eight weeks. To qualify for maternity benefits, an employee had to work at least ten weeks, a provision known as the "magic ten" requirement. Stella had worked nine weeks, long enough to qualify for regular unemployment benefits, but not for maternity benefits. She was deemed ineligible for the "regular" unemployment benefits because she had been pregnant, and she did not qualify for maternity benefits because she had not worked long enough.

Challenging the Status Quo

Stella appealed the denial of her maternity benefits claim to the administrative body that dealt with unemployment insurance appeals. She sought advice from a legal aid clinic, where she was advised by a law student to consider relying on the Canadian Bill of Rights, which applied to federal laws like the Unemployment Insurance Act, promising protection against discrimination based on race, national origin, colour, religion, or sex. It also promised individuals the right "to equality before the law and the protection of the law." However, in the eighteen years before Stella's case, the Supreme Court had struck down only a single law based on the Bill of Rights. So it was surprising, and perhaps optimistic, that the law student would suggest this legal argument.

According to political scientists Leslie Pal and F.L. Morton, who interviewed Stella and wrote a detailed account of her case, it was Stella who suggested the Bill of Rights argument to the lawyer she obtained for her appeal. Out of a job, denied unemployment benefits, and home with a newborn baby, Stella did not have the money to hire a lawyer. She went to the Vancouver Community Legal Assistance Society and met lawyer Allan MacLean, who reluctantly agreed to take on her case despite his misgivings about the longshot Bill of Rights argument. In order to appeal the unanimous decision against her, Stella also needed a union to sponsor her. The Service, Office and Retail Workers Union of Canada agreed, and she then joined the union.

Likely to the surprise of almost everyone involved, the judge who heard Stella's appeal agreed with her Bill of Rights argument. The Unemployment Insurance Commission appealed this decision to the Federal Court of

Appeal. By this time, Stella's case was gaining notoriety in the BC press and among women's groups. MacLean was able to convince a young feminist lawyer named Lynn Smith, the chair of the Vancouver Community Legal Assistance Society, to join Stella's legal team. Smith would go on to have a stellar career as a law professor, dean of the Faculty of Law at the University of British Columbia, and judge of the British Columbia Supreme Court. She wrote the landmark decision overturning the ban on assisted suicide in Canada.

The Federal Court of Appeal allowed the appeal and rejected Stella's argument that the act violated the right to equality before the law. Justice Louis Pratte wrote that, even assuming Stella had been discriminated against, it was not because of her sex. He asserted that if the law treated people differently, it was not because they were women as opposed to men, but because they were pregnant as opposed to not pregnant.

The only avenue left for Stella was an appeal to the Supreme Court of Canada. However, as the backing for her case grew, Stella herself seemed to lose interest in the case. She was in the midst of a family crisis: Her marriage was falling apart and would eventually dissolve, with her husband returning to the United States with the couple's young son. Moreover, Stella did not seem to like being a symbol of a growing feminist movement. She did not give interviews or permit herself to be photographed. Professors Pal and Morton report that she claimed not to share the hard-line feminism of some of her supporters.

Stella did agree to allow MacLean to appeal her case to the Supreme Court. This required money. The Vancouver Status of Women created a Stella Bliss Fund, which was supported by several unions and women's groups. John Nelligan of Ottawa, a recent past president of the Canadian Civil Liberties Association, brought gravitas to Stella's legal team when he agreed to serve as lead counsel at the high court on a pro bono basis.

The appeal was heard by seven of the nine Supreme Court judges over two days in June 1978. Unfortunately for Stella, the two judges who did not participate in the case were the two most likely to be sympathetic to her argument — Chief Justice Bora Laskin and Justice Wishart Spence — though their presence would have been unlikely to alter the court's decision.

A Terse Dismissal

In October, the high court delivered a unanimous decision rejecting Stella's appeal. The twelve-page judgment was terse and technical, never once mentioning Stella by name. She was reduced to "the appellant." Justice Roland Ritchie found that the Unemployment Insurance Act did not discriminate based on sex. In a memorable and oft-repeated statement, he wrote that "any inequality between the sexes in this area is not created by legislation but by nature."

The decision was seen as an example of formal equality, of treating "likes alike": equal treatment for those in the same or similar situations and different treatment for those in dissimilar situations. According to this view, Stella was not discriminated against under the law, because she was treated the same as other pregnant persons. The court did not acknowledge that only women could become pregnant. That would require looking at the impact of the law on a vulnerable group, which is the approach of substantive equality. Substantive equality would eventually be embraced by the Supreme Court, but it would take the enactment of the Canadian Charter of Rights and Freedoms and the mobilization of women's groups for that to happen.

Providing Fuel for the Fire

The loss was deeply disappointing to Stella and to her supporters. The judgment, and particularly the cavalier and offensive language used by Justice Ritchie, infuriated and galvanized women's groups across the country. The *Bliss* judgment was handed down during a time of constitutional discussions about the enactment of a constitutionally entrenched charter of rights. In September 1980, the federal government created a Special Committee of the Senate and the House of Commons on the Constitution, and nearly a hundred groups participated and gave testimony before the committee. Women's groups were particularly influential, and the name Stella Bliss was frequently invoked by them and other groups.

"Stella Bliss" became a rallying cry for advocates of a strong and expansive protection of equality in the Charter. Her case was described as notorious, and it was a fresh and open wound. It also struck a worrisome note about the Supreme Court's ability to deal with equality and other constitutional protections. There was a prevailing feeling that the court could not be trusted, and that the text of the Charter needed to give judges instructions that were as specific and expansive as possible. Stella's case motivated equality advocates to shape the wording of the Charter's equality guarantee (section 15) — "Every individual is equal before and under the law and has the right to the equal protection and equal benefit of the law without discrimination and, in particular, without discrimination based on race, national or ethnic origin, colour, religion, sex, age or mental or physical disability." And thus avoid the sort of reasoning used by the Supreme Court in her case.

Stella Retreats

The case took a toll on Stella. Her marriage had ended. To escape the attention in Vancouver, she left Canada for a while. When she returned, she settled in Victoria, where she worked in a consulting firm and ran several businesses of her own, although not the antique shop that she'd dreamed about as a young woman in England. From time to time she popped up in the local media. In 1981, the *Victoria Times Colonist* reported that she'd won a poetry contest. In 1984, she wrote a lengthy letter to the editor explaining how tough it was for women to qualify for unemployment insurance. In 1986, she wrote another letter to the editor responding to an article about a plan to build an overpass. Both letters were intelligent, sharp, and logical. After the 1986 letter, there was no further mention of Stella in the media, although references to her case continued. Stella reportedly died of brain cancer in Victoria in 1997, at the age of fifty-six. She lived long enough to see the Supreme Court formally overrule her decision.

Bliss Abandoned

The Canadian legal system works on the basis of precedent. Lower courts must follow the decisions of higher courts, unless they have been overruled. This creates certainty and predictability in the law. Courts, especially the Supreme Court of Canada, do not easily overrule their prior decisions. It was thus notable when, only a decade after *Bliss*, the Supreme Court explicitly overruled the decision.

In *Brooks v. Canada Safeway* (1989), the Supreme Court had harsh words for the decision it had rendered just over a decade before. The chief justice stated, "Over ten years have elapsed since the decision in *Bliss*. During that time there have been profound changes in women's labour force participation. With the benefit of a decade of hindsight and ten years of experience with claims of human rights discrimination and jurisprudence arising therefrom, I am prepared to say that *Bliss* was wrongly decided or, in any event, that *Bliss* would not be decided now as it was decided then."

The high court recognized that "combining paid work with motherhood and accommodating the childbearing needs of working women are ever-increasing imperatives." It recognized that these burdens fell on women. And it finally recognized what the courts in *Bliss* had refused to: that discrimination on the basis of pregnancy is discrimination based on sex.

PART II

THE CHARTER OF RIGHTS AND FREEDOMS

5

The Most Famous Name in Canadian Constitutional Law: David Oakes

The name Oakes is probably the most recognized name in Canadian constitutional law. Every judge in the country would know it, as would almost every one of Canada's 140,000 lawyers. Every first-year law student learns "the *Oakes* test." However, few of these legal professionals know Oakes's first name, let alone who he was and how his name came to be associated with the Charter and Canadian constitutional law. David Edwin Oakes was a young man from London, Ontario, who found himself enmeshed in Canada's criminal justice system just as the Canadian Charter of Rights and Freedoms came into force in 1982. Through chance and timing, the Supreme Court made his last name famous.

A Thursday Night Outside the Barn

On December 17, 1981, David Oakes was sitting in his car with a female companion outside the Barn Tavern in London. The temperature that Thursday evening hovered between –6 and –10 degrees. The Barn, a popular tavern that featured live music, dancing, and a $4.99 all-you-can-eat buffet, was a favourite for workers on their lunch break, families on a budget, and high school students looking for a place that would serve them a beer or two.

At the time, David was an unemployed construction worker in his early to mid-twenties. After injuring his shin and kneecap in an industrial accident, he'd had surgery, which had left him with a lot of pain. He was also embroiled in a dispute with worker's compensation and had consulted a lawyer.

A London police constable rapped on the window of the car and asked David to get out. He searched David and found eight one-gram vials of cannabis resin (hashish oil) in his pants pocket. The police arrested David and took him to the police station. They searched him again and found $619.45 cash on him. When he was told he was being charged with possession of a narcotic for the purpose of trafficking, David replied, "If that's the way it is, then that's what I'll have to face." David said he had originally purchased ten vials of hashish oil the day before for $150, and that the hashish oil was for his own use, to control the pain from his surgery. David claimed the cash was from a worker's compensation cheque.

Cannabis was legalized in Canada in 2018, but back in 1981, it was treated as a narcotic — a dangerous drug whose possession could attract serious criminal consequences. Under the Narcotic Control Act, the mere possession of cannabis could result in imprisonment for up to seven years, and if a person was found guilty of trafficking, they could face up to life imprisonment. Most people arrested with cannabis were unlikely to face such stiff prison sentences, but they remained a possibility. This was David's first offence, so he qualified for a lesser penalty of a fine up to $1,000 or up to six months' imprisonment, or both. He was convicted of possession of cannabis and sentenced to pay a fine of $300.

David's bigger problem was that the London police had charged him with possession of cannabis for the purpose of trafficking. Section 8 of the Narcotic Control Act presumed that anyone who unlawfully possessed a narcotic was selling it. It imposed a burden on the accused to prove they were not in possession for the purpose of trafficking. This type of clause was known as a "reverse onus" clause because it placed the onus of disproving an element of the crime on the defendant — the reverse of most crimes, where the onus of proving each element lies with the prosecution.

After a finding that he had been in possession of the narcotic, David brought a motion to challenge the constitutional validity of section 8 of the Narcotic Control Act.

History of the Case

The timing of David's case was significant because he was charged with illegal possession before the enactment of the Charter but still benefitted from its protections. *Oakes* began at the Ontario Court of Justice, where in 1982 the judge found that the reverse onus of the Narcotic Control Act violated the presumption of innocence contained in section 11(d) of the new Charter. That section provides that "any person charged with an offence has the right ... to be presumed innocent until proven guilty according to law in a fair and public hearing by an independent and impartial tribunal."

That was not the end of the analysis, however. Section 1 of the Charter guarantees the rights set out in the Charter "subject only to such reasonable limits prescribed by law as can be demonstrably justified in a free and democratic society." This means that the rights contained in the Charter — like the presumption of innocence in section 11(d) — are not absolute. They are subject to "reasonable limits." The question was, how would courts apply this "reasonable limits" requirement?

At trial, David was found guilty of possession, but he was acquitted on the more serious charge of possession for the purpose of trafficking. The judge said there was not a sufficient "rational connection" between possession and presumed trafficking. Therefore, section 8 of the Narcotic Control Act was not a reasonable limit under section 1 of the Charter.

The Crown appealed the decision to the Ontario Court of Appeal, which dismissed it in 1983. By this time, David's case had started to attract serious media attention. Canada's Minister of Justice Mark MacGuigan stated that he was not ready to rewrite the provisions of the Narcotic Control Act until the Supreme Court ruled on the issue. Soon after, the Crown appealed to the Supreme Court.

The case did not come before the Supreme Court until March 1985. Chief Justice Brian Dickson determined it would be heard by seven of the court's nine judges. The number of judges that sit a case is determined by the chief justice and can be five, seven, or all nine, depending on the complexity of the case.

No intervenors participated in the appeal. Intervenors are non-parties, who are not involved in the facts of the case itself but are interested in the legal issues the case has raised. They can be public interest organizations, like the Canadian Civil Liberties Association or the Criminal Lawyers' Association, or provincial attorneys general. Section 1 applies to every other section of the Charter, so it can potentially be at issue in every Charter case. If the Supreme Court were ever to decide to revisit "the *Oakes* test," there would likely be thirty intervenors or more knocking at the high court's door, seeking to intervene.

It's a Win! The Making of the *Oakes* Test

The Supreme Court ruled unanimously in David's favour. Chief Justice Brian Dickson wrote the majority decision, affirming that section 8 of the Narcotic Control Act violated section 11(d) of the Charter and could not be justified by the "reasonable limits" provisions set out in section 1.

The court then set out a several-part test for determining "reasonable limits." To begin, the court will examine whether the challenged legislation serves a "sufficiently important purpose." This threshold is a low one and almost always has been met. Next, the court will determine whether there is proportionality between the legislative measure that is being proposed and the government's objective. Here, Chief Justice Dickson set out a three-step test. First, there must be a rational connection between the law and its objective. Second, the law must not infringe upon a right more than is necessary to achieve its goal. Finally, the court balances the negative effects of the law against its positive effects.

From that day forward, the test for reasonable limits under section 1 became known as the *Oakes* test. It instantly became a fundamental component of Canadian constitutional law and the most cited case in the Charter era. It has been used in more than 1,700 written judicial decisions. It continues to help determine whether government actions breaching Charter protections can be justified. On the twenty-fifth anniversary of the Charter in 2007, a panel of experts voted *Oakes* the most influential case of the Charter era. The *Oakes* test influenced the drafting of the South African Constitution in 1996, as well as the constitutional law of other countries, such as Israel.

What Happened to David Oakes After the Case?

Because the Supreme Court of Canada had found section 8 of the Narcotic Control Act to be inconsistent with the Charter, and therefore to no force or effect, David would not be tried on the trafficking charge. The threat of prison was lifted. He had won his case, but he still had a criminal record for the possession conviction, which he carried with him for life. It is not known how this impacted his life. It may have hampered his ability to get certain jobs or to travel to the United States.

David remained in London until 2011, working as a cable installer, foreman, and staff supervisor. There is no indication that he ever had any further interactions with the criminal justice system. He preferred not to talk about his case, and rarely spoke to the media. Around 2011, he moved to Alberta, where he worked as a network installer and phone technician.

In 2012, David gave a rare interview to *The Lawyers Weekly* at a Calgary steakhouse. He reiterated what he had told the police in December 1981 when he was arrested: The cannabis oil was to help him deal with the pain he was suffering from an industrial accident. For good measure, he rolled up his pants leg to reveal a badly scarred shin and kneecap from the accident. Three decades later, David was still bitter about his dispute with workers' compensation, believing that his drug charge had affected its outcome. As for the landmark case that bears his name, David Oakes characterized it as "a pain in the ass."

6

A Boy with a Kirpan: Gurbaj Singh Multani

When Gurbaj Singh Multani moved to Canada at age eleven, he may have been a bit nervous about starting at a new school, making new friends, and learning a new language. But he certainly could not have expected that he would become the centre of a province-wide controversy. For almost five years, Gurbaj was swept up into a legal and political battle over his right to exercise his religious beliefs in a Quebec public school. In the end, he would secure an important win at the Supreme Court of Canada, but only after he was forced to withstand intense scrutiny and discrimination from the Quebec media and members of the public.

Moving to Montreal

Gurbaj was born in 1989 in Punjab, India. His family's move to Canada was spurred, at least in part, by an incident of religious discrimination in their home city of Amritsar. Gurbaj and his family adhered to Khalsa, an orthodox sect of Sikhism. Sikhs are a religious minority in India, with Hinduism being the dominant religion.

Gurbaj's father, Balvir Singh Multani, moved to Montreal on his own in 1996, and Gurbaj joined him in 2000. At the time, Quebec had a relatively small Sikh population of around eight thousand, with most Sikhs in Canada living in either British Columbia or Ontario. Gurbaj's prior schooling had been in English, and it probably would have been easier for him to enrol in an English school. However, Balvir saw the move as an opportunity for his son to learn both French and English. Gurbaj enrolled at École Sainte-Catherine-Labouré, a French public school in the LaSalle neighbourhood of Montreal. The school had a special "welcome class" that was intended to help integrate new immigrants into Quebec and teach them French as a second language.

By the time Gurbaj started at the school at the age of twelve, he had been initiated as an orthodox Sikh (also known as joining the Khalsa). Initiation represents a commitment to the Sikh faith. As part of their religious commitment, initiated male Sikhs adhere to a dress code that includes wearing a set of religious symbols commonly referred to as the Five Ks: (1) the kesh (uncut hair); (2) the kangha (a wooden comb); (3) the kara (a steel bracelet worn on the wrist); (4) the kaccha (a special undergarment); and (5) the kirpan (a metal dagger or sword). This fifth item, the kirpan, would become a subject of much controversy over the next six years.

Incident in the Schoolyard

Gurbaj wore his kirpan to school for a few months without incident. In fact, it seemed that staff and fellow students were unaware that he wore the small dagger under his clothing each day.

On November 19, 2001, Gurbaj was playing in the schoolyard when his kirpan fell out of his clothing. He picked it up, but not before a parent saw the dagger and reported it to the principal. Gurbaj soon found himself in the principal's office, where he was told he would need to remove the kirpan. Not wanting to abandon an important aspect of his faith, Gurbaj decided to go home and discuss the issue with his parents.

Gurbaj was held out of school while his parents worked on a resolution with the school board, the Commission scolaire Marguerite-Bourgeoys. Gurbaj could have returned to school at any time if he had abandoned his religious practice of wearing the kirpan, but he and his parents stuck to their convictions, attempting to reach a reasonable solution without having to abandon their religious beliefs.

On December 21, they came to a compromise — the school board would allow Gurbaj to wear the kirpan to school as long as he complied with a series of conditions, including keeping the kirpan sewn into a sealed cloth pouch under his clothes. However, this compromise needed to be ratified by the school's governing board before Gurbaj could return. Unfortunately for Gurbaj and his family, getting this agreement ratified would not prove to be a straightforward task.

Community Backlash

After the winter holiday break, Gurbaj was kept out of school for another month while waiting for his accommodation to be approved by the board. During this time, the school provided a tutor, who worked with Gurbaj at his home.

On February 12, 2002, the school's governing board refused to ratify the compromise, taking the position that, regardless of any safeguards taken, wearing a kirpan violated the school's code of conduct, which prohibited weapons and dangerous objects. This decision amounted to an absolute prohibition on wearing kirpans in the district's schools.

The board's decision was not made in isolation. Hundreds of parents pressured the board to ban kirpans, expressing concerns that they claimed were related to safety, though there had never been an instance of violence involving a kirpan in a Canadian school. In reality, the parents' fears were largely driven by a lack of understanding about Sikhs, and sometimes animus toward them, which had been exacerbated by local and world events in the early 2000s. The initial incident, when Gurbaj dropped his kirpan, took place just two months after the September 11 attacks in the United States. In the months and years following the attacks, there was a significant rise in Islamophobia, as well as racism directed at other groups, including Sikhs.

Administrative Appeal and a Short-Lived Win for the Multanis

After the decision of the governing board banning kirpans in district schools, the Multanis appealed to a review panel provided for under the school board's procedures. The panel unanimously upheld the kirpan ban on March 19, 2002. At this point, Gurbaj had been out of school for four months. After the review panel's decision, the board stopped sending a tutor to Gurbaj's home.

The Multanis had exhausted all routes of appeal within the school board. Their only remaining option was to challenge the kirpan ban in court. They retained Julius Grey, a renowned Montreal constitutional and human rights lawyer.

On March 25, 2002, Balvir Singh Multani filed a challenge in the Superior Court of Quebec, made both personally and on behalf of Gurbaj. Balvir asked the court to declare that Gurbaj had the right to wear his kirpan to school if it was sealed and sewn inside his clothing. He argued that these proposed measures would represent a reasonable accommodation of Gurbaj's freedom of religion and equality rights under the Charter, and under the Quebec Charter of Human Rights and Freedoms. Because the court challenge would take time and Gurbaj had now been out of school for more than four months, he also asked the court to make an immediate order allowing Gurbaj to wear his kirpan to school in accordance with the proposed measures.

On April 16, 2002, the court granted the interlocutory injunction allowing Gurbaj to return to school. At least until a final decision was rendered, Gurbaj would be allowed to wear his kirpan, as long as the dagger was sealed and sewn into his clothing, as had initially been proposed by the school board.

While Gurbaj may have been excited to return to school the next day, he did not receive a warm welcome. A police escort led him into the school as a group of parents stood outside, shouting racial insults at him. Still, Gurbaj said it felt good to be back at school and to see his classmates — though many of them stayed home. More than thirty parents kept their children out of school in protest. Quotes from these parents show that their concern was not just about safety. "We're talking about integration here," one parent said. Others were frustrated that newcomers to Quebec were not following the dominant social and cultural practices, and they were worried that Sikhs were "flexing too much legal muscle."

A month later, the superior court declared that Gurbaj had the right to wear his kirpan to school so long as he complied with a set of conditions similar to those he had previously agreed to. When asked if he was nervous about going to school after the court's ruling, Gurbaj responded, "When someone is fighting for his rights, he isn't scared."

A Disappointing Result from the Court of Appeal

Just ten days after the court issued its decision, the school board and the attorney general of Quebec announced that they would be appealing to the Quebec Court of Appeal. Balvir planned to continue the legal battle, but knew the ordeal had been hard on his son. Gurbaj finished the school year at École Sainte-Catherine-Labouré, but over the summer his family announced that he would be transferring to Greaves Academy, an English private school that would allow Gurbaj to wear his kirpan. Discussing the decision, Balvir said, "My son was in a depression all year. We don't want to send him into a new depression." Lawyer Julius Grey said that if their court challenge was successful, the family planned for Gurbaj to return to public school.

The Quebec Court of Appeal heard the case a year later, on June 9, 2003. The Multanis were joined by the World Sikh Organization, which participated as an intervenor. It took another nine months for the court to render its decision, which was finally released on March 4, 2004.

In a disappointing result for the Multanis and other Sikh residents of Quebec, the court of appeal reversed the superior court's decision and declared that the prohibition of kirpans in schools was constitutional. The court agreed that Gurbaj's religious belief was sincere, and that the board's decision was a limit on his religious freedoms, but said this limit was justified under section 1 of the Charter. The reasoning in the decision stated that the kirpan was a dangerous object, and that the accommodations proposed by the superior court would reduce safety standards at Quebec schools. The

Montreal teenager Gurbaj Singh Multani in the rotunda at the Supreme Court of Canada in Ottawa, Thursday, March 2, 2006.

court of appeals also endorsed the idea that allowing Sikh students to wear the kirpan would lead to other students bringing weapons to school in order to defend themselves.

Victory for Gurbaj and a Win for Sikh Students

From early on, Gurbaj and Balvir were prepared to take their case to the Supreme Court if they needed to. Now that possibility had become a reality. They appealed to the Supreme Court, and the case was heard on April 12, 2005, almost three and a half years after Gurbaj had dropped his kirpan in the schoolyard. A grade seven student when it all began, Gurbaj was now halfway through high school.

The World Sikh Organization again intervened in the case. They were joined by three other intervenors: the Canadian Civil Liberties Association, the Canadian Human Rights Commission, and the Ontario Human Rights Commission.

The Supreme Court of Canada unanimously overturned the school board's zero-tolerance kirpan policy, finding that the policy was an unjustified infringement on Gurbaj's freedom of religion, protected by section 2(a) of the Charter, which guarantees "freedom of conscience and religion." Writing for five of the eight judges, Justice Louise Charron found that Gurbaj's right to freedom of religion had been infringed because his religious belief was sincere, and that the board's decision resulted in a non-trivial interference with his ability to act in accordance with his belief. This was the easy part.

The more contentious issue was whether the infringement of Gurbaj's right to freedom of religion could be justified under section 1 of the Charter. Applying the *Oakes* test (chapter 5), Justice Charron found that ensuring a reasonable level of safety in schools was a pressing and substantial objective that met step one of the *Oakes* test. She emphasized that the objective was to maintain a *reasonable* level of safety, rather than maintaining absolute safety, and this framing would have important implications for the final step of the *Oakes* test, the proportionality analysis. Next, Charron concluded that the decision to ban kirpans in schools had a rational connection to the objective of maintaining safety, because the kirpan did have the potential to cause injury, even if such an incident was unlikely.

It was in the final step of the *Oakes* test — the minimal impairment analysis — where Justice Charron found that the complete ban of kirpans was unjustified. Under this step, the school board's decision did not need to be the absolute least intrusive option available to the board, but it did need to fall within a range of "reasonable alternatives." Charron rejected a number of arguments advanced by the school board claiming that kirpans were inherently dangerous. She said the risk of another student bringing a kirpan for violent purposes was quite low with the safeguards proposed by the superior court. (This is particularly true considering all the other sharp objects that are easier to obtain in a school, such as scissors and pencils.)

Justice Charron also pointed to the fact that Sikhs had been living in Canada for over a hundred years, yet there were zero reported cases of violence involving kirpans. Finally, she said the safety measures needed to fit the context at hand. In schools, teachers had the opportunity to form long-term relationships with students, monitoring their behaviour and anticipating potential issues. Charron concluded that kirpans were not inherently dangerous, and that the complete ban on them failed to meet the minimal impairment requirement of the *Oakes* test.

Finally, Charron stressed the importance of making reasonable accommodations for peoples' religious practices. Allowing Gurbaj to wear his kirpan demonstrated to him and others the importance of religious freedom and respect for minorities in Canadian society. The court declared the school board's kirpan ban null and inoperative.

Aftermath

A lot changed for Gurbaj over the course of his legal saga. It had begun when he was just twelve years old, but by the time the Supreme Court issued its final decision, Gurbaj was seventeen and about to graduate high school. After graduating in 2006, he completed CEGEP at the English-language John Abbott College in Montreal while working forty hours per week at Park'N Fly. In a 2008 interview with the *Montreal Gazette*, Gurbaj recounted a funny story:

> The supervisor on the night shift said to me, "Do you wear one of those things, too, (a kirpan) like that Sikh kid who got in all that trouble?"
>
> I said what do you mean "like that Sikh kid?" — I am that Sikh kid. I'm him!
>
> And he said, "Holy s--t! It's a small world!"

During the same interview, Gurbaj said he wanted to stay in Quebec. In the end, he wasn't able to. Gurbaj studied accounting at Concordia University, but it was difficult to find work in Quebec without being fully bilingual — an issue he faced as a direct result of his legal battle. "I wanted to learn French and that was the reason why I went to a French school. Since the case went through for six years, I wasn't able to attend a French school. By the time it was done, I was graduated from high school without being fully bilingual."

By 2020, Gurbaj had moved to Sudbury, Ontario, to work for the federal government. Despite the challenges he faced along the way, Gurbaj said he was glad to have helped establish an important right for all Canadians.

7

Teaching Hate in High School: Jim Keegstra

Canada has long been known as a country that champions diversity. Multiculturalism has been official federal government policy since 1971, and the 1982 Canadian Charter of Rights and Freedoms guaranteed equality rights against discrimination based on race, national or ethnic origin, colour, religion, sex, age, or mental or physical disability under section 15. In addition, the Charter guarantees freedom of expression under section 2(b). But Canada also has a history of hate that it has not been able to erase. Jim Keegstra forced the Supreme Court of Canada to determine the limits of freedom of expression and the scope of protection from hate speech.

Jim Keegstra from the Outside

James "Jim" Keegstra was born in 1934 in the southern Alberta town of Vulcan. Jim and his twin brother, John, were the youngest of seven children born to recent immigrants to Canada from Holland who were hard hit by the Great Depression. Jim's childhood was marked by financial instability and frequent moves. Amidst this uncertainty, religion was a constant stable force in his life. His parents had been members of the Dutch Reformed Church, but like many early immigrants to Canada, they eventually joined a new church. They were drawn to evangelism and fundamentalism, which emphasized emotion, faith, and a literal interpretation of the Bible.

In 1956, at the age of twenty-two, Jim married Lorraine, and they would have four children together. Jim worked hard to support his family. He initially worked as a mechanic, completing an apprenticeship in 1957. Soon after that, however, he decided to become a teacher. Jim enrolled at the University of Alberta at Calgary (now the University of Calgary), completed a two-year certificate program, and then did four years of summer courses to upgrade his degree to a Bachelor of Education, graduating in 1967. Throughout his schooling, Jim worked as a mechanic and a teacher to support his family.

After sojourns in Red Deer and Medicine Hat, the family moved to Eckville in 1967. Eckville is a small town outside of Red Deer with a population of roughly eight hundred people. With his degree in hand, Jim had been hired for a permanent position at Eckville's high school.

Jim taught social studies. His class was popular among students because it was relatively easy, and he entertained the class with jokes and discussions. He would often allow class discussion to veer away from the lesson plan, which the students enjoyed. At the same time, Jim was a strict disciplinarian who was known to whack students with his pointer if they misbehaved. He earned the nickname "the Pointer Prince" among students. His disciplinary style landed him in trouble in 1971, when he was charged with assault for hitting a grade nine student so hard that the student went home with welts on his back. The judge acquitted Jim, saying it was a "reasonable" use of his authority as a teacher.

Jim came to school early every morning to prepare his lessons and offer help to students. He got along especially well with one group of boys, helping them fix their cars and offering them life advice. Many people in the community viewed Jim as a good role model for students — he was a churchgoing man who did not drink or smoke. Jim and Lorraine would sometimes even open their home to those in need, including ex-convicts from the local jail.

While working as a teacher, Jim also became the mayor of Eckville. He was first elected as a town councillor, and then stepped in as interim mayor when the incumbent mayor fell ill. In the next election, in 1981, Jim was elected as mayor after running unopposed. Just one year later, the Board of Education fired Jim when they discovered he was ignoring the board's social studies curriculum, instead teaching his own version of social studies — one centring around his belief that Jews were evil.

Developing Antisemitic Beliefs

Jim Keegstra believed in a vast, all-encompassing Jewish conspiracy. Although many people in Eckville saw him as a good teacher and role model, Jim was in fact a deeply hateful man. He believed that Jews secretly ran the world, and that they wanted to destroy Christianity. In Jim's view, this Jewish conspiracy controlled global finance, media, and even most churches. He thought the Holocaust was a hoax manufactured by the Jewish conspiracy for sympathy, and that depressions, wars, and revolutions had been manufactured to meet the conspiracy's needs. He believed that most of the modern Christian world had been duped and he was one of the few people who knew the truth. He took it upon himself to teach this "truth" to his students.

Jim's hatred of Jews had developed over almost thirty years. He first learned about them when he was a child, reading about them in the Bible and in antisemitic pamphlets. His mother taught him that Jews were atheists because they rejected Christ. Jim admitted that he'd met very few Jews as a child — just his father's tailor and a few cattle buyers. Jim was also exposed to antisemitic views through Social Credit, a conservative political movement that his parents supported. The Social Credit movement in Canada had a long history of antisemitism.

The development of Jim's antisemitic views turned from a passive matter into an active one in his adulthood. Jim consumed a vast amount of antisemitic literature. By the late 1950s to early 1960s, when Jim was in his mid- to late twenties, he had reached his conclusions about the Jewish conspiracy.

Inside the Classroom of a Holocaust Denier

For more than ten years in Eckville, Jim imparted his antisemitic fantasies to classrooms full of impressionable students. There were no textbooks in his class. According to him, Jews had manufactured history, which then made its way into textbooks. Jim's students were expected to complete their assignments based only on notes from his lectures. One student said she received a failing mark on her essay after she did research at the library. Another student, who cited an encyclopedia, received a grade of 55 percent and the comment "Where did you get this? Built up by the Jewish press."

Jim taught his students that Jews were "treacherous," "subversive," "sadistic," "money-loving," "power hungry," and "child killers." If students didn't share the same views in their assignments, their grades would suffer. Jim's lessons followed a basic pattern: Jews were the source of the world's problems, and we would be better off without them. From a sampling of essays written by students in Jim's class, several students wrote positively of Hitler and agreed that "we should get rid of the Jews."

Jim Loses His Job and an Election

In late 1981, Jim received a series of written warnings from the school board superintendent. There had been a complaint from a parent, and Jim was told to stop teaching outside of the school curriculum. In October 1982, another parent filed a complaint after discovering that their son's social studies notebook was filled with notes about a Jewish conspiracy.

On December 7, 1982, the Board of Education voted 11–2 to fire Jim for continuing to teach his antisemitic conspiracy theories. While many people in Eckville supported the Board's decision, others supported Jim. Ninety-four students, almost half the school, signed a petition demanding that he be reinstated.

Jim appealed his dismissal, but the court upheld his firing as fair because he had failed to comply with written notices. Of course, Jim felt that the appeal hearing was a farce, and that it had been orchestrated by the Jewish conspiracy.

The Department of Education conducted its own investigation and concluded that Jim's teaching certificate should be revoked. Now unemployable as a teacher, he returned to the local garage to work as a mechanic.

Eckville residents demanded that Jim step down as mayor, with 240 of the 375 eligible voters signing a petition calling for his resignation. He refused to step down and was supported by town council in a 4–2 vote. However, he lost the next election a few months later, in October 1983.

Criminal Charges and Trial

After losing his job and the election, Jim was charged under the Criminal Code with the offence of "wilfully promoting hatred against an identifiable group." This was the beginning of a legal battle that would last more than ten years.

The hate speech section of the Criminal Code had been controversial since it was enacted in 1970, and Jim would become the first person successfully convicted under it. The recent enactment of the Charter in 1982 gave Jim the ammunition he needed to take his case all the way to the Supreme Court of Canada.

Jim hired Doug Christie, a lawyer from Victoria, British Columbia, who would go on to become notorious. While some described Christie as a defender of free speech, others pointed out that he only seemed interested in defending the speech of one particular group. Over the course of his career, Christie represented a long list of Holocaust deniers, neo-Nazis, and white supremacists, including Holocaust denier Ernst Zündel; Nazi prison guard Michael Seifert; and John Ross Taylor, the leader of the white supremacist Western Guard Party. But before becoming Jim Keegstra's lawyer, Christie was relatively unknown.

Before the trial, Jim applied to have his charges quashed on the basis that the hate speech provision of the Criminal Code violated his Charter right to freedom of expression, and that the section that provided a defence of truth violated the presumption of innocence. In November 1984, the Alberta Court of Queen's Bench rejected his application, and his case proceeded to trial. In July 1985, the jury convicted Jim of promoting hatred against an identifiable group, and he was fined $5,000. But the Alberta Court of Appeal overturned Jim's conviction, accepting his arguments that the Criminal

Jim Keegstra (left) leaves the Red Deer, Alberta, courthouse with his lawyer, Doug Christie, and a legal assistant on April 9, 1985.

Code provisions violated his Charter rights. The case was heading to the Supreme Court of Canada.

The Crown Takes the Battle to the Supreme Court

The Supreme Court heard Jim's case on December 5, 1989, amidst significant public attention. Numerous groups sought to participate in the hearing, and the high court granted intervenor status to the Canadian Jewish Congress, the League for Human Rights of B'nai Brith Canada, InterAmicus, the Women's Legal Education and Action Fund, and the Canadian Civil Liberties Association. The attorneys general of five other provinces also participated.

A year later, in December 1990, the Supreme Court issued its decision. In a close 4–3 ruling, the court sided with the Crown and found that the hate crimes provision of the Criminal Code was constitutional. Jim could indeed be prosecuted for wilfully promoting hatred against an identifiable group, in this case Jews.

The *Keegstra* case made an important pronouncement about the values underlying the guarantees of the Charter. Based on these values, a prohibition on the promotion of hatred was found to be a justified limit on freedom of expression in Canada.

Chief Justice Brian Dickson wrote for the majority, and Justice Beverley McLachlin (who would become chief justice a decade later, in January 2000) wrote a dissenting opinion. All of the judges agreed that hate speech and the promotion of hate propaganda were indeed protected as "expression" under section 2(b) of the Charter.

Chief Justice Dickson wrote that any attempt to convey meaning is considered expression under section 2(b). Expression that promotes hatred, as vile as it may be, is therefore protected. Because the hate speech provision of the Criminal Code placed a limit on protected expression, Dickson found it to be an infringement of Jim's freedom of expression rights. However, that didn't mean antisemites had free reign to spread their hate in Canada. The government could still place reasonable limits on the expression of hate propaganda, as long as those limits were justified in a free and democratic society. Dickson identified the objective of the hate speech provision as preventing the harm that flows from hate propaganda, including the pain suffered by members of the target group and the exacerbation of racial, religious, and ethnic tensions in Canada. To reach this conclusion, Dickson conducted a deep exploration of the different harms caused by the promotion of hatred. He placed particular emphasis on the dignity and self-worth of individuals who were the target of hate propaganda.

In her dissent, Justice McLachlin prioritized an unrestricted marketplace of ideas. In contrast, Dickson's approach prioritized the rights of those targeted by hate speech. Whereas Dickson spoke of a "uniquely Canadian" approach under section 1, McLachlin's views on freedom of expression were more closely aligned with the American conception of unfettered free speech. Dickson's "uniquely Canadian" approach to freedom of expression prevailed and remains the law today.

More Visits to Court and Jim's Final Years

The Supreme Court sent Jim's case back to the Alberta Court of Appeal, which ordered a new trial. Jim's second trial started on March 9, 1992, and lasted four months. This time, Jim represented himself in court. He was found guilty again, and the judge fined him $3,000. He once again appealed to the Alberta Court of Appeal, which ordered a third trial. The Crown appealed this decision to the Supreme Court of Canada, which restored Jim's conviction but again sent the case back to the Alberta Court of Appeal. Finally, the *Keegstra* case came to an end on September 26, 1996, when the court of appeal gave him a one-year suspended sentence and two hundred hours of community service.

Throughout thirteen years of fighting against his conviction, Jim remained steadfast in his hatred of Jews. One trial judge concluded that Jim could never be rehabilitated. Speaking outside the courthouse in 1992, Jim summed up why he kept appealing the court's decisions: "I've been found guilty, but I'm not guilty. A person who's not guilty should at least try to fight." Jim no doubt saw his countless losses in court as further evidence of a Jewish conspiracy.

Throughout his legal battle, Jim worked as a mechanic, and then later as a farmer with his twin brother, John. He and Lorraine eventually moved to Red Deer, where Jim worked as a custodian at an apartment building. Lorraine died in 2013, and Jim died just over a year later at the age of eighty.

Hate Speech and Antisemitism in Canada Since *Keegstra*

The *Keegstra* case is seen as a landmark victory vindicating Canada's anti-hate laws and the state's commitment to protect minority groups from hate. However, for members of Canada's Jewish community and other groups targeted by hate, *Keegstra* remains largely a symbolic victory. Although the Supreme Court upheld the constitutionality of Canada's anti-hate laws, the offence continued to be difficult to prosecute. In the decade that followed, just two criminal cases applied the provision.

Criminal law has not proven to be an effective tool in stopping antisemitic hate in Canada. More than three decades after *Keegstra*, antisemitism continues to be a prevalent issue. The past few years have seen an increase in the number of reported antisemitic incidents, including harassment, vandalism, and violence. *Keegstra* notwithstanding.

8

Canada's Most Notorious Child Pornographer: Robin Sharpe

John Robin Sharpe was an unsavoury poster child for freedom of expression. An unabashed user of child pornography and creator of pornographic stories about children, he rose to infamy by being at the centre of the storm over the limits of Canada's child pornography laws. He brought together a strange alliance of anti-pornography feminists and cultural conservatives against him. He had few defenders except for the staunchest of civil libertarians. In the end, his legacy is one of a child pornographer who became a sexual predator.

Robin's Early Years and Embrace of Counterculture

Robin Sharpe was born in Kelowna, British Columbia, during the Great Depression to working-class parents of English origin. Robin spent most of his life in Victoria. His family were strict Anglicans, and his religious upbringing influenced his childhood perceptions of right and wrong. Compared to other children around him, Robin felt governed by a sense of "hypermoralism" and was riddled with a sense of guilt for committing certain actions throughout his childhood and early adolescence. This feeling influenced his perception of sexuality and sexual relationships, connecting his childhood experiences to his pursuits as a writer in his late adulthood.

Robin's educational and professional history is diverse and unclear. He was a "jack of all trades" and took on many odd jobs in his youth. He decided to attend university and was able to do so through a bursary provided by the Imperial Order Daughters of the Empire, a charitable organization that focuses its welfare efforts on middle-class British immigrants. He intended to pursue architecture but decided political science and economics were more aligned with his interests.

After graduation, Robin worked as a town planner. He then ran a freelance home renovation business. He taught social studies and economics as a college instructor for four years. Robin's interest in political and social issues went beyond his teaching experience, and he did not shy away from expressing his political opinions. He was especially vocal when it came to the law and its relationship to personal choice. He was a strong proponent of the legalization of drugs, championing minimal government interference in people's use of psychedelics and other narcotics. He believed that federal legislation regulating and criminalizing narcotics impacted people's freedom of conscience under the Charter of Rights and Freedoms.

Robin married, had two children, divorced, and later came out as gay when he was in his thirties. He was a known member of the "countercultures" of the 1960s and 1970s. He was active in the punk scene of the West Coast and was known by many of the emerging bands of the time, whose members remembered him as a generous man with a keen interest in music and leftist politics. Robin seemed to have found his community, and to be flourishing in it.

Detention and Arrest

After his retirement, Robin began travelling, using his frequent travels across Asia as inspiration for his writing. Much of his writing was private and unpublished, and it was these works that brought him to court on charges of child pornography in the 1990s.

Canada lacked detailed legislation criminalizing the possession of child pornography until 1993. Initially introduced by Justice Minister Kim Campbell in 1991, the new Criminal Code provisions broadened the criminalization of child pornography to include possession of pornographic material in all forms, private or public.

Robin's seven-year-battle with the legal system began in April 1995, when he was detained by U.S. Customs officials in Seattle. He was on his way back to Canada from a trip to Sri Lanka when airport security flagged him for possession of marijuana he'd picked up during a layover in Amsterdam. Searching his belongings, Customs also found computer disks with fictional pornographic stories featuring young boys (referenced throughout the case law as the "*Boyabuse* stories") and about ten photographs of nude boys who were described as being in their late teens. U.S. Customs officials briefly detained Robin, but then released him.

Robin boarded a Greyhound bus bound for Vancouver, which was stopped by Canada Customs officials at the Peace Arch border crossing in Douglas, British Columbia, about forty minutes outside Vancouver. This was years before 9/11, and security was lax. Canada Customs officials were generally disinterested in Canadians returning from the U.S. In those days, it was possible to cross the border without ID. But Canada Customs took an interest in Robin because they had been tipped off by their American counterparts at the Seattle airport. Customs officials found the suspect photos and computer disks, and transferred Robin to the Surrey police station, where he was processed, held overnight, and released.

After that, nothing happened for over a year, and Robin assumed he was in the clear. However, in the interim, his case had been transferred to a special unit of the Vancouver Police Department dedicated to stopping the spread of child pornography.

When it landed on the desk of Detective Noreen Waters, the case immediately caught her attention. She obtained a search warrant for Robin's apartment, and on May 13, 1996, she led a team of three police officers who came knocking on the door of Robin's Kitsilano neighbourhood apartment at 7:55 a.m. During the search they seized photo albums of naked young boys, books, and more of Robin's writings. Robin was arrested, handcuffed,

Child pornography advocate Robin Sharpe attempting to avoid media by ducking into a store after leaving the British Columbia Supreme Court in Vancouver on Monday, July 19, 2004.

and taken to the police station. He was charged with two counts of possession of child pornography and two counts of possession of child pornography for the purposes of distribution or sale.

Robin contacted lawyers, who thought his case was relatively straightforward, with a predictable outcome. They advised him to plead guilty to the four charges laid against him. Robin disagreed and decided to go to trial, arguing that the charges, particularly those related to his *Boyabuse* stories, violated his Charter right of freedom of expression. He believed he was well within his rights to write and publish his explicit literary work, and he was prepared to stand his ground all the way to the Supreme Court of Canada.

Attracting Attention and Notoriety

After Robin's arrest, he began to attract media and public attention. A local television reporter showed up at his apartment and surreptitiously filmed him and his building. The local tabloid newspaper called him a "pervert," and posters about him started appearing in his neighbourhood, including in his building. This was but a prelude to the media storm to come.

Representing himself at the British Columbia Supreme Court, before Justice Duncan Shaw, Robin challenged the constitutionality of the child pornography law. Justice Shaw faced the tough legal task of balancing Charter rights with public concerns for children's safety. In his assessment of the facts, and with expert evidence on child pornography, Justice Shaw found that a conviction for simple possession of child pornography violated Robin's freedom of expression under the Charter. He said there was no evidence that the production of child pornography would be reduced if the Criminal Code's provision on simple possession was upheld. He therefore found that provision unconstitutional, and he declared it invalid.

Justice Shaw's decision, delivered on a Friday in mid-January, unleased a firestorm of criticism from the public and the media. In a time when most Canadians still watched television news, the decision was the lead story across the country, and it was front-page news in the weekend papers. It became the target of derision on op-ed pages and talk radio shows. Justice Shaw himself was the target of vilification and hate. He received death threats. The police provided security for him and his home. The volume and fury of the media and public reaction exceeded that of any court decision in Canada.

The decision sparked both public and political outcry. Justice Shaw was disparaged in the media as being "out of touch with Canadian values" and presenting a danger to children. The Reform Party — then the Official Opposition in Parliament — demanded that Minister of Justice Anne McLellan invoke the notwithstanding clause and override Justice Shaw's decision. Minister McLellan argued that the government would continue to defend the constitutionality of the child pornography provision on appeal, but it would not intervene in the legal process by invoking the notwithstanding clause.

The British Columbia Court of Appeal upheld Justice Shaw's decision. The British Columbia Civil Liberties Association had intervened to support Robin's freedom of expression claim, arguing that government should not censor or sanction expression. The strongest argument against Robin's conviction was the argument against criminalizing thoughts. The Civil Liberties

Association argued that the criminal law could be used to punish expression that incited or prompted harm or violence, but it could not be used to punish ideas that were simply not publicly accepted. It asserted that "such a blanket law 'bears the hallmarks of tyranny.'" The court of appeal agreed in part, concluding that criminalizing simple possession of child pornography, regardless of the content, was too broad and potentially violated an individual's Charter rights.

The court of appeal released its decision on Canada Day in 1999. Once again, the Canadian public was puzzled by the court's choice to protect Robin's freedom of expression rights over protecting children from exploitation and harm. The court of appeal decision, like the trial judgment, brought attention to the limits of freedom of expression and its potential for government control through criminalizing certain ideologies and forms of expression.

Reaching the Highest Court in Canada

The Crown appealed the decision to the Supreme Court of Canada, which heard the case on January 18, 2000. It was one of the first cases presided over by the new Chief Justice Beverley McLachlin, who was known as a champion of freedom of expression. She had written a dissent in the famous *Keegstra* case (chapter 7), and she would have found Canada's anti-hate laws unconstitutional as impermissible restrictions on freedom of expression.

The Supreme Court unanimously upheld the constitutionality of the child pornography provisions of the Criminal Code. In a decision that surprised many, Chief Justice McLachlin wrote for a majority of six justices, identifying two constitutional problems with the legislation. The first problem was that the law captured written materials (like Sharpe's *Boyabuse* stories) and visual representations (i.e., drawings or paintings) created by and held by a person for their exclusive personal use. The second problem was that the law captured photos or recordings created by or featuring a person that do not depict unlawful sexual activity and are held by the person exclusively for their private use. The justices expressed concern about the right to private possession and the possession of material depicting lawful sexual activities. But instead of striking down the legislation as unconstitutional, as is the usual practice in such cases, the high court "read in" these two exceptions to save the legislation, in other words declaring that the exceptions were now part of the law. Interestingly, a minority of three justices wrote an opinion that would have radically overhauled Canadian freedom of expression law by excluding child pornography altogether from protection under the law.

The public reaction to the court's decision was much more muted. The media, government officials, and many politicians had prepared for the high court to strike down the legislation as unconstitutional, as the courts below had. By taking the unusual step of reading in exceptions to the law, Chief Justice McLachlin had not only saved the problematic legislation but also staved off a media and political frenzy. With the Supreme Court having cured the constitutional issues with the legislation, there was nothing for government or parliamentarians to do. The story of the court's decision died within a few days.

Proposed Legislative Changes

The Supreme Court's decision set in motion a plan to amend the criminal law's approach to child pornography. In 2004, the Liberal government introduced a bill that would limit the statutory defence of artistic merit, to close any loopholes in existing legislation. The arts and literary communities in Canada sharply criticized the bill, asserting that it bordered on censorship because of the implications that determining the scope of "public good" would have on the legal perception of artistic works and expression. The bill died when Parliament was dissolved in 2004.

In the new Parliament, Minister of Justice Irwin Cotler introduced a new version of the bill. This time, the statutory defence of artistic merit was amended to a defence of legitimate purpose, meaning that the content in question had to pass a two-fold test: It must serve a legitimate purpose of administering justice, or a legitimate purpose to medicine, science, art, or education; and it could not pose any undue harm to children. The bill was passed into law and came into effect in 2005, giving those charged with simple possession of child pornography a legal defence of "legitimate purpose."

Retrial and New Offences

The Supreme Court ordered a retrial of Robin's convictions at the British Columbia Supreme Court, where the case was heard once again by Justice Shaw. At trial, Justice Shaw acquitted Robin of the charges of possession of written pornographic material. He found that Robin's written works did not counsel or advocate the commission of sexual crimes as set out in the Criminal Code and that they had artistic merit as literary works. Robin was therefore sentenced based only on his conviction for possession of pornographic photographs. He was ordered to serve 120 days of house arrest in his home in Victoria. Many people criticized this light sentence, not seeing it as sufficient penalty for Robin's actions.

Robin was now a convicted sex offender. He was required to register under Canada's National Sex Offender Registry and to report to the registry's offices if he moved or planned to travel. He had gained a reputation as "Canada's most notorious child pornographer" — and the media attention that came with it.

The Supreme Court battle was not the end of Robin's interaction with the Canadian legal system, however. In 2004, he was charged with indecent assault, gross indecency, and sexual assault in relation to an individual who was a minor at the time. Robin was acquitted of the sexual assault charge but convicted of the other two. He was sentenced to two years less a day, which he had served by the time the decision was appealed to the court of appeal. Once more, Robin was in the news as a sexual predator.

Robin seemed unable to keep out of trouble. In 2006, he was in the news again because he was wanted on a Canada-wide warrant. Now seventy-three years old, he had failed to comply with the requirements of the National Sex Offender Registry. His legal battles continued.

In 2008, Robin sought out a fresh start in Montreal and found a new community there where he lived for the last few years of his life. He remained in Montreal until his health deteriorated. Suffering from liver-related illnesses, he returned home to Victoria to seek treatment and be near his family in his last days. He passed away in 2015.

9

Championing LGBTQ Expression: Jim Deva, Bruce Smyth, and the Little Sister's Bookstore

Jim Deva and Bruce Smyth were partners of forty-two years who found themselves and their Little Sister's bookstore at the centre of a high-profile case regarding censorship, freedom of expression, and equality. In their battles in and outside the courts, the duo challenged homophobia and government censorship. Little Sister's became not only an iconic LGBTQ institution, but also a symbol of how ordinary people can stand up to government power.

Love in the Supermarket

Bruce Smyth and Jim Deva met in the grocery department at Hudson Bay Northern Stores in the Northwest Territories in 1972. Jim was from rural Alberta and was spending the summer up north while he was pursuing his Bachelor of Education degree at the University of Calgary. Bruce was from Winnipeg. When the two first met, Jim was uninterested in Bruce and requested a transfer to another section of the store in order to avoid him. But over time, the two became friends and then roommates. Bruce did not know Jim was gay until Jim came out to him during a car ride. Bruce was so shocked that he drove the car into a ditch, but he was quickly overwhelmed with joy because he was attracted to Jim. The two became romantic partners, and would soon become business partners as well, after they moved to Vancouver in the mid-1970s.

Little Sister's Is Born

The duo decided to open a bookstore in Vancouver with their friend Barb Thomas because they were frustrated by the lack of gay, lesbian, and queer reading material available at mainstream book shops. Jim recalled how important books on sexuality were for him when he was growing up, as they provided him with a sense of direction and worth during a confusing and complicated time in his life. Jim and Bruce wanted to cultivate a community where people from all walks of life could come together and feel like they belonged.

In 1983, Little Sister's Book & Art Emporium opened at 1221 Thurlow Street, in an old residential house. Jim and Bruce lived in the home and operated the bookstore from the upper level. Despite the lack of both heat and water in the building, Jim and Bruce quickly made it feel like home. At the time, it was customary for gay bookstores to have literary names such as Oscar Wilde, but the duo wanted their bookstore's name to be more fun. After pondering, they decided to name it after a grey cat that used to roam the aisles. The cat, named Little Sister, was known for her feisty and determined attitude, which mirrored Jim's and Bruce's personalities.

Little Sister's was quickly viewed as a safe haven for members of the LGBTQ community. It sold gay and lesbian erotic books, sexual health books, books on coming out, and other queer and trans literature, as well as gifts, clothes, and intimate adult toys. Little Sister's was more than just a bookstore; it was a community that cultivated a safe space for people to learn about their sexuality, ask questions about coming out to their families, and build a collective identity.

Not everyone welcomed Little Sister's. There were haters out there, and the bookstore was bombed three times between 1987 and 1992, causing damage to the property. Although it was never explicitly confirmed that the attacks were motivated by homophobia, the political climate and harmful societal norms at the time support the belief that the attacks were motivated by anti-gay hate. In 1996, Jim and Bruce moved the bookstore to 1238 Davie Street, where it remains to this day.

While the bombings were recognized as specific acts of terrorism, Jim felt like he was always living in a state of terror because of his vulnerability as an openly gay man. The 1980s and 1990s were a time when LGBTQ persons faced discrimination and harassment despite the advancement of gay rights in Canada. In 1981, Toronto police arrested three hundred men during a raid on four bathhouses for "indecent acts" in a bawdy house, and the following day a crowd of three thousand stormed the police precinct, as they believed the actions of the police were homophobic and anti-gay. The HIV/AIDS epidemic was at its height in the 1980s and further stigmatized LGBTQ individuals, especially gay men.

The Charter of Rights and Freedoms was enacted in 1982, with section 15 protecting equality rights, but discrimination on the basis of sexual orientation was not explicitly enumerated. In 1995, the Supreme Court of Canada did recognize sexual orientation as an "analogous ground" that was protected under section 15.

Although Jim and Bruce experienced homophobia, they put their fears on the back burner in order to keep Little Sister's alive. Despite public opposition to the bookstore, they were determined to create a space where being gay did not have to be taboo.

Little Sister's Becomes a Target of Big Brother

Homophobia and terrorist attacks on Little Sister's were not the end of Jim and Bruce's problems. In 1985, Canada Customs seized the store's Christmas order at the border. Jim and Bruce were devastated, as they needed these shipments for the bookstore to survive. Little Sister's imported 80 to 90 percent of its erotica material from the United States, which caused ongoing tensions between the couple and Canada Customs. In addition to erotica, the sexual magazines also included HIV/AIDS education and safe-sex materials, which were especially important in the 1980s and 1990s because they provided gay and queer individuals with necessary information to protect themselves during the HIV/AIDS epidemic.

Between 1984 and 1994, Little Sister's bookstore identified over 260 items that were detained by Canada Customs because they were deemed "obscene" materials. However, some of these materials had already been ruled admissible when imported by mainstream bookstores. The internal inconsistencies in what materials were being deemed "obscene," and thus prohibited, raised red flags for Jim, Bruce, the staff at Little Sister's, and supporters of the bookstore. While Canada Customs officers had the power under the Customs Act to determine whether an item was "obscene," Jim and Bruce were concerned about the arbitrary nature of the officers' power, since there were no consistent guidelines provided to determine the appropriate tariff classification on materials. The definition of "obscene" comes from section 163(8) of the Criminal Code, which defines obscene items as "any publication a dominant characteristic of which is the undue exploitation of sex, or of sex and any one or more of the following subjects, namely, crime, horror, cruelty, and violence." The bookstore continued to have most of its orders stopped at the border, where Canada Customs would delay, confiscate, prohibit, destroy, and misclassify Little Sister's imports.

The ongoing tensions with Canada Customs severely impacted Little Sister's operations and finances. Moreover, because the Customs legislation placed the onus on the importers to prove their materials were not obscene, it was very difficult for Jim and Bruce to reclaim their materials. Initially, the bookstore held demonstrations to protest the actions of Canada Customs, because they could not afford a legal battle against the government. However, after much reflection, Jim decided that more needed to be done. He believed he had a civic duty to fight the government, and that the fight to stand up for what he believed in was about more than the bookstore at that point. Both Jim and Bruce wanted to accomplish more than just gaining their seized items, so they decided to challenge Customs' decisions in court.

Little Sister's Versus Big Brother

In 1990, Jim and Bruce, alongside the BC Civil Liberties Association, filed a lawsuit claiming that the Customs legislation violated their section 2(b) rights to freedom of expression and their section 15(1) rights to equality under the Charter. The case was plagued by delays; it did not go to trial at the British Columbia Supreme Court until October 1994.

The trial spanned thirty-six days over the course of three months, and it took the judge, Justice Kenneth Smith, nearly a year to write his decision. Some viewed the constant delays in the trial as the government's attempt to bury Little Sister's in legal fees to force them to drop the case. Little Sister's incurred $250,000 in legal costs. In order to survive, the store's longtime manager, Janine Fuller, held fundraisers and book sales to raise funds to alleviate some of the legal debt. Despite the numerous obstacles in Little Sister's way, Jim and Bruce refused to back down.

In 1996, Justice Smith ruled that Canada Customs was arbitrarily applying the Customs Act and Customs Tariff, which constituted discrimination, but he rejected that the Customs legislation itself was unconstitutional. He found that while the legislation did violate freedom of

Jim Deva, co-owner of Little Sister's bookstore in Vancouver, April 13, 2006.

expression, it was justified under the *Oakes* test as a "reasonable limit" under section 1 of the Charter.

Disappointed with the outcome, Jim and Bruce — alongside the Civil Liberties Association — appealed Justice Smith's decision to the British Columbia Court of Appeal. In a 2–1 decision, the court of appeal affirmed the trial decision. The majority held that the spread of obscene materials, whether hetero- or homosexual, would be harmful to society, and thus the Customs legislation was a justified infringement on freedom of expression.

Little Sister's Appears Before All Nine Supreme Court Judges

Despite their exhaustion and increasing legal debt, Jim and Bruce refused to back away from pursuing their case and applied for leave to appeal to the Supreme Court of Canada. The Supreme Court agreed to hear their case, which was argued before all nine judges in March 2000. Little Sister's was represented by legendary constitutional litigator Joseph Arvay, who was a paraplegic. As Arvay argued the case from his wheelchair, the case really had the feel of David challenging the Goliath of the Canadian state.

David did not quite slay Goliath that day, but Little Sister's wounded the state and obtained a partial victory over Canada Customs. As in the courts below, a majority of the Supreme Court ruled that Canada Customs had violated Little Sister's section 2(b) freedom of expression rights, but found that the infringement was justified under section 1 of the Charter. However, the court struck down the provision of the Customs legislation that had placed the burden of proving that seized material was not obscene on Little Sister's.

Addressing Little Sister's equality claim, the majority of the court found that the Customs legislation was not in itself discriminatory, because the obscenity definition did not result in differential treatment based on sexual orientation. However, the majority recognized that Little Sister's had experienced adverse treatment from Canada Customs that impacted their "legitimate sense of self-worth and human dignity." Moreover, the court agreed that Canada Customs had treated homosexual materials different from heterosexual ones. Despite this, the court ultimately decided that the Customs legislation — both on its face and in its effects — did not create a basis for differential treatment on the grounds of sexual orientation. The Supreme Court of Canada majority found that Canada Customs had not infringed Little Sister's section 15(1) rights to equality. The court chastised Canada Customs but upheld the constitutionality of most of the legislation.

Little Sister's could claim a small but not insignificant victory in the court's decision to strike down the reverse onus provision that had required importers like it to prove that their seized material was not obscene. Henceforth, Canada Customs would have to prove that any material it was seizing was obscene.

A Short-Lived Victory

Despite not getting the full outcome they desired, Jim and Bruce were immensely grateful. After the decision, Jim stepped outside and stood on the Supreme Court stairs. He was amazed by the thirty or so lawyers and community activists around him and overwhelmed with gratitude and humility that they were here because they believed in the same cause as he, Bruce, and Little Sister's did.

Their victory was short-lived. In 2002, Little Sister's filed an appeal against a decision to seize several imported titles set to be delivered to the bookstore. After the Supreme Court decision, Canada Customs had implemented new guidelines on their screening procedures, but Little Sister's felt the changes would lead to more, rather than fewer, seizures. Under the new system, Little Sister's imports remained a target of Customs' delays and seizures. Little Sister's launched an entirely new legal battle against Canada Border Services Agency (formerly Canada Customs), which ended in 2007 when Little Sister's ran out of money for the lawsuit.

Jim and Bruce's Legacy

In September 2014, Jim tragically died after falling off a ladder in his backyard. He was just sixty-five years old. He was remembered as a kind-hearted man who cared for the marginalized and worked tirelessly to advance the goals of equality. Prior to his death, Jim was awarded the Community Hero of the Year Award from *Xtra*, an LGBTQ magazine. Jim didn't consider himself a hero. He wanted people to remember him as someone who empowered others to be active in fighting for what they believed in. In 2016, the Jim Deva Plaza was opened during Pride festivities in Vancouver as a memorial to his legacy. The plaza is located next to the famous rainbow crosswalks at Davie and Bute streets, and features a unique pink megaphone sculpture that symbolizes Jim's legacy as an advocate for free speech and gay rights.

Two years after Jim's death, Bruce decided to sell his share of Little Sister's. Jim was gone, and Janine Fuller had taken medical leave. Bruce decided to hand the store over to their longtime friend, Don Wilson, who continues to operate the store today. Bruce had planned to spend his free time in Mexico with friends and family, but after a week in Puerto Vallarta, he passed away at St. John Hospice following a battle with polycystic kidney disease and macular degeneration.

The two founders had passed, but Little Sister's lives on, a mecca for Vancouver's LGBTQ community. Little Sister's fulfilled Jim and Bruce's hopes and dreams when they moved to Vancouver and opened a store named for a spirited cat.

10

Even Prisoners Have the Right to Vote: Rick Sauvé

Rick Sauvé, a former hippie turned outlaw biker turned prisoner's rights advocate, was sentenced to life in prison for first-degree murder in the Port Hope 8 biker case of 1979. Like all prisoners, he was denied the right to vote. Through his legal challenge, Rick reminded Canadians that prisoners are still part of Canadian society, and they want to and have the right to participate in the political process.

Rick's Early Life and Cultural Influences

Richard "Rick" Sauvé was born into a working-class French-Canadian family. He and his ten siblings grew up in Cobourg, Ontario. After grade ten, Rick secured a job at the Davidson Rubber factory in Port Hope. At age twenty-one, he married his sixteen-year-old girlfriend, Sharon, who was five months pregnant and gave birth to a daughter in January 1974. The marriage encountered difficulties, with Sharon struggling to adapt to motherhood and feeling trapped in a relationship where she no longer loved her husband.

In the 1960s and 1970s counterculture movement, there was a complex and somewhat paradoxical connection between hippies and outlaw motorcycle gangs. The counterculture ethos embraced by hippies promoted peace, love, and an anti-establishment attitude. Biker gangs were also anti-establishment and rejected traditional values, but they were much more confrontational, and at times violent. During this time, groups such as the Hells Angels and Satan's Choice were popularized by Hollywood in movies like *The Wild One* and *Easy Rider*.

Joining Satan's Choice

After being fired from Davidson Rubber in 1975, Rick found a factory job and became the president of the local steelworkers union. His marriage was strained, and in 1977, Rick decided to join the Peterborough chapter of the Satan's Choice Motorcycle Club, finding a greater sense of belonging in the company of his biker "brothers" than with his wife. Rick was sponsored by his friend, Satan's Choice member Merv Blaker.

Rick soon clashed with William "Heavy" Matiyek, the sergeant-at-arms of the rival Golden Hawk Riders. Matiyek, known as the "town bully" in Port Hope, regularly carried a shotgun and a handgun. In July 1977, while Rick was at work, Matiyek shot at his house, forcing Sharon and their daughter to seek shelter. Outraged, Rick confronted Matiyek with a baseball bat. Matiyek apologized for the shooting incident and admitted to being heavily under the influence of drugs when he attacked the Sauvé residence.

Shootout at the Queen's Hotel

On the night of October 18, 1978, Rick received a call from a local drug addict, informing him that Matiyek was at the Queen's Hotel and wanted to meet Rick urgently. Fearing a violent confrontation, Rick attempted to round up fellow Satan's Choice members to accompany him. Unable to reach many local members, he contacted Merv Blaker from the Peterborough chapter, and later called the Toronto chapter for support as well.

Arriving at the Queen's Hotel with Blaker, Rick could feel the tension in the air. He sat down at the table with Matiyek, who was visibly intoxicated and brandished a handgun at Rick, threatening him and preventing him from leaving. Rick's fellow Satan's Choice biker gang member Gary "Nutty" Comeau arrived, as did Lorne Edgar Campbell, who had previously beaten Matiyek in a fight. When Matiyek reached for his gun, Campbell shot him three times. It was chaos. Rick and the other bikers fled the hotel. Rick and Blaker headed to Satan's Choice's Toronto clubhouse and later to the home of another biker. Matiyek was pronounced dead on arrival at the hospital.

At the time of the shooting, Rick had been in Satan's Choice for about a year.

Sauvé's Arrest and Trial

In December 1978, Rick was arrested on charges of conspiracy to commit murder. The charges were later increased to include first-degree murder. He was twenty-six years old and faced the possibility of life in prison. He was prepared to accept a plea bargain and plead guilty to a lesser charge, but the Crown attorney wanted all of the accused to accompany their guilty pleas with a statement that killing Matiyek had been a premeditated act. The accused bikers — known as the Port Hope 8 — rejected the deal. Although Campbell testified that he had shot Matiyek in self-defence, the jury convicted Rick and Comeau of first-degree murder, and they were sentenced to life imprisonment. Four other Satan's Choice members were convicted of second-degree murder.

Rick displayed no emotion at the sentencing, but he later broke down in tears in front of his wife and daughter, acknowledging the likelihood that he might never see them again. He was twenty-seven.

Rick's Life in Prison

Rick began serving his sentence at Millhaven Institution, a maximum-security prison in Bath, Ontario, about thirty minutes from Kingston. Less than a decade old at the time, Millhaven would later become home to many infamous inmates, including Paul Bernardo (the "Scarborough Rapist" and "Schoolgirl Killer"), Bruce McArthur (the serial killer of homosexual men in Toronto's Gay Village), Omar Khadr (a Canadian who had been convicted in the U.S. of terrorism for fighting with the Taliban in Afghanistan as a teenager), and other members of the Port Hope 8. The prison was popularized by the Tragically Hip in their song "38 Years Old," about a prisoner escape.

Rick wasn't prepared for prison. He had no concept of what happened inside. He was scared, and he didn't know if he would ever get out. During his first three weeks at Millhaven, he saw three inmates killed by other prisoners, and during his full four and half years there, he saw a total of twelve prisoners killed by others. He also claimed that the prison guards routinely beat the prisoners. Rick thought about giving up and committing suicide. He also pondered escape.

In 1983, Rick was transferred to Collins Bay Institution, a multi-level facility in Kingston. During his time there, Rick converted to Buddhism, renounced his former lifestyle, and became a pacifist. He practised transcendental meditation and refused the material possessions allowed inmates, such as a radio, a TV, or books. Despite his rejection of materialism, he held on to one luxury: alcohol. Using the fresh fruit he was provided as a religious accommodation, Rick brewed moonshine in a hole in the wall of his cell.

At Collins Bay, Rick earned his high school diploma, a BA in psychology from Queen's University, and an honours BA in criminology from the University of Ottawa. In May 1987, at age thirty-four, Rick attended his convocation at Queen's University, wearing his convocation gown and hat along with handcuffs and chains. He was then marched out by police and taken back to Collins Bay.

Rick and Sharon got divorced while he was in Collins Bay. The split was a long time coming. In 1989, Rick started to date Michele Bradley, a criminology student from the University of Ottawa who became infatuated with him when her criminology class visited Collins Bay to study him as an example of a "lifer" prisoner. Rick and Michele married in 1990 at the Collins Bay prison chapel.

Launching the Challenge for the Prisoner's Right to Vote: *Sauvé I*

In 1983, a year after the Charter of Rights and Freedoms came into force, Rick launched a constitutional challenge to the law that disqualified prisoners from voting in federal elections, initiating a ten-year legal battle with the federal government. Rick argued that the Canada Elections Act violated section 3 of the Charter, which says: "Every citizen of Canada has the right to vote in an election of the members of the House of Commons or of a legislative assembly and to be qualified for membership therein." Parliament had taken the right to vote away from prisoners. That was clear. The question was whether that deprivation met the "reasonable limits" of section 1 of the Charter.

Rick lost his challenge at the Ontario Superior Court on the basis that the exclusion of criminals from voting was justified as necessary to reinforce the concept of a "decent and responsible citizenry" in a liberal democracy. The Ontario Court of Appeal reversed this judgment. All nine judges of the Supreme Court heard the appeal on May 27, 1993. Surprisingly for a case of such importance, the Supreme Court delivered its decision immediately, in a brief three-paragraph judgment ruling in Rick's favour. The high court held that the restriction on prisoners' right to vote in the Canada Elections Act was too broad and failed the *Oakes* test.

Rick's victory was short-lived. The federal government responded by amending the law to deny the right to vote only to those inmates serving a sentence of two years or more — Parliament's attempt to tailor the limitation to make it "reasonable" so that it would pass the *Oakes* test. Rick launched another challenge to the legislation, which became known as *Sauvé II* (and his first case thereby becoming known as *Sauvé I*).

Sauvé II

By the time the Supreme Court decided *Sauvé II*, it was 2002, nearly nineteen years after Rick had started *Sauvé I*. Again, all nine judges heard the appeal. This time, however, the court was sharply divided, ruling 5–4 in Rick's favour. Writing for the majority, Chief Justice Beverley McLachlin declared that the right to vote is a fundamental democratic right, essential to the functioning of a free and democratic society, and that the government failed to demonstrate the reasonableness of the new limit on that right. The majority stated that a prohibition on prisoners voting was neither proportional nor rationally connected to any valid social objective, and therefore could not be saved by section 1 of the Charter.

Rick Sauvé, 2017.

The four justices in dissent argued that the country's highest court should defer to Parliament's judgment in cases like *Sauvé II* that involve a clash of social or political ideologies. They accepted the justification offered by Parliament in defence of the restriction on prisoners' right to vote and would have upheld the law as constitutional.

Nevertheless, after nearly twenty years, Rick had won the right to vote for himself and for all prisoners. His victory gave his fellow prisoners hope for community engagement. Around election time, they would read the newspapers, watch television, and discuss the political parties and their platforms. By securing the right to vote, inmates could now express their ideas through the ballot box, instead of only in hallway conversations.

A New Life

In 1995, at the age of forty-two, Rick was released on parole, having served sixteen years in prison. After his release, he sought to mentor prisoners to reject criminality as a way of life. Soon after his release, Rick began working with St. Leonard's House LifeLine and PeerLife Transition Services in

Windsor, Ontario, helping to prepare "lifers" like himself to successfully transition from a correctional environment to life on parole. He provided individual counselling, release planning, and parole hearing assistance. Rick assisted at over four hundred parole hearings and has presented workshops for both the Parole Board of Canada and the Correctional Service of Canada.

Rick developed and ran a variety of institutional self-help groups within the prison system. He created a program for prisoners whose crimes involved gang culture that is delivered at Collins Bay and other prisons in Ontario. He frequently speaks to community groups, high schools, universities, and youth at risk. He has also made presentations to media and parliamentary committees and written articles for several publications and journals.

In 2017, Rick was awarded the Ed McIsaac Human Rights in Corrections Award by the Office of the Correctional Investigator. The award honours those who demonstrate a lifelong commitment to improving corrections and protecting the human rights of the incarcerated. In receiving the award, Rick became the first prisoner to be honoured.

Private Life

Rick is now a grandfather in his seventies. He lives outside Lindsay, Ontario, with his wife, Michele, and a variety of cats. Like many retirees, Rick works around the home and in his garden. He also designs and builds custom cabinetry. He is proud of the case that bears his name and the precedent it established, but it came at a cost for him and for his family. His grandchildren always knew that their grandfather had been in prison, but when they studied his case in school, they felt stigmatized.

Rick has journeyed a long way from the twenty-six-year-old Satan's Choice biker, giving up almost everything from his former life. Except one thing: He still rides a motorcycle.

11

Abortion Crusader: Dr. Henry Morgentaler

One of his biographers called Henry Morgentaler "a difficult hero." His detractors might have preferred "an unrelenting villain." Dr. Morgentaler was Canada's most famous abortionist and crusader for women's access to abortion. He often provoked strong emotions. He landed before the Supreme Court of Canada three times, forever changing Canadian law and guaranteeing women the right to abortion across the country.

A Childhood Interrupted

Henryk "Henry" Morgentaler was sixteen years old when the Nazis overran his hometown of Lodz, Poland, in 1939, confining all Jews to the Lodz ghetto. Henry's father was sent to a concentration camp, where he perished, while his older sister was deported to her death at Treblinka. Henry and his younger brother, Mike, were deported to Auschwitz with their mother. Prodded forward by Nazi guards as they exited the train, the two brothers were separated from their mother and never saw her again. Selected for work rather than the gas chambers, Henry and Mike were sent to the notorious Dachau concentration camp. The brothers were liberated by American troops on April 29, 1945. Henry was twenty-two, weighed just seventy pounds, and had no teeth left.

Henry located and later married his high school girlfriend, Chava (Eva) Rosenfarb, a survivor of the Bergen-Belsen concentration camp. Henry, Mike, and Chava, with Chava's surviving family, moved to Feldafing, Germany. Henry aspired to become a doctor and attended a German university on a scholarship from the United Nations Relief and Rehabilitation Administration.

Still in ill health, Henry was hospitalized with jaundice from viral hepatitis when he received his acceptance to medical school at Marburg-Lahn University.

Becoming Dr. Morgentaler

Henry set his sights on practising medicine in North America. The Canadian government had a longstanding anti-Jewish immigration policy, well documented by Irving Abella and Harold Troper's book *None Is Too Many: Canada and the Jews of Europe 1933–1948*. Canada accepted former Nazis and their collaborators more willingly than Jews who had survived the horrors of the Holocaust. Despite the odds, Henry and Chava immigrated to Montreal in 1950. Henry completed medical school in 1953 at the Université de Montréal and began his general practice in 1955 after obtaining Canadian citizenship.

Henry was struck by how much religious beliefs shaped public policy on reproductive health and limited his patients' access to contraception and abortion. As a member and then president of the Humanist Fellowship of Montreal, he advocated before Parliament's Standing Committee on Health and Welfare on behalf of the Humanist Fellowship to speak out against Canada's laws that made abortion illegal.

As news of Dr. Morgentaler's view on abortion were publicized, women sought his help with unwanted pregnancies. At first he refused because he feared losing his medical licence. But once he finally agreed, he never turned back.

Police Raid the Morgentaler Clinic

By 1969, Dr. Morgentaler's practice centred on family planning, IUD insertions, oral contraceptives, vasectomies, and abortions. Attitudes toward sex, contraception, and abortion were changing. Justice Minister Pierre Trudeau famously remarked, "The state has no place in the bedrooms of the nation." Trudeau's omnibus criminal law reforms in 1969 made hospital-based abortions legal, but only with the consent of at least three doctors and if the woman's health or life was at risk. However, hospitals were not required to offer abortions, and Dr. Morgentaler saw how board-approved hospital-only abortions meant women in conservative communities and provinces would be denied meaningful access. Convinced that private abortion clinics were needed to bridge these gaps, he opened such a clinic in Montreal.

The first of many police raids occurred on June 1, 1970. The police arrested Morgentaler, clinic staff, and patients. They were later released. Morgentaler was defiant and continued his work performing abortions.

On August 15, an undercover police officer posing as the husband of a woman seeking an abortion arrested Dr. Morgentaler before the procedure began. Other plainclothes officers arrested patients and staff, who were taken to the police station along with Morgentaler. Dr. Morgentaler spent two nights in police custody. This time, he was formally charged with illegally performing abortions. Protests began immediately. People picketed outside Montreal's Palais de Justice and across Canada in support of Morgentaler.

Morgentaler's First Criminal Trial

The public discourse on abortion was changing. Dr. Morgentaler's first criminal trial took place in 1973, the same year that the United States Supreme Court decided *Roe v. Wade*, recognizing a woman's constitutional right to an abortion. Dr. Morgentaler went on the offensive to capture public sentiment. He openly admitted to performing over five thousand abortions in violation of section 251 of the Criminal Code, and he called on other physicians to break the law. He held press conferences in French and English and badgered cabinet ministers. He had CTV film a consenting patient's abortion procedure, which audaciously aired on Mother's Day. The program galvanized anti-abortion sentiment, and protests began in front of Morgentaler's clinic.

Antisemitic sentiment also reared its head with placards like "Remember Auschwitz."

Morgentaler chose lawyer Claude-Armand Sheppard, the former president of the Quebec Civil Liberties Union, to defend him. The trial began in October 1973 before Associate Chief Justice James K. Hugessen. Morgentaler faced six counts of performing illegal abortions in violation of section 251 of the Criminal Code. Sheppard raised the common law defence of necessity. The validity of the defence became a main issue in this and subsequent cases. Morgentaler and Sheppard requested a French-speaking jury, taking a risk that, although predominantly Roman Catholic, the French-Canadian jurors would be moved by testimonies of "real problems of real people in real circumstances."

The defence's gamble paid off. After a four-week trial, the jury reached a not guilty verdict.

The Crown immediately appealed Morgentaler's acquittal, and on April 26, 1974, the Quebec Court of Appeal unanimously reversed the lower court's decision. However, instead of ordering a new trial, the court of appeal substituted a guilty verdict and returned the matter to the trial judge for sentencing. This was highly unusual. Justice Hugessen then sentenced Dr. Morgentaler to eighteen months in jail, followed by a three-year ban from performing abortions. However, Justice Hugessen delayed the jail term to allow Dr. Morgentaler's appeal to the Supreme Court of Canada.

Supreme Court, Round I, 1974

Chief Justice Bora Laskin, a liberal and civil liberties–oriented judge, presided over the Supreme Court. Justice Laskin's liberal leaning, and the potentially persuasive effect of *Roe v. Wade*, gave Morgentaler some optimism. However, the more conservative judges were inclined to uphold Parliament's decision on the limits of abortion. In April 1974, in a 6–3 decision, the Supreme Court confirmed the Quebec Court of Appeal's decision and reinstated the guilty verdict.

Parliament responded by changing the law to prohibit an appellate court from ever again substituting a guilty verdict after a jury acquittal. However, Dr. Morgentaler's sentence stood, and he turned himself in to the authorities.

Dr. Henry Morgentaler at a news conference in Halifax, Nova Scotia, in 1989. Morgentaler told reporters that he performed seven abortions in his Halifax clinic and challenged the Nova Scotia government to prosecute him.

Prison and Another Acquittal

Dr. Morgentaler, now fifty, began his prison term in Montreal's Bordeaux Prison. After two months, he was transferred to the Waterloo prison, a lower-security prison in the Eastern Townships, where he suffered abuse. He was dragged from his cell and thrown in solitary confinement as punishment for sleeping with his bare feet uncovered. The guards forced him to strip naked. Eventually, Dr. Morgentaler's prison time was cut short when he suffered a heart attack and was transferred to a nursing home on doctor's orders.

While he was in jail, a jury acquitted Morgentaler of another round of charges for illegally performing abortions. However, this time, the Quebec Court of Appeal upheld the jury acquittal, ruling that the common law defence of necessity applied to section 251 of the Criminal Code and that the trial judge had erred in law by failing to instruct the jury on that defence.

Expanding Across Canada: New Tensions and Money Problems

With the goal of expanding abortion access, in 1983, Dr. Morgentaler opened clinics in Winnipeg and Toronto and announced plans for a Halifax clinic. Police repeatedly raided the Winnipeg clinic and arrested staff, including on opening day. The Toronto clinic became the site of near constant pro-life, anti-abortion protests and was also raided by police. All of it was a financial drain on clinic resources. At the same time, tensions arose between Dr. Morgentaler and some of the women's groups that were financing his legal defence. Some feminists were unhappy that he had become the central figure in the broader feminist movement for abortion rights.

Money became a serious problem in the 1980s. Dr. Morgentaler's medical licence was suspended, and he faced mounting legal debt. Some supporters questioned his spending to furnish his clinics. Even the Canadian Abortion Rights Action League, which consistently supported Dr. Morgentaler and raised funds for legal fees, had concerns that he was misspending the money on non-essentials.

Supreme Court, Round II: A Historic Decision

Two juries had already acquitted Dr. Morgentaler, when a third jury, in Ontario, acquitted him and two other doctors of illegally performing abortions. It seemed no jury in Canada would convict him for performing abortions. Nonetheless, the Ontario Court of Appeal set aside Morgentaler's acquittal and ordered a new trial. Once again, Morgentaler appealed to the Supreme Court of Canada. Ontario's government agreed not to shut down Morgentaler's Toronto clinic pending the appeal.

Seven Supreme Court justices heard the appeal over three days in October 1986. Two differences from the 1974 case proved critical. First, effective in 1982, the Canadian Charter of Rights and Freedoms had constitutionalized a broad array of rights, including the section 7 "right to life, liberty and security of the person and the right not to be deprived thereof except in accordance with the principles of fundamental justice." Second, also in 1982, Prime Minister Pierre Trudeau had appointed Justice Bertha Wilson, the first female Supreme Court justice.

This time, the court went to the heart of the matter, declaring the Criminal Code prohibition on abortion unconstitutional and vacating the charges. Never again would Dr. Morgentaler or his colleagues face criminal charges and jail. The 5–2 decision was a whopping 156 pages long, with four sets of reasons.

Chief Justice Brian Dickson and Justice Antonio Lamer issued the lead decision. They declared that attaching criminal penalties for women who choose not to carry pregnancies to term, and the systemic, bureaucratic delays for an approved hospital abortion, infringed women's security of the person. This infringement did not accord with principles of fundamental justice as required under section 7. Nor did it meet the *Oakes* reasonable limit test. Similarly, the concurring opinion of Justices Jean Beetz and Willard Estey found that the inherent delays in the procedural requirements for an approved abortion would likely endanger women's lives and health and were manifestly unfair.

Justice Bertha Wilson's concurring opinion was a decision for the ages. Rather than delve into academic and procedural reasoning, she found that the right to liberty guaranteed by section 7 gave women a positive right to choose whether to access abortion services. Further, she wrote, the threat to women's psychological and physical security posed by section 251 of the Criminal Code infringed section 7 rights. She stated: "Liberty in a free and democratic society does not require the state to approve the personal decisions made by its citizens; it does, however, require the state to respect them ... The question then becomes whether the decision of a woman to terminate her pregnancy falls within this class of protected decisions. I have no doubt that it does."

Justices William McIntyre and Gérard La Forest dissented, finding that section 7 did not create new rights and that "the solution [to the abortion question] in this country must be left to Parliament."

The deed was done. There was now no law restricting abortion.

Supreme Court, Round III: Challenging the Maritimes

Parliament twice tried and failed to fill the abortion regulation void left by the Supreme Court's striking down of Criminal Code section 251. Then

Nova Scotia enacted legislation making it a provincial offence to perform abortions and several other medical procedures outside of hospitals. Many thought the legislators were seeking to curtail Dr. Morgentaler's plans for a Maritime-based private clinic. Once again, Dr. Morgentaler took up the challenge, opened a Halifax clinic, was charged, and wound up before the Supreme Court of Canada.

The Supreme Court's 1993 decision held that Nova Scotia's law was outside the provinces' constitutional jurisdiction, stating that "only the federal government, through the Criminal Code, can legislate access to abortion." Morgentaler had won his third and final victory at Canada's highest court.

Battles and Honours

Dr. Morgentaler continually pressed ahead to ensure women's access to abortion. When a firebomb destroyed the Toronto clinic, he opened a new one. He opened a clinic in Fredericton, New Brunswick, and sued the governments of Prince Edward Island, Nova Scotia, and New Brunswick over access to and payment for abortions.

Dr. Morgentaler showed no sign of slowing down. He continued to attract media attention and magnetize anti-abortion protests. When Western University awarded him an honorary degree in 2005, it triggered protests, a petition signed by twelve thousand people, and the withdrawal of $2 million in donor funds. Dr. Morgentaler responded at the award ceremony, saying, "Well-loved children grow into adults who do not build concentration camps, do not rape, and do not murder."

Protests continued to follow Dr. Morgentaler even after his retirement in 2006 following heart bypass surgery. The announcement in 2008 that he was receiving the nation's highest honour, the Order of Canada, again ignited protest. The Canadian Conference of Catholic Bishops decried that honouring Dr. Morgentaler undermined the Order's significance. Some previous recipients returned their medals, and picketers protested outside the ceremony.

On May 29, 2013, Dr. Henry Morgentaler died of heart failure in his home in Toronto, surrounded by family members. He was ninety years old. He had been relentless in championing abortion rights.

12

A Woman Who Would Not Submit: Chantale Daigle

Most constitutional challengers are involved in long, expensive litigation that can take years or even decades. Chantale Daigle's interaction with the legal system lasted a matter of weeks. It was brief, intense, and extremely stressful, but she vindicated not only her own right to control her body, but the right of all women to do so.

An Ordinary Woman Thrust into an Unordinary Situation

Chantale Daigle was born in 1968 in Chibougamau, Quebec, a mining town of less than ten thousand people about a six-hour drive north of Quebec City. Her parents were divorced and living in different cities by the time Chantale moved to Montreal as a young woman. Chantale had a close relationship with her parents and her two brothers and one sister. She considered herself something of a free spirit.

Chantale was twenty-one when she met twenty-five-year-old Jean-Guy Tremblay at a Radio Shack electronics store in Montreal. She was working as a restaurant server at the time, led an active life, and dreamt of one day owning her own restaurant. After a couple months of dating, under pressure from Jean-Guy, Chantale quit her restaurant job and started a day job as a receptionist. Soon afterward, in February 1989, Jean-Guy moved in with Chantale. Chantale's siblings started to notice concerning changes in her behaviour. She didn't seem to be her usual enthusiastic self. Even her voice sounded different. Jean-Guy was jealous and controlling, abusive and sometimes violent.

A few months into their relationship, Jean-Guy insisted that Chantale stop using contraceptives. She discovered she was pregnant in March 1989. The two had been together for four months. During the early stages of her pregnancy, Jean-Guy became physically violent. In early July, after five months of living together, Chantale left Jean-Guy and returned to Chibougamau to live with her father.

Bodies as Battlegrounds

A year before, in 1988, the Supreme Court had struck down Canada's restrictive abortion law in *Morgentaler*. But it had not also recognized that women had a right to control their own bodies and make their own reproductive choices. Only Justice Bertha Wilson would have gone that far, but she was the lone female voice on the court at the time.

Chantale arranged to have an abortion at the hospital in Sherbrooke, about an eight-hour drive from Chibougamau. At this point, her story was not that different from those of other young women who found themselves with an unwanted pregnancy after leaving an abusive relationship. But Chantale soon found herself in an unprecedented situation, with Jean-Guy trying to exert control over her body.

The Interlocutory Injunction

When they broke up, Jean-Guy had made it clear that he would not pay child support for any baby. Chantale had told him that she would not carry her pregnancy to term. She did not expect him to put up much resistance. Chantale underestimated just how controlling Jean-Guy was.

One morning in July, Chantale was en route to Sherbrooke for a doctor's appointment, accompanied by her brother Mario and sister-in-law, when they crossed paths with Jean-Guy's car. Mario instinctively pulled over at a telephone booth. Although it is unclear whom he called, he learned that a bailiff had delivered an interlocutory injunction, effective between July 7 and 17. An interlocutory injunction is a temporary order from a judge prohibiting someone from doing something. In this case, it prohibited Chantale from getting an abortion. Such an order had never before been issued in Canada. If Chantale proceeded with the abortion, she would be liable for a $50,000 fine and up to two years imprisonment.

Chantale was determined to challenge the injunction, and a court date was set for July 17. Journalists began bombarding Chantale. Overnight, she felt, her private life had become public. Jean-Guy was receiving similar attention, but he did not seem to mind. He once phoned Chantale's brother to share the news that his photo was on the front page of the *Journal de Montréal*.

The night before her court appearance, Chantale slept in a tent in a campground near Val d'Or. She was so confident she would win, she rebooked her abortion appointment for July 19.

Surprised by the Courts

Things did not go as planned for Chantale on July 17. Something that stood out to her was that neither side called witnesses. There was a clear discrepancy between her expectations of the legal system and the framing of her case by legal experts. Her individual circumstances and the domestic violence she faced were not the focus. *Tremblay v. Daigle* became about the legal question of the rights of a fetus.

Justice Jacques Viens of the Superior Court of Quebec upheld the interlocutory injunction. The court relied on section 1 of the Quebec Charter of Human Rights and Freedoms, which states that "every human being has a right to life, and to personal security, inviolability and freedom." The appearance of the words "human" and "person" throughout the Quebec Charter was cited as evidence that the legislature intended to differentiate between these categories, and that fetuses count as humans, with a positive right to life in the meaning of section 1.

Chantale's lawyer, Daniel Bédard, was quick to propose to Chantale that they appeal the judgment. However, a 3–2 majority of the Quebec Court of

Appeal dismissed the appeal. It upheld the lower court's decision that a fetus had a positive right to life under section 1 of the Quebec Charter. The majority held that the rights of the fetus outweighed any potential constitutional right for Chantale to access abortion services.

A Race Against the Clock

Time was of the essence for Chantale. She was twenty-one weeks pregnant. If she had any hope of getting an abortion within the medically recommended time of twenty-four weeks, her lawyers had to get the Supreme Court to hear the case on an expedited basis. This was an unprecedented race against the clock. It was July and the Supreme Court was on summer recess. Most of the judges had left Ottawa and were scattered around the world. Justice Beverley McLachlin was travelling in Europe. Justice Antonio Lamer was said to be on his yacht, somewhere near the Statue of Liberty.

Chief Justice Brian Dickson recalled the judges after Chantale's application was filed on July 27, 1989. On August 1, five members of the court

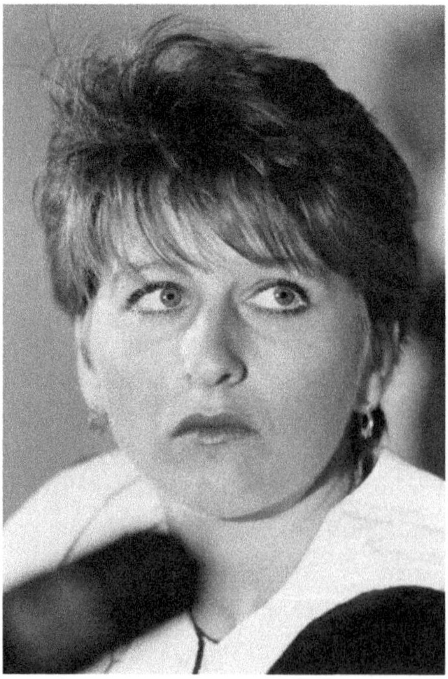

Chantale Daigle.

convened at the Supreme Court in Ottawa to decide whether to hear the appeal. Anti-abortion protestors congregated outside the building to hold a "mock baby shower," complete with baby toys and an overhead airplane toting a banner that read, "Garde ton enfant — keep your baby." The Supreme Court agreed to hear Chantale's appeal. The hearing was scheduled for August 8, 1989, which fell during her twenty-third week of pregnancy.

The Supreme Court granted intervenor status to the Canadian Abortion Rights Action League and the Canadian Civil Liberties Association (supporting Chantale) and the Campaign Life Coalition, REAL Women of Canada, and Canadian Physicians for Life (supporting Jean-Guy). Although intervention as a procedural tool had been on the upswing since 1987, the number of non-government intervenors in this case indicated the importance that different civil society groups attached to Chantale Daigle's dilemma.

Secreting Away to Boston

Chantale was reaching a breaking point while she was waiting for the Supreme Court to decide whether to hear her appeal. She was inching dangerously close to the twenty-four-week mark of her pregnancy, after which provinces would not offer access to abortion unless the woman's health was in danger.

On the day her notice for application to appeal was filed with the Supreme Court, Chantale was thrown a lifeline by a non-profit organization: la Coalition pour l'avortement libre et gratuit, which translates roughly to "the Coalition for Free Abortion." The coalition raised $8,000 for Chantale's cause through a pro-choice demonstration in Montreal on July 27, 1989. Lise Gratton and Marie-Paule Lanthier — two counsellors at the Montreal Women's Health Centre — used the funds to arrange for Chantale to obtain an abortion in Boston. Now she just had to get there.

In a scene that could have been taken from a dystopian Margaret Atwood novel, Chantale set out for Boston by car with Gratton and Lanthier on July 30. To avoid being recognized, she was decked out in a punk disguise, which included cutting her hair and dyeing it red and green. When questioned by a border patrol agent about why a suitcase in the trunk contained a stethoscope and syringes, one of the women responded that the tools belonged to a cousin they were visiting. This explanation satisfied the agent.

In contempt of the rulings by the Quebec Superior Court and the Quebec Court of Appeal, Chantale had an abortion at a Boston hospital on July 31, 1989 — the day before the Supreme Court's leave to appeal hearing. Chantale did not tell her lawyers. However, somehow, the Quebec government became aware of her procedure. Gratton reported that in the few weeks leading up to Chantale's abortion, there had been clicking noises on the telephone line at the Montreal clinic, which made her suspicious that the phones were wiretapped by police, who had been tipped off by an anonymous informant.

Government lawyers opted to sit on the information about Chantale's abortion until midway through the Supreme Court hearing, stirring suspicion that they hoped the appeal would be dismissed as moot when the news was sprung on the bench.

The Supreme Court Elects to Speak

Midway through the day, after Jean-Guy's lawyers had made their submissions, Daniel Bédard approached the bench apologetically to inform them that Chantale had obtained an abortion in the United States. He was reportedly flustered and angry, given that he had just learned the news himself from Quebec government lawyers during the lunch break. He told the judges, "I am not asking for understanding. I am not saying this is acceptable behaviour."

The question before the court then became whether to hear the appellant's submissions on its merits, irrespective of this development. Chief Justice Dickson, who had pressed for the expedited appeal decision and hearing, was livid and wanted to dismiss the case. Justice Beverley McLachlin implored Dickson and her colleagues to put themselves in Chantale's shoes; she was desperate. Dickson and his colleagues were swayed and returned to the courtroom to continue the case.

After deciding to proceed with Chantale's appeal, the court was, once again, faced with the fetal rights question. It had sidestepped this issue in

Morgentaler and in a later case brought by Joseph Borowski, an anti-abortion activist from Saskatchewan. It could not avoid it now.

A unanimous Supreme Court allowed Chantale's appeal the same day as the hearing but did not provide their reasons until a few months later. The court held that the Quebec Charter and Civil Code did not confer legal status onto fetuses and that the injunction therefore had no legal basis. By implication, the same principle applied to the Canadian Charter of Rights. The Supreme Court also held that there is no legal right or recourse for fathers of unborn fetuses to veto a woman's choice not to carry a pregnancy to term. The decision made national and international news, including the front page of *The New York Times*.

Escaping to Crescent Street

After the hearing, journalists flocked to Chantale's mother's house, where Chantale hid in a closet. She phoned one of her lawyers, Lucien Cliche, in tears, claiming she felt like a prisoner. Cliche drove to pick Chantale up that evening, and they stayed at the Grand Hôtel in Montreal, en route to Ottawa, where Chantale had press conferences scheduled the following day. Chantale and Cliche both fondly remember meandering down Crescent Street that night, near the spot that once housed Frank Roncarelli's famous restaurant. At some point, Daniel Bédard joined them and, according to Chantale, asked her why she had not told him about her abortion. She responded lightly, "Because it was none of your business, Mr. Bédard."

Life After Court for Chantale and Jean-Guy

Jean-Guy could have pursued contempt charges against Chantale and sought a fine or argued that she should be jailed for disobeying the court order against her. He elected not to. Since then, Jean-Guy has popped up in the news from time to time. He served a five-year prison term in Alberta for attacking two women in Calgary. He was convicted fourteen times for violence against women in Quebec and Alberta and was declared a long-term offender by the courts.

A year after her victory at the Supreme Court, Chantale wrote a book documenting her struggle, *Le seul choix, le mien* (*The Sole Choice Is Mine*).

She had moved back to Chibougamau and said she had a restored sense of peace and was pursuing her goal of owning a restaurant someday. Chantale has now virtually disappeared from the public sphere. She reportedly still lives in Chibougamau, but changed her name to escape her past notoriety.

Chantale is a middle-aged woman today. She is the mother of four children. In 2023, a miniseries about Chantale's case aired on Crave. It was called *Désobéir*, French for "Disobey."

13

The Right to the Basic Necessities of Life: Louise Gosselin

Louise Gosselin grew up in difficult circumstances, and things did not get easier for her in adulthood. Chronic physical and psychological health problems made it hard for her to find and keep a job. She qualified for social assistance but received significantly reduced benefits because of her youth. The amount was not enough to live on. Louise's case forced the Supreme Court of Canada to confront the question of whether the Charter imposes a positive obligation on the government to provide certain rights, like the right to a basic livelihood.

Louise's Family and Childhood

Louise was born in 1959 in Quebec. Her parents separated in 1971, when she was twelve. Because her mother was ill, Louise was sent to live in a foster home. When she turned eighteen, she returned to live with her mother in Longueuil, Quebec, for most of the next ten years.

Louise had many health problems growing up — both physical and psychological. They made school difficult, and she was unable to finish high school. As an adult, she had a hard time finding a stable job, although not for lack of effort. She held many jobs over the years, but they never lasted very long. As a result, Louise received social assistance most of her adult life.

Benefits Under Thirty

In the 1980s, Quebec provided social assistance under the Social Aid Act, which first came into force in 1970. The province's social assistance scheme was intended to be based on financial need, but it offered different benefits depending on whether someone was over or under thirty years old. People thirty and over received a higher amount if they lived on their own and a lower amount if they lived with their parents. Those under thirty received the lower amount regardless of their living circumstances.

Quebec, like most of North America, experienced a severe recession during the early 1980s. As a result, unemployment skyrocketed. It was much higher for people aged eighteen to twenty-four than for other adults, and even higher for young people with fewer than eight years of education — they had an unemployment rate of 40 to 60 percent. In 1984, in response to the problem of youth unemployment, the Quebec government created programs they hoped would provide people under thirty with skills and education so they could find long-term employment. However, some critics thought the province was really just trying to save money, rather than incentivize young people to work. In addition, some argued that the two-tier social assistance scheme was based on stereotypes that painted people on social assistance as lazy and unmotivated to work. Louise was proof that this stereotype was untrue; there was nothing she wanted more than to be able to work and gain independence.

Caught in a vicious cycle of poverty, Louise tried many times to escape it, each time falling back onto the reduced benefits amount of $170 per month. It was almost impossible to survive on that amount. She suffered from severe anxiety and depression, which led to addiction and an attempted suicide.

In October 1986, a change to the rules in her mother's apartment building forced Louise to move out of the one-bedroom unit. When not living at her mother's house, it was even harder for her to make ends meet on the low social assistance benefits. At times she lived on the streets, or in rooming houses where she faced harassment. Even when she was able to find affordable accommodations, they were not nice places to live. One basement apartment she rented was full of bugs, badly lit, and unheated. It was so cold, Louise's feet were blue all winter and her ankles hurt so much that she had trouble walking. At another point, when her rent was $170 per month — the same amount as her welfare payment — Louise was forced to live with someone who provided her with room and board in exchange for sex.

Her financial instability took an extreme toll on her physical and mental well-being. Louise had to budget very carefully to afford food, and it was a constant source of anxiety. She often had to forgo meat, fruit, and vegetables, and a nutritionist said she consumed only 50 percent of the recommended doses of vitamins and minerals. Louise suffered from malnutrition, which caused anxiety, lack of concentration, and instability.

Living in such a dire financial situation also made it difficult for Louise to find a job. When she did, she would be overcome with fear at the thought of getting fired and returning to her reduced benefit amount. It was a self-fulfilling prophecy, as the fear would debilitate her and she would end up losing the job. Louise also struggled with drug and alcohol addiction, but she attended Alcoholics Anonymous to help control her addiction so she could work.

Over the years, Louise tried her hand at many jobs. She worked as a cook, a restaurant server, and a nurse's assistant. She loved animals, and in 1987 she was very excited to start a new job as a salesperson in a pet store. However, she had to leave after a few weeks because she suffered from severe allergies to the animals.

After that, Louise went back to receiving reduced benefits. She was soon being treated in a psychiatric hospital for two months. When she got out, she found an apartment for $235 per month. Her benefits were now $188 per month, and she worked as a cleaner to make up the gap.

In 1988, Louise enrolled in the Remedial Education Program, which raised her benefits to almost the amount received by those thirty and over. When she turned thirty in July 1989, her monthly benefits finally rose to $739 per month.

Class Action

In 1986, Louise worked with a lawyer named Jean-Pierre Villaggi to challenge Quebec's social assistance scheme by starting a class action lawsuit against the Quebec government. Referring to section 15(1) of the Charter, the equality provision, which had come into force in April 1985, they claimed that the social assistance scheme was discriminatory on the basis of age. Later, they added a claim that the failure of the government to provide young people with the minimum funds needed to survive was a violation of their right to security of the person under section 7 of the Charter.

The class action weaved its way very slowly through the courts. The trial court rejected Louise's claims in 1992. She appealed to the Quebec Court of Appeal and was met with another disappointing outcome. In 1999, the court of appeal held that Louise's Charter rights had not been violated. However, one judge dissented, providing a glimmer of hope that Louise's argument might succeed if she appealed to the Supreme Court.

One Last Attempt to Secure Rights for the Poor

The Supreme Court agreed to hear Louise's case. In the lead-up to the hearing on October 29, 2001, the case garnered significant media attention across Canada. Social assistance was a hot topic not just because of Louise's Charter challenge, but also because Jean Chrétien's Liberal government had been trying for more than seven years to reform Canada's welfare system. While many advocacy groups were fighting for better social assistance programs, other people were strongly opposed to the idea. Newspapers ran editorials with titles such as "Social Assistance Isn't a Right" and "Sadly, a Case Rooted in Laziness."

Between leave being granted and Louise's case being decided, the Canadian Charter of Rights and Freedoms celebrated its twentieth birthday. Critics of the Charter questioned why unelected judges were able to make decisions that had such far-reaching impact on Canadian society, and equality rights were a major focus of their criticism. Louise's case was an important opportunity for the Supreme Court to either expand or set limits on the Charter's protections of equality and security of the person.

When the Supreme Court released its ruling on December 19, 2002, it was a disheartening result for Louise and the other class members. The court held that the two-tier social assistance scheme was constitutional.

No Positive Obligation on Government ... but ... Maybe One Day?

Although Louise lost her case at the Supreme Court of Canada, there was a silver lining: A majority of judges agreed that, in the future, such a claim might succeed. They said it was possible that one day section 7 might place positive obligations on the government. Section 7 states that "Everyone has the right to life, liberty and security of the person and the right not to be deprived thereof except in accordance with the principles of fundamental justice."

However, the majority's decision was a huge blow to the hopes of Louise and others who had been fighting to help bring thousands of Canadians out of poverty.

In a 5–4 decision, Chief Justice Beverley McLachlin, writing for the majority, held that none of the rights claimed by Louise had been infringed. All four dissenting judges found that the social assistance scheme discriminated against those under thirty. Justices Louise Arbour and Claire L'Heureux-Dubé further found that the scheme deprived Louise and those under thirty of their right to security of the person.

Chief Justice McLachlin was keenly aware that the case would have massive economic and political implications if Louise succeeded. Not only was the lawsuit claiming damages of $389 million, but if the court found that the Charter had been violated, it would impose a positive obligation on governments across Canada to establish social assistance schemes that met a baseline level determined by the court. The common theme across McLachlin's analysis for both section 7 and the equality guarantee of section 15 was that she felt the evidence given at trial was "frail" and didn't justify such enormous implications. The main hangup was the fact that Louise Gosselin had been the only member of the class to testify at trial — none of the other estimated 75,000 class members came forward to share their experiences.

Turning to the section 7 security of the person claim, McLachlin noted that no Supreme Court case thus far had established section 7 as placing positive obligations on the state. She left open the possibility, saying that "one day s. 7 may be interpreted to include positive obligations." But today was not that day. McLachlin again emphasized her view that the evidentiary record was insufficient.

Justice Louise Arbour's dissent focused squarely on the positive obligation of the state to provide social assistance under section 7 of the Charter. Whereas the majority had merely left open the possibility, Arbour was willing to say definitively that section 7 contained a positive dimension. Justices L'Heureux-Dubé and Arbour both said there was no question that Louise's physical and psychological integrity had been breached. They underscored that living with the constant threat of poverty was psychologically harmful, and that the amount of $170 per month was barely above the $152 per month required to receive proper nutrition — never mind other living expenses. As a result, they found that Louise's section 7 rights had been breached.

Justice Arbour's dissent was powerful, but it did not help Louise and others receiving social assistance — it was merely the expression of the minority on the court.

The Aftermath for Louise

Louise was disappointed but not surprised by the high court's decision. She was proud of the work she and her lawyers had done, noting that she thought her case had influenced the Quebec government's decision to abolish the two-tier scheme in 1989.

Louise was forty-three years old, and it had been seventeen years since she launched the class action lawsuit in the Superior Court of Quebec. She continued to be unable to work due to her health problems. She was now living on $716 per month, the maximum benefit at the time for a single person who was not working. Offering some words of optimism, Louise said, "What counts is to not lose hope, to continue to believe in the value that we live in a democratic society."

A few years later, Louise said the Supreme Court ruling confirmed to her that "some people want the poor to stay poor." As of 2005, she was still receiving social assistance and living in a tough neighbourhood in Montreal. "I try to survive," she said.

Social Assistance in Canada

For those receiving social assistance in Canada, the direct and immediate impact of the *Gosselin* ruling was anti-climactic — it simply upheld the status quo. Today, twenty-three years later, nearly one million single adults in Canada continue to be stuck in a cycle of "deep poverty," earning on average just $11,700 per year.

Justice Louise Arbour stepped down from the Supreme Court two years after the *Gosselin* judgment. Justice Claire L'Heureux-Dubé retired from the court the same year as the decision. In the more than twenty years since, the court has not come close to embracing a positive obligation on the state to protect life, liberty, or security of the person under section 7 of the Charter.

14

Canada's Dominatrix: Terri-Jean Bedford

Black is a common colour in Canadian courts. Judges wear black robes and lawyers wear black gowns. The uniforms of the justice system are meant to project equality, but they also reflect uniformity and conformity. Although black is her trademark colour, nobody would ever accuse Terri-Jean Bedford of conformity. She stormed the Supreme Court of Canada clad head to toe in black leather spandex, with gloves and a riding crop, and marched out with a momentous legal victory for sex workers in Canada.

Becoming Terri-Jean Bedford

Terri-Jean was born in Collingwood, Ontario, in 1959. She grew up in abject poverty, and when she was six, the Children's Aid Society arrived at her parents' small farmhouse and took little Terri-Jean away. She had never attended school and had twice been brought to the hospital for malnutrition. She was adopted by a Windsor family, the Bedfords.

Terri-Jean grew close to her adoptive father, but she suffered physical and verbal abuse at the hands of her adoptive mother. When she was twelve, the

Bedfords sent her away to an all-girls' convent school. From there, she moved from group home to group home until she was sixteen. During this time, she began to dabble in both drugs and sex work. At sixteen, Terri-Jean moved into an apartment in downtown Windsor with the help of a social worker.

For the next few years, Terri-Jean worked as a sex worker in massage parlors, on the streets, and in live-in arrangements in clients' homes. Throughout her time as a sex worker, and especially on the streets, she was often subjected to physical, sexual, and verbal abuse. She repeatedly found her security and her life at risk from clients and from "boyfriends" acting as pimps. Nevertheless, she created a lucrative career as a sex trade worker, eventually running her own escort service with at least eighteen employees.

In 1986, Terri-Jean's escort service in Windsor was raided by police. She was charged with multiple offences relating to the operation of a common bawdy house. At the time, the courts and legislation defined a bawdy house as a place where "prostitution" or "acts of indecency" occurred often and on a regular basis. Terri-Jean was convicted and spent fifteen months in prison.

By 1993, now thirty-four years old, Terri-Jean had moved into a home in the leafy suburbs of Toronto. Amidst the middle-class suburban life of malls, commuters, and shuffling kids to hockey and soccer games, she operated Madame de Sade's House of Erotica, a space for cross-dressing, role play, domination, and more. Many security measures were in place: She conducted checks on potential clients, hired a security guard, and never accepted intoxicated clients. For the entire duration of Madame de Sade's operation, there were never any violent or abusive incidents against Terri-Jean or any of her employees. On September 15, 1994, police raided "the Bondage Bungalow," as Terri-Jean's business was later dubbed by the press. Once again, she was charged with unlawfully keeping a bawdy house.

A six-year, highly publicized and expensive legal battle ensued and made Terri-Jean Bedford the "most famous Canadian dominatrix." She was also fighting her case in the media. In interviews, she often appeared in full leather garb, carrying her signature riding crop. She was once featured spanking a client's bottom in a promotional poster for a fundraiser for her trial.

Terri-Jean was convicted at trial, and her appeal to the Ontario Court of Appeal failed. This time, there was no prison sentence; Terri-Jean was simply fined $3,000. But she was left with extremely costly legal bills. At the court of appeal, she was represented by Osgoode Hall law professor Alan Young, who, six years later, would call on her to be the named applicant in what would become Canada's ground-breaking challenge to Canada's prostitution laws.

The Sex Trade Before *Bedford*

Selling sex for money was not illegal in Canada. However, many activities related to prostitution had long been outlawed under the Criminal Code, most notably communication for the purposes of prostitution, keeping a common bawdy house, and living off the avails of prostitution. Before the decision in *Bedford*, working in the sex trade, especially as a woman, was extremely dangerous. Between 1994 and 2003, at least seventy-nine sex workers were killed in Canada while engaging in prostitution activities, of which 95 percent were women. This number does not include sex workers who disappeared and have not been found and may very well have been murdered. A survey conducted in the mid-1990s showed that three-quarters of sex workers in Vancouver had experienced violence over the previous six months.

When men, often "johns" (clients), were arrested under the communication section, 70 percent had their charges stayed because courts could send them to "john school," where they would learn the dangers of the sex trade; if they completed the course, the charges were dropped. In contrast, 68 percent of women, mostly sex workers, who were charged under the same section were found guilty. They had no "john school" equivalent to save them. Forty percent of women charged under the provision, compared to 5 percent of men, were given prison sentences.

Police intervention and investigation often focused on the sex worker rather than on violent or abusive clients. Police said the threat of violence from clients was too great to have undercover agents pose as sex workers to catch johns. The laws in place at the time forced women to operate alone and in the dark.

The *Prostitution Reference*

In 1990, the Supreme Court held that both the bawdy house and communication provisions of the Criminal Code were constitutional, in a case known as the *Prostitution Reference*. Two justices, the only women on the court at the time, disagreed. Supreme Court decisions bind all courts below them, as well as governments and police. They can be changed only by the Supreme Court itself, and the court does not easily change course.

One lawyer set out to get the high court to change course.

Alan Young: Constitutional Pioneer

Osgoode Hall professor Alan Young assembled and led the legal team that set out to overturn the *Prostitution Reference* and have these laws declared unconstitutional. Young had made a career of defending Canadians' rights to liberty. For him, *Bedford* was the "culmination of a twenty-year litigation strategy to challenge all the consensual crimes dealing with hedonistic activities." These included challenges to the criminalization of cannabis and of consensual sex work.

As a constitutional litigator, Young had an acute sense of how and when a constitutional challenge should be launched. The team would challenge the prostitution legislation by claiming a section 7 infringement. Instead of focusing on the dangers of potential imprisonment, as in the *Prostitution Reference*, they would tackle the issue of security of person as it related to the dangers created by these laws. The legislative framework pushed sex workers to work on the streets; they were prevented from hiring protection and could not properly screen their clients.

Launching the Challenge

Young enlisted his former client Terri-Jean Bedford along with two other former sex workers, Amy Lebovitch and Valerie Scott, as the plaintiffs in the challenge to the sex work laws. The challenge was argued before Justice Andrea Himel at the Ontario Superior Court of Justice in Toronto in the fall of 2009. Justice Himel released her decision in late 2010, deciding in favour of the sex workers. She declared that the provisions preventing communication, bawdy houses, and "living off the avails" were unconstitutional and made it impossible for women to work in the sex trade, itself a legal activity, without putting themselves in serious danger. Justice Himel declared that thirty days after her decision, the laws would become invalid.

Terri-Jean was ecstatic, speaking to reporters in her typical spiked heels and leather clothes. Justice Himel was later caricatured in the media, slashing a whip through the Charter. The government appealed the decision and applied to have the suspension of the court's order extended until the appeal decision was delivered. The unconstitutional laws would stay in force for the moment.

The case was brought to the Ontario Court of Appeal, and its decision was released in March 2012. The court of appeal usually sits in panels of three judges, but in matters of national importance that are likely to be taken to the Supreme Court, it will sometimes sit in a panel of five judges. It did so in *Bedford*. The judges' decision was a setback for Terri-Jean and her co-plaintiffs. While the court did find that the three provisions deprived sex workers of their security of person, the majority found that the communication law did so in a manner consistent with the policy objectives of the law.

Terri-Jean Bedford talking to reporters at the Supreme Court of Canada in Ottawa after learning Canada's highest court struck down the country's prostitution laws in their entirety in a unanimous 9–0 ruling.

The harm it caused was not disproportionate to the objectives it sought to meet. Furthermore, the judges chose not to strike down the "living off the avails" provision, instead specifying that the law applied only in circumstances of exploitation.

Terri-Jean and the rest of the team were unsatisfied with this result. They appealed the decision, and the Supreme Court agreed to hear their case.

Storming the Supreme Court

The Supreme Court is a very formal, conservative institution. The high ceilings of its Great Hall give it the feel of a cathedral. There is a dress code for lawyers and judges. While there is no formal dress code for visitors, unofficially it is a place where formal dress — jackets, ties and collared shirts, and blouses — prevails. When Terri-Jean came to the Supreme Court, the staff, the judges, and the media had never seen anyone like her, clad in her trademark black spandex and riding crop. Terri-Jean made the point that the country's highest court belonged to all Canadians, including sex workers and dominatrixes.

In 2013, the Supreme Court ruled unanimously in favour of Terri-Jean and sex workers: The court declared all three provisions unconstitutional. In her decision, Chief Justice Beverley McLachlin emphasized that prostitution is a legal activity. The government had argued that, like many trades, there are dangers associated with the sex trade that workers agree to take on by choosing that line of employment. But McLachlin recognized that for many, this job was not a choice. Even when it was a choice, the government's laws impeded sex workers from putting in place protection for themselves and imposed dangerous conditions on them. As McLachlin put it, "the violence of a john does not diminish the role of the state in making a prostitute more vulnerable to that violence."

The bawdy house provisions were struck down because their effect on Scott, Lebovitch, and Terri-Jean's security of person was grossly disproportionate to the objective of the laws. The government had sought to prevent the public nuisance that comes with brothels. But the court ruled that preventing public nuisance was not worth exposing sex workers to the added danger of street work.

The communication laws were also found to be grossly disproportionate. Again, their goal was to prevent public nuisance, to stop sex workers from accosting the public. But the Supreme Court ruled that this goal was not sufficient justification to prevent sex workers from screening clients or communicating with each other to stay safe.

The "living off the avails" laws were struck down because they were overbroad. While the purpose of the law was to stop pimps from exploiting sex workers, it did not distinguish between exploitative behaviour and potentially helpful behaviour. A trusted security guard or driver was treated no differently than a parasitic pimp. The court found that the positive effects of the law did not outweigh the negative ones and that there were better ways to achieve the legitimate goals the government had set out without forcing sex workers into dangerous conditions.

The *Prostitution Reference* was overturned. Terri-Jean and the team had won.

When the decision was released, Terri-Jean met with reporters, once again sporting her leather suit and riding crop. At the time, the Senate was going through a significant expenses scandal involving many senators. She joked that Prime Minister Stephen Harper had offered her a job as a whip to keep the Senate in line.

Moving to Parliament

The Supreme Court gave Harper's Conservative government a year to decide how to act. The government could have done nothing: let the decision stand, effectively decriminalizing safe sex work in Canada. Instead, it chose to enact new legislation. Six months after the decision, Minister of Justice Peter MacKay introduced Bill C-36 in Parliament. If the bill passed, it would be a criminal offence to procure sex work. The government wanted to adopt the "Nordic model," which sees sex workers as victims and their clients as criminals. Furthermore, a section was added outlawing "material benefit from sexual services," essentially mirroring the "living off the avails" prohibitions from the previous version of the law. To the government's credit, they included a subsection to alleviate a concern that Amy Lebovitch had raised in relation to her partner, by protecting those who are in "legitimate living arrangements" with the sex worker.

Amy Lebovitch and Valerie Scott testified against the bill before the Standing Committee on Justice and Human Rights. They explained how the new provisions were just as unconstitutional as the old, forcing sex workers to work alone and in hiding. Scott likened the provisions to the banning of alcohol during prohibition: "Prohibition enriched organized crime, kept the police busy, added risks that weren't there before, and criminalized the actions of a significant percentage of the population." The same applied to restrictions on sex workers. Both advocates believed the provisions should be struck down and no new legislation should be introduced in its place.

Parliament did not heed their warnings: Bill C-36 came into effect in early December 2014 and is still the law in Canada today. In 2023, a judge of the Ontario Superior Court of Justice upheld the constitutionality of the new law.

Life After *Bedford*

All three women gained public notoriety after the case. Valerie Scott and Amy Lebovitch continued their advocacy work. Their lawyer, Alan Young, passed away in 2024.

Though the government's response was disappointing, Terri-Jean, Lebovitch, and Scott's work was not entirely in vain. After the legislative change, women went from representing 42 percent of those charged with sex-trade related crimes to only 5 percent, showing the shift in focus from sex worker to johns. Furthermore, the total number of sex-trade-related crimes reported was more than halved, from 2,904 in 2010 to 1,298 in 2019. However, this was mostly because communication offences were no longer as prominent, dropping from 89.8 percent of sex-trade-related crimes to only 10.3 percent. Still, between 2015 and 2019, thirty-five sex workers were killed. The homicide rate for sex workers before and after the enactment of Bill C-36 has stayed relatively constant, at around eight women per year.

In 2022, Terri-Jean published her memoirs about her life and her legal battles and was working on turning them into a play. She has now retired from the sex work industry.

15

The Right to Die with Dignity: Sue Rodriguez

For a time, Sue Rodriguez was one of the most recognizable figures in Canada. Most people achieve fame for their actions in life; Sue captured public attention for her public fight to seek assistance in dying. She lost her battle at the Supreme Court of Canada, but nonetheless obtained medical help to end her life, thus spawning a twenty-year debate over the right to medical assistance in dying (MAID). The debate continues today.

An Idyllic Upbringing with a Tragic End

By her own account, Sue had a happy and carefree childhood. Susan ("Sue") Jane Shipley was born in 1950 in Winnipeg and spent most of her childhood in a well-to-do suburban Toronto neighbourhood. Her grandfather was a wealthy businessman and Sue was brought up in affluence. She went to summer camps, had dance and piano lessons, and spent time at her family's lakeside cottage.

During Sue's teenage years, life for the Shipleys took a dark turn. The family experienced a series of tragic events over a period of five years: In

1963, her Aunt Virginia died in a house fire along with three of her four children. Another aunt, Elizabeth, died in 1968 of a brain aneurysm. For Sue, the most tragic of all was the slow death of her father from alcoholism when Sue was seventeen.

After Sue's father died, her grandparents gave her a modest allowance for a few years. When they died, they donated their entire estate to the Virginia Military Institute. For the first time, Sue was on her own.

Starting a New Life in San Diego

Sue completed two years of an early childhood education program at Seneca College in Toronto. When she was twenty-one, she married a mechanic. The marriage did not last long, and the two were divorced in 1975. Perhaps seeking a fresh start, Sue moved to San Diego in 1976. She had been to California before, and it was the perfect place for someone like Sue who lived a healthy, active lifestyle. She loved skiing, hiking, and rock climbing and once ran a half marathon. She was not particularly career-focused, preferring to spend time on her hobbies. In San Diego she held many different jobs, including cross-country ski instructor, lab technician, and event coordinator.

Sue met her husband, Henry Rodriguez, while she was working at the University of California, San Diego. Henry was a shy, quiet man five years younger than Sue. He was attracted to her strength and decisiveness. They married in 1981, and their son, Cole, was born in 1984. They soon moved to Saanich, British Columbia, a community north of Victoria. It was in Saanich that Sue's life would begin to fall apart.

Sue's ALS Diagnosis

Sue and Henry separated in February 1991. Although Henry initiated the split, both of them acknowledged that their relationship had had longstanding problems. Then Sue lost her job. Around the same time, she started experiencing a strange twitching in her fingers. She saw a neurologist, who found nothing wrong with her. Given all that was going on in Sue's personal life, he attributed her symptoms to anxiety. Her symptoms continued to worsen throughout the spring and summer of 1991. The twitching got more severe, and she developed pain in her shoulder. She knew something was wrong.

Sue found a new doctor, who sent her for tests at the University Hospital in Vancouver. On August 22, 1991, just hours after the tests were complete, the doctor told Sue that she had amyotrophic lateral sclerosis (ALS), also known as Lou Gehrig's disease. At the age of forty-one, she faced almost total paralysis and a life expectancy of just two to five years. Alone on the ferry ride back to Victoria, Sue felt panicked, in a state of shock.

ALS is a fatal neurological disease with no cure. As the disease progressed, Sue could expect to get weaker, eventually becoming fully paralyzed. She would lose the ability to walk, to talk, and even to swallow and breathe on her own. Throughout this process, her mind would remain fully intact, and she would be aware of everything that was happening. Having ALS is often described as being a prisoner in one's own body. Sue lived an active and independent life, and she couldn't see what her place in the world would be if she could not move. Over the next month, Sue felt "profoundly tense and depressed."

Henry moved back in with Sue, and they took the house off the market. They had discussed getting back together prior to Sue's diagnosis, and now it was an easy decision. But the move didn't work out. Sue eventually moved to the basement to ease tensions between them.

Deciding to Die

At first, Sue was determined to fight her ALS. She tried a number of experimental and alternative treatments, but none were successful. Her symptoms continued to worsen. By April 1992, Sue had accepted that she could not fight her disease. One evening in April, she attended a meeting of the ALS Society. Surrounded by other ALS patients, she saw what the future held in store for her.

That was the night Sue decided to die by suicide. She did not hesitate or debate the morality of her decision. She wanted to stay with her son, Cole, for as long as she could. At the same time, she did not want to leave him remembering her as incapacitated, and she wanted to spare herself a humiliating end.

Sue decided that the right time for her to go would be when she lost her voice; at that point, she would lose control over whether she lived or died.

However, she realized that by that time she would likely also have lost the physical ability to kill herself. She would not be able to move her hands or arms, or even to swallow on her own. She decided to seek the assistance of a doctor.

In deciding to end her life, Sue did not realize the magnitude of the legal battle that lay ahead of her.

The Right to Die Society

Sue's family doctor was appalled when she asked for his thoughts on euthanasia. So was the next doctor Sue tried. Instead of the empathy she expected, Sue was met with the harsh reality that she was asking these doctors to commit a crime. Although suicide had been decriminalized in Canada in 1972, section 241(b) of the Criminal Code still made it a criminal offence to help someone to die by suicide, punishable by up to fourteen years in prison.

Not knowing how to proceed, Sue got in touch with the Right to Die Society of Canada in August 1992. There she met John Hofsess, who would soon turn "Sue Rodriguez" into a household name across Canada. John had founded the Right to Die Society Canada in 1992, just a few months before meeting Sue. He convinced Sue to go public with her story. Sue said that without John, she probably would have died privately, without making any public statements or launching a legal challenge. There were many doctors who would have acted outside the law and assisted Sue in dying privately.

Launching the Legal Challenge

Sue and John hired lawyer Chris Considine, who had handled several high-profile cases and he was eager to take on the first legal challenge to the prohibition on assisted suicide.

Sue filed an application to the Supreme Court of British Columbia asking for a declaration that section 241(b) of the Criminal Code was unconstitutional and that any doctor assisting her in dying by suicide would not be committing a criminal offence. Sue's argument was based on three Charter provisions: that section 241(b) violated her right to liberty and her right to security of the person guaranteed under section 7 of the Charter; that it resulted in "cruel and unusual" treatment in violation of section 12; and that the prohibition discriminated against people with disabilities in violation of section 15, the Charter's equality guarantee.

A court date was set for December 17, 1992.

Sue launched her challenge to the assisted suicide law not just in the courts but also in the media. When it came to publicity, John was both skilled and well connected. Sue's story was covered by newspapers, magazines, and television networks across the country. John even arranged for a documentary crew to follow Sue and document her legal battle. Despite the attention her case would receive, Sue was a rather private person. In particular, she tried her best to maintain Cole's privacy.

In December 1992, after taping a CBC interview, Sue met Svend Robinson, the NDP member of Parliament for Burnaby-Kingsway, who would become one of her strongest supporters and closest friends. Svend was Canada's first openly gay member of Parliament. Having watched many close friends die of AIDS, he became an advocate for physician-assisted suicide

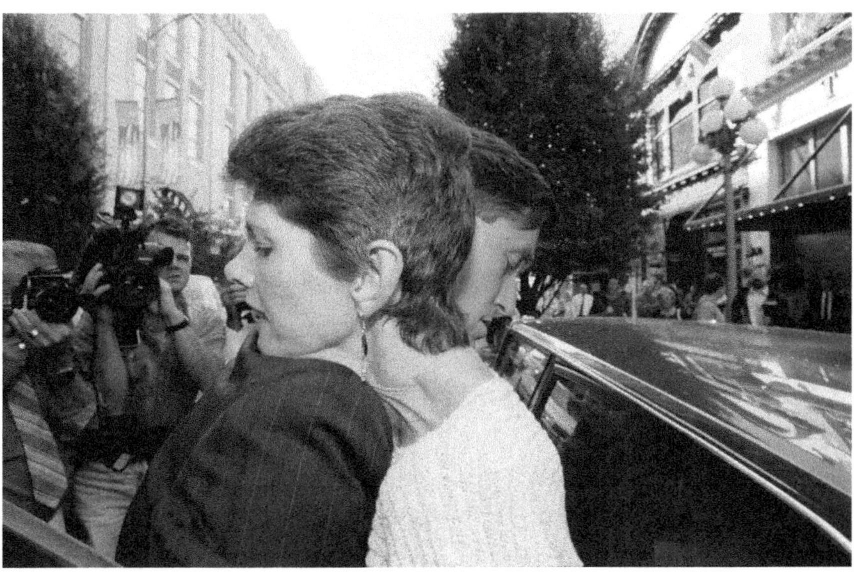

Sue Rodriguez supported by MP Svend Robinson as he helps her out of a car on the way to a press conference in Victoria, British Columbia, in 1993.

and was a political consultant for the Right to Die Society. Sue and Svend hit it off from the start, and their friendship would grow into something very special.

The Trial: Sue's "Plea for Help"

At the trial, Justice Allen Melvin heard expert witnesses, Sue's personal testimony, and presentations from two intervenors: the Pro-Life Society of British Columbia and the Pacific Physicians for Life Society. Both groups opposed Sue's request. The pro-life groups argued that the prohibition on assisted suicide was constitutional and further that Sue's request was morally wrong.

Sue described her legal challenge as "a plea for help." She told the judge: "I want to be in charge of my life and my death. I just feel an inner guidance tells me that it's the right thing to do and I should be allowed to do it." Sue went into detail on what ALS would do to her body — her airways would close down, she would become unable to swallow, and she would eventually die of choking, asphyxiation, or pneumonia.

Sue disliked talking about what ALS would do to her — not because she was scared, but rather because she did not want to look like she was seeking sympathy or pity. She found it painful to face the intervenors. She was not seeking to impose her beliefs on anyone else; she just wanted control over her own life and death. She asked why these groups were fighting against her right to autonomy and self-determination.

After a long day in court, Sue left to attend Cole's school Christmas concert. She spent the next weeks creating happy holiday memories for Cole — since it could be their last Christmas together.

Two Negative Decisions and a Rift in the Legal Team

Twelve days after Sue appeared in court, Justice Melvin dismissed her application. He upheld section 241, finding that Sue's Charter rights to security of the person, equality, and freedom from cruel and unusual treatment or punishment were not infringed because the law did not discriminate against people with physical disabilities. Even if any of Sue's Charter rights were infringed, Justice Melvin said that infringement would be justified under section 1 of the Charter because the prohibition on assisted suicide protected the welfare of vulnerable people.

Sue filed a notice of appeal almost immediately.

In late January 1993, John Hofsess wrote a front-page article attacking the pro-life groups for intervening against Sue in court. Even though Sue had not seen the piece, John signed it with her initials. It was not Sue's style to openly attack other people's beliefs, and she told John so.

The British Columbia Court of Appeal heard Sue's case over two days in February 1993 and dismissed her appeal just a few weeks later. Sue and Svend received news of the judgment by phone. Sue held a press conference that same morning, announcing that she would appeal to the Supreme Court of Canada.

Reporters also learned that a doctor had come forward to help Sue, although they did not know his name. Sue intended for the details of her death to remain confidential. However, John could not resist speaking on the matter. Later that day, he was quoted as saying that Sue's death would not take place in secret, and that all information would go public at the time of her death. This time, Sue and Svend both felt that John had taken things too far in his attempts to engage the media and spur public debate. They announced that they would be severing their relationship with him and the Right to Die Society.

Sue's Battle Reaches Canada's Highest Court

By the time the Supreme Court of Canada heard Sue's case on May 20, 1993, her condition had worsened significantly. It now took all her energy just to make it through the day, and she required assistance to complete basic tasks like eating. While she could still speak, it was very difficult for her.

For just the second time in Canadian history, the Supreme Court allowed live television coverage from inside the courtroom. Sue watched the proceedings from home. Given the importance of her legal challenge, nine groups representing the spectrum of opinions on the right to die were granted intervenor status in the case.

The Supreme Court took just seven hours to hear the case, and four months to deliver a decision. This was quick by Supreme Court standards;

the judges realized both the importance of the issue and that time was of the essence for Sue.

Between the hearing and the decision, Sue celebrated her forty-third birthday. She felt broken down and knew she would be ready to die at any moment. Regardless of what the Supreme Court decided, she had a doctor who was ready to help her die. The original doctor was out of the country, but Sue and Svend had found another who was willing to help. This time, they kept the doctor's identity a close secret, not revealing it to anyone.

The Supreme Court delivered its decision on September 30, 1993. In a 5–4 decision, the court upheld the prohibition on assisted suicide. Sue received the news over the phone while she was with Svend and her lawyer, Chris. They held a press conference later that day. Sue's words were barely audible, but her message was clear: "I hope that Parliament will act."

A Court Divided

The majority decision, written by Justice John Sopinka, dismissed each of Sue's Charter claims in turn. Sopinka concluded that the prohibition on assisted suicide both deprived Sue of personal autonomy and caused her physical pain and psychological stress; however, this infringement of her right to security of the person accorded with the principles of fundamental justice because it was not arbitrary or unfair. Sopinka pointed to both moral considerations and the potential for abuse if there was an exception to the law for the terminally ill. He maintained that Sue's section 12 right to be free from cruel and unusual treatment or punishment was not engaged because the prohibition on assisted suicide did not constitute "treatment" in the meaning of section 12. On Sue's section 15 claim, he simply found that any potential infringement of her equality rights would be justified as a reasonable limit under section 1.

Four judges dissented, writing in separate opinions that the prohibition on assisted suicide was unconstitutional. Chief Justice Antonio Lamer found that it infringed Sue's section 15(1) equality rights and that the infringement was not justified under section 1. He wrote that the law placed a burden on people with physical disabilities by limiting their ability for self-determination. The law then failed to meet the minimal impairment requirement in Lamer's analysis of section 1. An absolute prohibition on assisted suicide was over-inclusive in that it achieved its objective of protecting vulnerable persons but also placed a burden on people like Sue who showed no evidence of vulnerability. Such a burden could not be justified in a free and democratic society.

Justice Beverley McLachlin (with Justice Claire L'Heureux-Dubé concurring) agreed with the majority's conclusion that the assisted suicide prohibition infringed Sue's section 7 rights to liberty and security of the person. Unlike Sopinka, she found that this infringement did not accord with the principles of fundamental justice and subsequently could not be justified under section 1. Analyzing the issue on an individual level as it related to one person, Sue Rodriguez, McLachlin placed more weight on the principles of autonomy, self-determination, and dignity than on society's interests in preventing abuse.

Sue Dies by Physician-Assisted Suicide

Sue lived for just four and a half months after the Supreme Court's decision. She spent much of this time alone in bed. She had almost completely lost the ability to speak, and breathing and swallowing were difficult. On her last public outing, she attended Chinese New Year's festivities in downtown Victoria with Cole and Svend.

When she decided it was time to die, Sue gave one last interview to the documentary crew, saying, "I would rather end it now, while I'm able to speak and be clear about what I want. I know it's right for me, and I feel I've done all I can to contribute to life and it's time for me to move on."

Sue died on February 12, 1994, with the assistance of an anonymous doctor. Sue, Svend, and the doctor met in Sue's home, and Sue died in Svend's arms. Sue had asked to have her ashes buried under a fig tree. She didn't want a funeral or a ceremony, just a small gathering of close family and friends.

The Continued Fight for the Right to Die in Canada

Sue knew the Supreme Court would one day have to revisit their decision. Although she lost her court battle, she opened the floor for a public debate about end-of-life issues in Canada. Speaking about how she wanted to be remembered, Sue said, "I would like to go down in history saying I had something to do with the laws being changed and creating a more compassionate society as a result."

Over the next twenty years, Parliament debated six bills seeking to decriminalize assisted suicide, though none passed. Other countries made more progress on the issue in that time. By 2010, five countries and three U.S. states had passed legislation allowing some form of assisted dying.

As Sue predicted, the Supreme Court did indeed revisit its decision, twenty-three years later in *Carter v. Canada* (2015). This time, Beverley McLachlin presided over the case as Chief Justice, and her focus on individual autonomy and self-determination prevailed, granting others what Sue Rodriguez had been denied: the right to die with the help of a doctor at a time of their choosing.

16

Trial Within a Reasonable Time: Elijah Askov

Elijah Askov was a "rounder" — a repeat customer in the criminal justice system. His name has become associated with the chronic delay that plagues the Canadian justice system. The Supreme Court of Canada's 1990 decision in his case triggered "an *Askov* crisis," resulting in more than 51,000 charges being dismissed in 27,000 individual cases by the Crown prosecution in Ontario alone. Then followed "*Askov* motions" seeking to dismiss cases for unreasonable delay in violation of the Canadian Charter of Rights and Freedoms.

Elijah's Background and Trouble at Fran's

Elijah Anton Askov was born in Bulgaria in 1946. He immigrated to Canada in 1966, at the age of twenty. Elijah and his wife, Mary, had two sons, and in the 1970s, the Askovs lived in downtown Toronto. In the late 1970s or early 1980s, they moved to Scarborough, where they lived in a two-storey, semi-detached home. Elijah worked at San Francesco Foods, a family-owned restaurant near Dufferin Street and St. Clair Avenue West famous for its veal sandwiches. He would make the thirty-minute drive into Toronto to work evenings at the restaurant.

Elijah's restaurant job was not the Askov family's only source of income. Elijah had a long criminal record dating back to 1966, the year he arrived in Canada. His wife also had a criminal record, which included convictions for theft and possession of stolen property.

Just four years after he arrived in Canada, Elijah was involved in a high-profile burglary-turned-murder at Fran's, a popular Yonge Street restaurant. The case took many bizarre turns and would go on to become Toronto's most expensive homicide investigation. It also turned into one of the most expensive trials in city history as the Crown brought in more than a hundred witnesses from across Canada and the United States.

At trial, Askov, Nicholas Popovic, Radko Govedarov, and Sreto "Lucky" Dzambas were convicted of murder. They appealed to the Ontario Court of Appeal, and eventually to the Supreme Court of Canada in 1975. Radko and Lucky's convictions were upheld, while Elijah and Nick were granted new trials due to a technical point of law regarding the definition of "burglary." In his second trial, Elijah pled guilty to being an accessory to murder.

Even with the trials over, the saga was not finished. Both Radko and Lucky escaped from prison in separate high-profile incidents. In a final strange turn, Nick had a deportation order against him but was mistakenly released from jail in 1976 before appearing at the immigration proceeding.

Elijah continued his criminal exploits after the Fran's robbery-murder. In 1981, he was caught with twenty-eight pounds of hashish and sentenced to eighteen months in jail for possession for the purpose of trafficking.

Background on the Main *Askov* Case

By November 1983, Elijah had completed his drug trafficking sentence and was back to the world of crime. But while he was serving his sentence, there had been a major change to the criminal justice system — the Charter of Rights and Freedoms had been enacted. With the Charter in force, Elijah's next arrest would lead to a seven-year legal battle that defined "the right to be tried within a reasonable time" in Canada.

The case, commonly known as *R v. Askov*, involved four men who were co-accused in an extortion plot: Elijah, Ira Ralph Hussey, Sam Gugliotta, and Eddie Melo. Eddie Melo was a boxer of some repute who had ties to organized crime in Montreal. The four tried to extort money from a Montrealer who booked nude dancers to work in clubs across Quebec and was expanding into Ontario. The police arrested the four following a meeting at a Hamilton club in November 1983. While he was out on bail and awaiting trial, Elijah was rearrested for committing break and enter. He was convicted and sentenced to two months of jail time and two years of probation.

Systemic Delays in Peel District

The proceedings for the *Askov* case were held at the Brampton courthouse, located in the District of Peel, outside Toronto. Peel was experiencing a substantial shortage of both judges and courtrooms, which had caused a significant backlog of cases. The delays in Peel were worse than anywhere else in Canada. A study had shown that cases in the Brampton courthouse were taking, on average, 607 days from the end of a preliminary hearing through to trial in the provincial court and 423 days for the superior court. For comparison, cases in New Brunswick took 152 days to reach trial in the provincial court and 72 days for the superior court. Other regions in Ontario were also experiencing significant delays, but none were as bad as Peel.

There were a number of starts and stops in the preliminary hearing in the case, which did not conclude until September 21, 1984. The trial was scheduled for over a year later, on October 15, 1985. This was the earliest possible date given the availability of judges and courtrooms in Brampton. But when October 15, 1985, rolled around, the trial did not start on time. The accused waited ten days before it became clear that the trial was not going to happen in the current sitting. It was pushed back another year, to September 2, 1986.

Motion to Stay Proceedings

The trial finally began on September 2, 1986. It had been almost three years since Elijah and his three co-defendants were arrested (thirty-four months, to be exact). When the trial started, the defence lawyers immediately asked for a stay of proceedings due to an unreasonable delay. A stay is a halt or an abandonment of the charges. This request was based on section 11(b) of the Charter, which says that any person charged with an offence has the right to be tried within a reasonable time.

Elijah was represented by Charles Barhydt, a young lawyer who had been practising for only a few years. Barhydt made some creative arguments to convince the trial judge that the thirty-four-month delay had breached the four men's Charter rights. Perhaps the judge, Justice Michael Bolan, had himself grown tired of the monumental backlog of cases at his courthouse, because he adopted Barhydt's argument and decided that the long delay was unconstitutional. Justice Bolan said the delay was caused by a "chronic shortage of institutional resources in the Judicial District of Peel." The judge ordered that the proceedings be stayed for all four men.

The Ontario Court of Appeal Finds the Delay Reasonable

The Crown appealed to the Ontario Court of Appeal, which overturned the decision, ordering that the stay be set aside and that the trial proceed. The court did not contest the trial judge's finding that Peel District lacked resources but said the delay was reasonable.

After their loss at the court of appeal, Elijah and his co-accused sought new lawyers who they hoped could secure them a win at Canada's highest court. Elijah hired Michael Code, and Hussey hired Clayton Ruby. Both lawyers had argued a number of cases at the Supreme Court, and they had worked together on many cases. Code went on to argue many more appeals at the Supreme Court and was appointed as a judge on the Ontario Superior Court of Justice in 2009. Ruby was one of Canada's most prominent criminal and civil rights lawyers.

A Victory Against Systemic Delays

With a team of high-powered lawyers backing them up, Elijah and the other men argued their case at the Supreme Court of Canada on March 23, 1990. It was one of Chief Justice Brian Dickson's last cases, as he retired on July 1, 1990, and Antonio Lamer became Chief Justice. The decision came on October 18, 1990, relatively quickly by the court's standards. Elijah and his co-accused had succeeded: The proceedings against them were stayed, and they were free to go.

In *Askov*, the Supreme Court developed a framework for determining whether a delay was reasonable. The court was unanimous in finding that the thirty-four-month delay in this case was unreasonable, but it was highly divided when it came to what the test for unreasonable delay should be. A five-judge majority defined the test, but there were four separate concurring opinions from the remaining judges, who disagreed with various aspects of the reasonableness analysis. This fragmented disagreement foreshadowed some of the issues that would arise in the aftermath of the *Askov* decision.

Justice Peter Cory wrote the majority decision. He first outlined the purpose of section 11(b), writing that there were two aspects to the right being protected: an individual aspect and a societal aspect. On an individual level, section 11(b) protected a person's liberty and security of the person. Because our criminal justice system has a presumption of innocence, a person should have the opportunity to clear their name at the earliest possible time. From a societal perspective, the public also has an interest in a timely trial, Justice Cory wrote, because it reassures the community that accused persons are treated fairly and that those who break the law are brought to justice.

With these dual purposes in mind, Justice Cory outlined the factors to be considered when determining whether a delay was unreasonable. The first was the length of the delay — longer delays would be more difficult to justify. The court would then determine the cause of the delay by looking at the conduct of the Crown and the accused, as well as systemic or institutional delays.

Given the facts of the *Askov* case, where the delay was caused largely by a lack of judicial resources, Cory focused most of his attention on the issue of systemic or institutional delays. He wrote that the right to be tried in a reasonable time is so important that a lack of resources cannot be used to justify delays. While there should be some leeway given to the government for funding issues, those who cause the delays (in this case, those setting the budgets) should ultimately bear the blame if cases are dismissed.

In order to determine if a systemic delay was unreasonable, Justice Cory said courts should look to comparable jurisdictions in Canada. Finally, he wrote, a delay was presumed to prejudice the accused, and the Crown should bear the burden of proving that there was no prejudice to the accused if they wanted to excuse the delay.

Applying this framework to Askov's case, Cory said the thirty-four-month delay was so long that it would require a very strong justification, even factoring in the six months of delay caused by Elijah asking for more time to prepare for trial. The major cause of the delay in this case, he said, was systemic. He found that Peel's times to trial were, on average, up to four times longer than other comparable regions in Canada. Moreover, Elijah's case took longer to get to trial than 90 percent of cases in Peel. In colourful language, Cory wrote: "This case therefore represents one of the worst from the point of view of delay in the worst district not only in Canada, but so far as the studies indicate, anywhere north of the Rio Grande."

Justice Cory did not stop at finding the delay in Elijah's case unreasonable. He added that, considering comparable districts in Canada, other delays of six to eight months might be unreasonable in Peel.

An Earthquake Hits the Legal System

The court's decision hit like a 7.0 earthquake, sending shockwaves throughout Canada's legal system that continue to reverberate today. In the first thirteen months afterward, 51,971 criminal charges were dismissed, stayed, or withdrawn in Ontario alone — an estimated 27,000 individual cases. The media had a field day. Politicians, prosecutors, and even the Supreme Court justices themselves immediately faced backlash after these purges. Within a few months, Howard Hampton, the attorney general of Ontario, announced that the provincial government would spend $10 million in emergency funding to hire more judges, Crown attorneys, and support staff.

The Supreme Court was clearly feeling the heat as well. In a highly unusual move, Justice Cory, speaking at an "ask a Supreme Court justice anything" panel at a legal conference in Cambridge, England, in July 1991, claimed *Askov* had been misinterpreted. Judges rarely speak about their cases, and Cory's remarks in response to a question from journalist Stephen Bindman raised eyebrows. As seen in cases like *Lavell* (discrimination against pregnant women), *Rodriguez* (assisted suicide), or *Bedford* (prostitution), it often takes decades for the Supreme Court to revisit its decisions. The Supreme Court took the opportunity to walk back some of its *Askov* decision just two years later, in *R v. Morin*.

The Aftermath for Elijah Askov

Although Elijah was free to go after the Supreme Court stayed his charges, it wasn't long before he was in trouble again. Less than a year later, he was arrested for drug trafficking after he sold cocaine to an undercover police officer. In May 1991, he was given a six-year sentence for the trafficking charges.

Elijah was released without serving his full sentence, but he was arrested again in 1993 for breaking and entering in Niagara. In 1995, back in prison, Elijah reflected on how his time in prison had made it difficult for him to adjust to life on the outside. He recalled a time when he found himself screaming at a streetcar driver who had politely asked him to move out of the way. Elijah was eventually able to compose himself, but his initial reaction was automatic. He said he had developed that behaviour in prison because "you want the next guy to worry about you. It's survival."

In 2003, Elijah was again convicted of possessing cocaine for the purpose of trafficking. His activities after that are unknown. If he is still alive, he would turn eighty years old in 2026.

The Continuing Plague of Delay

R v. Askov did not solve the problem of delay in the Canadian justice system. In 2016, the Supreme Court established a new framework for dealing with delay, lamenting that the justice system had come to tolerate excessive delay. The decision did not result in significant change, however, and in 2025, the Supreme Court was scheduled to yet again address the issue of unreasonable delay.

17

Equality in Substance: Mark Andrews

Mark Andrews was an unlikely poster child for the new equality protections of the Canadian Charter of Rights of Freedoms, which were deemed so potentially disruptive they were delayed for three years, until 1985, to come into effect. Women like the Famous Five and Stella Bliss, Chinese immigrants like Quong Wing, and Jehovah's Witnesses spurred the constitutional entrenchment of equality rights, but perhaps it took a white, male, Oxford-educated British citizen like Mark Andrews to make it easier for the Supreme Court of Canada to embrace a broader notion of equality under the Charter.

Mark's Early Years

Mark David Andrews was born in 1959 at a Royal Air Force (RAF) base in West Germany. Mark got used to moving around during his childhood because of his father's position in the RAF. He attended a variety of schools but ended up at Abingdon Senior School in Oxfordshire, England, graduating in 1978. Perhaps demonstrating a rebellious streak to go along with his determination, Mark once ran away from Abingdon, covering nearly sixteen kilometres on foot before his father found him and returned him to the school, but not before taking Mark home for tea. At Abingdon, Mark started rowing and became known for his prowess in the sport.

Mark joined the British Army for a short while, but he didn't want to follow in his father's footsteps. He left to attend Oxford University's Magdalen College, where he studied law (known as "reading law" in the United Kingdom). Oxford was an eventful time for Mark. In addition to his studies, he continued to participate in rowing competitions and often took home medals for winning races. In 1980 and 1981, he was a member of the men's eight rowing team that won the Cambridge–Oxford boat race along the Thames River. Mark also rowed for England in the World Championships, earning a Silver medal — something not many Canadian lawyers can brag about.

At Oxford, Mark met his future partner, Shelagh Scarth, a Canadian from Winnipeg who was one of the first women to win a prestigious Rhodes Scholarship. Shelagh and Mark met in 1979 while she was also reading law and rowing at Magdalen College. The couple made their first trip to Winnipeg in 1982 for Mark to meet Shelagh's parents. They then travelled overland to British Columbia, falling in love with the West Coast.

Starting Their Careers in Vancouver

The couple married in 1983, in the same chapel in Winnipeg where Shelagh's parents had wed thirty years earlier. The couple set their hearts on Vancouver and moved there after their wedding, ready to start their careers as lawyers in Canada. Both secured articling positions at top Vancouver firms. They completed their articles, passed the Law Society's exams, and satisfied the governing lawyers that they were of good character. Shelagh was called to the bar, but Mark was not yet a Canadian citizen, and the Barristers and Solicitors Act in British Columbia required that all lawyers be Canadian citizens.

Mark was fortunate to have supporters to help him challenge this requirement. He had articled at Russell & DuMoulin, a large, highly respected Vancouver firm. At six-foot-six, Mark was hard to miss. Even as an articling student, he must have made quite an impression on the lawyers at his firm, because they rallied behind him. First, they took his case to the Law Society of British Columbia, seeking an amendment to remove the citizenship requirement from the governing act. The governors of the Law Society rejected the positive recommendation made by a committee studying the issue. Next, Mark's colleagues brought his case to the membership at the annual general meeting. Again they were unsuccessful. The only recourse left was the courts. Meanwhile, Russell & DuMoulin decided to pay Mark the salary he would have been paid as an associate lawyer while he continued to work at the firm as an extended articling student.

Challenging the Law

Mark's Russell & DuMoulin colleagues also supported a legal challenge to the law. At the British Columbia Supreme Court, Mark's friend and colleague Geoff Cowper argued his case. They had the misfortune of drawing Justice Martin Taylor — a judge who himself was an English immigrant who had had to wait five years to qualify to be a citizen and then several more years to become a lawyer. He thought the requirement was necessary for immigrants to acculturate to Canada and rejected Mark's challenge. The next stop was the court of appeal.

In a judgment written by Justice Beverley McLachlin (who would later be appointed to the Supreme Court of Canada, eventually becoming its Chief Justice), the British Columbia Court of Appeal ruled in Mark's favour in May 1986. After the court's decision, Mark was called to the bar. He was now able to practise law, but he continued his larger legal challenge.

Justice McLachlin held that the citizenship requirement violated the right to equality under section 15 of the Charter of Rights and Freedoms and was not justified as a reasonable limit under section 1 of the Charter. Citizenship was not among the listed grounds of discrimination under section 15, but Justice McLachlin held that the list was not exhaustive and could expand to include other grounds, such as citizenship. The Law Society applied for and was granted leave to appeal the decision to the Supreme Court of Canada.

Taking Their Case to the Supreme Court of Canada

The Law Society's appeal was heard over two days in October 1987 before seven of the nine Supreme Court judges. Geoff Cowper had represented Mark by himself at the lower courts, but this time he was joined by another colleague, Stanley Martin. This was the first case the Supreme Court had heard dealing with equality rights under section 15 since that provision came into force in 1985. The stakes were high. In addition to the Government of British Columbia, the attorneys general of five other provinces intervened in the case. Other public interest intervenors, representing what became known as "Charter Canadians" or "equality-seeking groups," also participated. These included the Women's Legal Education and Action Fund, the Coalition of Provincial Organizations of the Handicapped, the Canadian Association of University Teachers, and the Ontario Confederation of University Faculty Associations.

All of the participants were concerned in one way or another with the approach to equality that the Supreme Court would take. Under the Canadian Bill of Rights, the Supreme Court had embraced a "formal equality" approach where it examined whether a law treated "similarly situated" groups the same. This was exemplified in cases like *Bliss* (1978) that had become notorious. Governments were concerned that the court would embrace too broad a vision of equality, potentially putting hundreds of their laws at risk. Equality-seeking groups were concerned that the court would continue to embrace formal equality, making it harder to challenge discriminatory action.

In February 1989, the Supreme Court ruled in Mark's favour and held that the citizenship requirement in British Columbia's Barristers and Solicitors Act violated section 15 of the Charter. The court expressly rejected an approach of formal equality, opting instead to embrace the concept of substantive equality, focusing on disadvantages experienced by historically oppressed groups.

The court held that the assessment of section 15(1) rights involves a two-step legal test. First, the impugned provision will violate section 15(1) if it creates a distinction that has the effect of imposing burdens or disadvantages on a group that are not imposed on others, or of withholding access

Lawyer Mark Andrews.

to opportunities and advantages that are available to other members of the community. Second, the distinction cannot be justified as a reasonable limit under the *Oakes* test.

Andrews after *Andrews*

After winning the case and being admitted to the bar, Mark had a long and successful career as a commercial litigator at Russell & DuMoulin, now known as Fasken. In an age where lawyers often go from firm to firm for various reasons, Mark remained loyal to the firm that had stood by him when he was blocked from becoming a lawyer. In 2004, he was named Queen's Counsel in recognition of his advocacy experience and skill. He was also made a fellow of the prestigious American College of Trial Lawyers, one of fewer than 350 Canadian lawyers to be so recognized. Because of his strong commitment to equality, Mark never shied away from representing unpopular clients.

Shelagh and Mark had four children and one grandson. Shelagh also had a successful legal career. She was a partner in the British Columbia firm Shrum, Liddle & Hebenton, which merged in the mid-1980s with McCarthy & McCarthy of Toronto to become McCarthy Tétrault. She was appointed as a "Master," a judicial officer now known as an associate justice.

Mark's Last Appeal

Mark returned to the Supreme Court as a lawyer on several occasions. In his final appearance, in December 2019, he was joined by the colleagues who had represented him before the same court more than thirty years before and had become his lifelong friends: Geoff Cowper and Stanley Martin. Strangely, the lawyer who had represented the Law Society of British Columbia was also participating. By this time, Mark was dying of brain cancer, but he was still on the top of his game as an advocate. When his allotted argument time was over, the judges allowed Mark to continue because they wanted to hear more of what he had to say. Mark passed away in March 2020, before the Supreme Court issued its decision in his last case.

After Mark's death, the Law Society of British Columbia created the Mark Andrews Excellence in Litigation Award to recognize strong advocates and litigators — a fitting tribute for the lawyer who forced the Law Society and the government to abandon their discriminatory policy.

18

Making Equality Real for LGBTQ People: Delwin Vriend

Delwin Vriend's story represents a shift in the history of LGBTQ rights in Canada and the development of equality rights under the Charter. In 1991, Delwin was fired from his job as a lab instructor and coordinator in Edmonton solely because he was gay. The Supreme Court decision in Delwin's favour was both a turning point for the recognition of LGBTQ rights in Canada and a flashpoint in the relationship between courts and legislatures.

Growing Up Gay in Alberta in the 1970s and 1980s

Delwin Vriend was born in Sioux Center, Iowa, in January 1966. His family moved to Edmonton when he was two years old. Delwin spent his childhood and teenage years in Edmonton, where his family were devout members of the Christian Reformed Church, a Calvinist branch of Christianity. The church's teachings emphasize the promotion of Christian values in education and political advocacy. It holds the position that homosexuality is incompatible with obedience to the will of God and is a sin.

In the 1970s and 1980s, Canada was not a particularly welcoming or safe environment for LGBTQ persons. In the 1960s, the RCMP had operated a nationwide surveillance regime, sending agents into known gay bars to photograph patrons. Officers would make sweeps of areas where gay men met, interrogating them and demanding the names of other gay men. Police collected the names of thousands of potentially queer people. The federal government even funded research that aimed to scientifically detect homosexuality. It was not uncommon for queer Canadians to lose their jobs because of their sexuality.

In the 1970s and early 1980s, police across Canada conducted raids of bathhouses and gay bars in an effort to clamp down on what was seen as morally reprehensible behaviour. Before the 1976 Olympics in Montreal, police violently raided multiple bathhouses in the city and arrested over a hundred men. They claimed to be "cleaning up" the city before the Olympics. The idea of gay existence as unclean and morally reprehensible was seen as justification for the use of bawdy house legislation to discriminate against queer Canadians and attack gay bars and bathhouses. In 1981, when Delwin was fifteen years old, police raided the Pisces Health Spa in Edmonton. They arrested fifty-three men in one night, sending a clear message to the queer community in Edmonton: You are not welcome here. This was the reality of queer existence as Delwin Vriend grew up.

Throughout his childhood, Delwin attended private Christian schools. It was obvious to him that the teachers were concerned he was gay. Delwin hid his sexual orientation from the people around him all through middle and high school and when he attended The King's College in Edmonton for his first year of university. He then transferred to Calvin University in Grand Rapids, Michigan, for "three hell years," where he completed his studies in physics and mathematics. In 1987, shortly after being hired as a lab instructor at The King's College, Delwin came out to his parents, who responded positively, accepting his identity. The same cannot be said for the administration at the university.

Discrimination and Termination

In 1987, The King's College had no explicit policy on homosexuality. Delwin was open and honest with his direct superior at work, choosing to reveal his sexual orientation. Delwin became an active member in Edmonton's LGBTQ community, joining the Gay and Lesbian Awareness Society (GALA), a group dedicated to promoting civil rights for LGBTQ Edmontonians and awareness of issues impacting the LGBTQ community.

The president of The King's College learned about Delwin's sexuality and, in February 1990, called him into his office to confirm it. Delwin later learned that an influential donor from southern Alberta had threatened to pull his funding from the school if Delwin was not fired. For the next year, in consultation with the board of directors and donors, the university began working on a policy that would prohibit LGBTQ people from being employed at the school.

Nearly a year after inquiring about Delwin's sexuality, the university's president asked him to resign. Delwin refused and was promptly fired. He was told explicitly that his termination was because of his sexuality.

Knowing full well that his unjust termination was a real possibility, Delwin had already consulted with a lawyer, Victor Leginsky. In June 1991, Delwin filed a complaint with the Alberta Human Rights Commission. Delwin did not set out to go to the Supreme Court; he simply wanted the Alberta government to protect him from discrimination, as it did other Albertans with its Individual's Rights Protection Act (IRPA).

Alberta's Human Rights Protection

The legislative framework for Alberta's human rights protection originated in 1972. The IRPA prohibited discrimination in public notices, accommodation, tenancy, pay, and employment practices based on certain specific grounds. In its original form, the IRPA set out that people are equal without regard to race, religious beliefs, colour, sex, age, ancestry, or place of origin. Notably, sexual orientation was missing from this list. In its preamble, the act made clear that Alberta sought to recognize the equal and inalienable rights of persons as the "foundation for peace and justice in our society," as a fundamental principle in Alberta and as a pressing matter of public policy.

Before Delwin's application to the Alberta Human Rights Commission, the IRPA had been amended to add gender, physical disability, and mental disability as specific protected grounds. The sections of the act prohibiting discrimination allowed the commission to accept only complaints based on these enumerated grounds.

In July 1991, the commission informed Delwin that he was unable to make a complaint under the IRPA because sexual orientation was not a protected status. The commission had been specifically directed by the Alberta government not to investigate cases related to sexual orientation.

Delwin was expecting this result. By 1992, he was the president of GALA. Working with GALA, the affiliated Gay and Lesbian Community Centre of Edmonton, and Dignity Canada Dignité, for gay Catholics and supporters, Delwin launched a Charter claim against the Alberta government challenging the constitutionality of the IRPA provisions that left Delwin without any recourse for the discrimination he faced. Specifically, they argued that section 15 of the Charter, which guarantees equality before and under the law as individuals within Canada, had been violated by the IRPA by excluding sexual orientation.

Delwin's case was no longer an individual claim. He was no longer fighting to get his job back; he was fighting for protection against discrimination for all LGBTQ persons in Alberta.

The Journey Through the Lower Courts

Justice Anne Russell heard Delwin's case at Alberta's Court of Queen's Bench in 1993 and delivered her decision on April 12, 1994. To that point, section 15 of the Charter had never been used successfully to counter discrimination against gay Canadians. Section 15 protects all Canadians against discrimination, but like the IRPA, it lists certain grounds (race, national or ethnic origin, colour, religion, sex, age, or mental or physical disability) that are specifically protected. Section 15 claims can be successful only if discrimination occurred based on one of the enumerated grounds — or any ground the court deems analogous. In 1995, the Supreme Court would recognize sexual orientation as an "analogous ground"; however, until *Vriend*, the Supreme Court had never found in favour of a LGBTQ person.

Justice Russell's decision came before the Supreme Court's 1995 decision, but she still found that homosexual people were analogous to the groups protected by section 15 of the Charter. She wrote that omitting sexual orientation from the IRPA reinforced stereotypes against gay people and perpetuated and tacitly endorsed discrimination in Alberta. She said the law had a differential impact on Delwin, and therefore his right to equality was infringed when he was denied the legal remedy offered to other disenfranchised groups. The judge cited the preamble of the IRPA, which sets out the purpose of the act as recognizing the inherent dignity and equality of people. She wrote that omitting sexual orientation "controverts the very principle [the act] purports to embody." The Alberta government had no justification for overriding these Canadians' rights, she ruled.

Delwin Vriend smiles at a news conference in Edmonton after the Supreme Court of Canada ruled that the government of Alberta must recognize sexual orientation under the Charter of Rights and Freedoms.

Justice Russell concluded that the only justifiable remedy in this case would be to "read in" sexual orientation to the act. Reading in is a remedy in constitutional cases, where judges will add certain terms to a statute to make it conform to the Constitution. In essence, because the Albertan government refused to add sexual orientation as a ground for protection under the IRPA, Justice Russell did it herself. She considered striking down the unconstitutional legislation as a whole but said that would do nothing to help Delwin and would put more disadvantaged people in danger.

Justice Russell's ruling was a big win for the Vriend team, but it would be short-lived. The provincial government appealed the decision to the Alberta Court of Appeal.

Setback at the Court of Appeal

Over the next year, in preparation for the appeal, Delwin changed his legal team, taking on Harvard Law graduate Douglas Stollery. He also recruited Sheila Greckol, one of the leading labour and human rights lawyers in Alberta, who took the case on a pro bono basis. Many intervenors joined the case during the appeal, including the Canadian Human Rights Commission, the Evangelical Fellowship of Canada, and Focus on the Family Canada.

The hearing before the court of appeal did not go well. The appeal was heard by three judges: Willis O'Leary, Constance Hunt, and the infamous John "Buzz" McClung. The grandson of Famous Five member Nellie McClung, Justice McClung was known for holding strong conservative views, as well as a surly disposition. When Sheila Greckol began her oral argument, Justice McClung turned his back to her, facing the wall of the courtroom. Douglas Stollery referred to the event as "unprecedented ... it was a sad day for the justice system."

Thus, it came as no surprise to Delwin's team when, on February 23, 1996, the court of appeal released its decision, allowing the government's appeal by a 2–1 margin. The reasons delivered in Justice McClung's judgment contained archaic stereotyping and moral grandstanding. He suggested that if the Alberta government were to validate and protect homosexual relationships, it would rebut "a millenia [sic] of moral teaching." He also stated that Justice Russell should have "exercised self-restraint" and not ventured into the territory of the legislature simply because human rights were involved.

Delwin was not deterred. Shortly after the decision was released, his team filed for appeal with the Supreme Court of Canada, and the court agreed to hear his case.

In Front of the Supreme Court

The atmosphere in the Supreme Court was very different than at the court of appeal. Although Delwin's legal team entered the courtroom to find religious pamphlets laid out which denounced the sin of homosexuality, they were treated with respect by the judges. The case attracted significant attention across the country; seventeen intervenors participated in the hearing. These included human rights organizations, religious groups, LGBT associations, and representatives of the governments of Canada and Ontario.

All nine justices heard the case, but only eight were involved in writing the decision. A week after the hearing, Justice John Sopinka passed away suddenly at the age of sixty-four. He was the first Supreme Court justice to die in office since Chief Justice Bora Laskin passed away in 1984. Delwin's legal team was scared that his death would spell the end for them, as they saw Justice Sopinka as their "swing vote." Their worries were unfounded. The court unanimously declared that the IRPA was in violation of section 15 of the Charter.

There was some disagreement among the judges as to the correct interpretation of section 15. Contrary to the majority, Justice Claire L'Heureux-Dubé said the focus of an equality rights analysis should be on uncovering the negative impacts discrimination has on individuals rather than on whether the individual fits into an enumerated or analogous ground. The Supreme Court criticized Justice McClung's decision and reaffirmed the courts' role as interpreters of the Constitution: Judges are not overstepping, or lacking in self-restraint, when they act to ensure that legislation conforms with our Constitution; indeed, that is the precise role of the courts.

Seven of the eight justices agreed with Justice Russell that the appropriate remedy was to read in sexual orientation to the IRPA. Reading in would ensure that the Charter and the original purpose of the IRPA were respected while maintaining the human rights legislation for the rest of Albertans. Only Justice Jack Major — an Albertan — disagreed with the majority. He believed the legislation should be struck down in its entirety. He suggested that reading in would be appropriate if it could be safely assumed that the legislature intended to resolve the under-inclusiveness of the act. However, the Alberta government had consistently refused to fix its omission. For that reason, he thought it best to strike it down and give the government the chance to draft sound legislation — or to use the notwithstanding clause to keep the IRPA in force as it stood before the decision.

When the decision was released in April 1998, there were immediate calls by Christian and conservative groups across Alberta for the government to use the Charter's notwithstanding clause to override the Supreme Court's decision. The Alberta government could have introduced legislation to keep the IRPA exactly as it was, notwithstanding its breach of equality rights. However, by mid-April, Premier Ralph Klein announced the decision not to use the override.

Delwin Vriend's journey through the courts was over. More than seven years after he had lost his job because he was gay, Delwin had won a huge victory for LGBTQ persons in Alberta, and indeed in all of Canada.

Vriend's Impact

During the case, the IRPA was renamed the Alberta Human Rights Act. Its content today remains much the same as it was in 1991, with one clear distinction: sexual orientation was added to the legislation in every relevant section. This didn't happen immediately. It took eleven years after the *Vriend* decision. Today, gay Albertans enjoy the same rights protection as other protected classes. If they face discrimination in housing, employment, or obtaining goods or services, they can file a complaint to vindicate their rights.

As for Delwin Vriend, he never applied to get his job back at The King's College. During the arduous eight-year process and the intense media scrutiny, he felt the need to change careers and to return to a relatively secluded life. He worked at the library at the University of Alberta for five years, then left Canada in 2000. Today, Delwin lives in Paris, where runs his own software and website consulting company.

19

Seeking Same-Sex Marriage: The Michaels

Michael Leshner and Michael Stark, known as "the Michaels," became the first same-sex couple to be issued a marriage licence in Canada. This historic event in June 2003 resulted in *Time* magazine naming them Canadian Newsmakers of the Year and paved the way for other same-sex couples to marry. Their legal victory was the culmination of decades of political advocacy and legal battles by LGBTQ advocates.

Michael, Michael, and "the Michaels"

Michael Leshner was born in Niagara Falls, New York, in 1948. The grandson of Jewish immigrants, Leshner faced challenges growing up gay in St. Catharines, Ontario. This led him to pursue higher education at the University of Toronto, where he earned a law degree in 1973. He then began working as an assistant crown attorney.

Michael "Mike" Stark, was born in Nova Scotia into a strict Catholic family. Growing up in rural areas in a military family, Mike found it difficult to come out until he was in his twenties. Stark, about ten years younger than

Leshner, moved to Toronto to study at Ryerson University (now Toronto Metropolitan University) and worked in graphic communication at a printing company.

Leshner and Stark met in Toronto's Gay Village in 1981. On May 23, the Victoria Day long weekend, Stark was supposed to go see a movie with a friend. She cancelled at the last minute, and Stark, having recently come out, decided to go out anyway. He found himself at the intersection of Church and Gerrard, at the entrance to Buddies, a well-known underground gay bar. He walked nervously around the block several times; he didn't want anyone to see him enter. He finally gathered up the courage to go in.

Leshner was far more confident in his sexuality. He lived in the neighbourhood, had several gay friends, and was much more established in his career. The young Stark, with his bubbly demeanour and short, curly hair, caught Leshner's eye. Leshner approached Stark and introduced himself. Aside from a very short-lived breakup that lasted only a few hours, they have been together ever since.

Homophobia in Canada

At the time, however, the gay community faced great discrimination. In February 1981, just months before the Michaels met, hundreds of police officers had raided four of Toronto's gay bathhouses in "Operation Soap." Nearly three hundred men faced criminal charges, either for being in a bawdy house or for operating one. Most of these charges were eventually dropped, and thirty-five years later, Toronto police issued an official apology. In a teary interview, Stark shared: "We could see we were living in a society where we were being held back because of our sexual orientation. Michael [Leshner] made it a mission: he wanted to see, in his lifetime, that those legal impediments be taken away."

In the early days, the couple took part in various protests and media interviews. They attended the first Gay Pride Parade in the summer of 1981. At that point, Pride parades were more a march and demonstration than the celebrations they have since become. There was virtually no goodwill between the police and the gay and lesbian community. Besides trying to shift public opinion and gain traction politically, Leshner opted for a legal strategy to advance the fight for equal rights. The right to marry, Leshner felt, was the "last piece in the puzzle" to gaining equality.

Leshner's Influence on Human Rights Efforts

In 1992, Leshner, employed by the Ontario government, gained attention for successfully advocating for himself and Stark before the Ontario Human Rights Tribunal. His argument focused on securing survivor pensions for gay individuals — and not only within the government; he also urged private companies to adopt similar policies. Leshner emphasized the need for social change and discouraged a victim mentality within the gay and lesbian community.

Leshner's efforts in 1992 influenced the Ontario New Democratic Party government of Bob Rae to propose the Equality Rights Statute Amendment Act (Bill 167) in 1994. The bill would have provided cohabiting same-sex couples with rights and obligations nearly equal to those of opposite-sex couples in a common-law marriage by amending the definition of "spouse" in seventy-nine provincial statutes. It would not have conferred same-sex marriage rights, however, because the definition of marriage is a matter of federal jurisdiction. There was strong public and political opposition to the bill, and it was defeated at the second reading, after the withdrawal of support from the Liberal Party.

Among the religious and conservative voices against the bill, Don Pennell of the Family Coalition Party of Ontario stated, "Homosexuals may choose to behave in a certain way but it is wrong for the government to legally sanction and support these choices. This legislation would have put heterosexual and homosexual relationships on virtually the same level, which is morally reprehensible and economically foolish."

In 1999, the Supreme Court of Canada ruled that the exclusion of same-sex couples from the definition of "spouse" when it came to benefits violated the Charter. This set the stage for a challenge on the prohibition of same-sex couples marrying.

Seven Same-Sex Couples Seek Same-Sex Marriage

In December 2000, at the Metropolitan Community Church of Toronto, Pastor Brent Hawkes initiated the publication of "banns of marriage" (i.e., the public announcement of an impending marriage). This prelude aimed at officiating wedding ceremonies for two same-sex couples, Kevin Bourassa and Joe Varnell, and Anne and Elaine Vautour, scheduled for January 14, 2001. Banns of marriage were recognized as a legally valid method for conducting a marriage without the necessity of a city-issued marriage licence. There was a legal void, since both processes required certification by the provincial registrar, setting the stage for a court case to force the registrar to certify same-sex marriages.

Throughout the year, additional same-sex couples, including Hedy Halpern and Colleen Rogers, joined the legal challenge. When he learned of his colleagues' intentions to advocate for the legalization of same-sex civil marriage, Leshner convinced Stark to marry him, prompting them to join the case. Leshner proposed to Stark in front of reporters.

The case began at the Ontario Superior Court in November 2001 and become known as *Halpern* because Hedy and Colleen were the first of the seven couples listed in the lawsuit. On July 12, 2002, the court ruled in

Michael Leshner (left) and Michael Stark (centre) hold their marriage licence after being married by Superior Court Justice John Hamilton (right) in Toronto on Tuesday, June 10, 2003.

favour of the couples. It mandated the extension of marriage rights to same-sex couples but decided to postpone the implementation of the ruling for a two-year period to give the legislature time to respond.

It was on to the Ontario Court of Appeal, which issued its decision on June 10, 2003. The unanimous ruling concluded that the exclusion of same-sex couples was a blatant violation of equality rights under the Charter and did not qualify as a reasonable limit under section 1. In addition, the court determined that there would be no suspension of the remedy for the general population: The newly established definition allowing same-sex couples to marry would come into effect immediately.

Making Same-Sex Marriage Legal

The Michaels became the first gay couple to be issued a marriage licence after the decision, while Bourassa and Varnell and the Vautours became the first legally recognized same-sex spouses, since their marriages were deemed legal as of the date of the original ceremonies. The Michaels' wedding took place immediately following the court of appeal's decision in *Halpern*.

The morning of June 10, 2003, was chilly but sunny in Toronto. The couple had been told a few days before that the decision would be coming out that morning. The Michaels hopped off the Bay Street bus, carrying their brand-new suits and wedding bands, and briskly walked over to Osgoode Hall (the home of the appeal court) with their lawyer to hear the decision on *Halpern*. Leshner was excited, sensing they were about to cross the finish line. Hoping for a positive outcome, the Michaels lined up three judges who were willing to officiate the wedding. There was no big announcement from the court. At about 10:00 a.m., paper copies of the ruling were handed out at the courthouse. Everyone flipped to read the last few pages. There it was — Ontario finally recognized same-sex marriage.

The next few hours were critical. The couple needed to marry before the federal government had a chance to appeal the decision, which could temporarily suspend the court's ruling. As Stark put it, "It was a move to get at least one couple married, so that at least there'd be one on the books." Immediately after the release of the decision, the Michaels picked up their marriage licence at Toronto City Hall and rushed back to the courthouse for their wedding ceremony. About thirty to forty people gathered in the small cloak room. The wedding had no flowers or decorations. It did have Leshner's ninety-year-old mother, in her wheelchair, grinning from the moment Stark and her son walked into the room until the couple exchanged their vows and rings. Leshner's mother, suffering from dementia, inspired by ceremony, began singing "O Canada" ... a few times.

The photo of the Michaels' first kiss as a married couple circulated around the world. If there had been social media, it would have gone viral. The story was covered by *The New York Times*, *Le Monde*, and even the state-owned *China Daily*. "It really sunk in how historic [that day] was," Stark told the CBC. "We knew it would be big, but we never really envisioned it would be as big as it was."

Two months later, the Michaels hosted a wonderful reception for family, friends, and special supporters — a truly beautiful, emotional experience. They went to California a few weeks later for a family wedding, then added an extra week for a honeymoon, accompanied, of course, by their schnauzer, Schmikey.

Response Inside and Outside of Canada

In the aftermath of *Halpern*, the federal government decided to accept the result reached by the Ontario Court of Appeal, and thus did not seek leave to appeal to the Supreme Court of Canada. *Halpern* was one of a series of same-sex marriage cases brought across Canada that succeeded in having the common law definition of marriage struck down as unconstitutional. In the two years following the decision, courts in seven of Canada's other nine provinces and one of its three territories also legalized same-sex marriage in their jurisdictions.

Instead of appealing these cases, the Liberal government produced a draft bill in July 2003 that would redefine marriage. Before proceeding with the introduction of the bill in Parliament, the government referred the bill to the Supreme Court, asking four questions about its validity. The Michaels were invited to participate as intervenors, along with the other *Halpern* couples, and did so. The decision in *Reference re Same-Sex Marriage* upheld the constitutionality of the bill, effectively allowing same-sex marriage in all provinces. The bill, passed into law as the Civil Marriage Act, allows for the marriage of same-sex couples while ensuring religious freedom by allowing officials of religious groups to decline to perform the marriage if same-sex marriage is against the beliefs of the religion.

In enacting the Civil Marriage Act in 2005, Canada became the fourth country in the world to legalize same-sex marriage, after the Netherlands, Belgium, and Spain. As of 2025, same-sex marriage is officially recognized in thirty-eight countries. More than sixty countries, however, continue to criminalize homosexuality; in twelve of them, being gay is an offence punishable by death.

The United States Supreme Court, which rarely pays much attention to Canada, treated *Halpern* as an exception. Two weeks after the Ontario Court of Appeal's decision, the U.S. Supreme Court issued a monumental decision of its own in *Lawerence v. Texas*, declaring laws that criminalized gay sex to be unconstitutional. The majority said the case had nothing to do with gay marriage, but Justice Antonin Scalia, in dissent, disagreed. Pointing north to Canada and invoking *Halpern* by name, Justice Scalia asserted that such was the natural conclusion of court interference in matters that should best be left to the people's democratically elected representatives.

Meanwhile, the Michaels gained prominence in Toronto, and even garnered international attention. *Time* magazine recognized the couple as Canadian Newsmakers of the Year in 2003, symbolizing "the year that Canada rethought what was taboo." In contrast, *The Globe and Mail*, in its selection of "Nation Builders of the Year," did not choose the Michaels, instead recognizing the judges involved in *Halpern* — Chief Justice Roy McMurtry and Justices Eileen Gillese and James MacPherson.

Not all Canadians supported the Michaels, however, with some labelling them a "sick aberration" in letters to newspapers. Others defended them. This division reflected public opinion polls indicating that Canadians were split on the acceptance of same-sex marriage. In 2003, the bishop of the Roman Catholic Diocese of Sault Ste. Marie contended that future Prime Minister Paul Martin would not be considered a true Catholic if his government endorsed same-sex marriage. Around the same time, the bishop of the Roman Catholic Diocese of Calgary suggested that then Prime Minister Jean

Chrétien might face damnation for acknowledging such marriages. Michael Leshner, calling these arguments "religious intolerance," responded, "I think the bishop has consumed too much mad cow.... The Charter of Rights takes precedence over the Bible."

Contemporary Conversations

The Michaels still live in Toronto. Like many other happily married couples, they have kept mementoes from their special day, with framed photos of the historic day hanging on the walls and collections of newspaper clippings. They now embrace their role as gay "ambassadors," spreading the word and acting as mentors and positive role models for the LGBTQ community and the greater society. Like many senior couples, they enjoy warm holidays to escape the cold Canadian winters. One thing they cannot escape, however, is the current political climate, especially in the United States. Leshner is deeply concerned about recent attacks on LGBTQ rights in several U.S. states. "It's all kind of forced. It doesn't seem to be part of the natural progression of issues," he commented. The couple fears that history is repeating itself, despite the social taboo they helped break two decades ago.

20

Unlikely Equality Militants: Joanne Fraser, Colleen Fox, and Allison Pilgrim

Joanne Fraser was living her dream of being a police officer. A mother on leave from the RCMP, she returned to work part-time through the force's job-sharing program. However, participation in the program came with an unexpected catch: lower pension benefits in retirement. This policy had a disproportionate impact on women, who were the vast majority of job-sharing participants. Together with RCMP members Allison Pilgrim and Colleen Fox, Joanne challenged the discriminatory policy. Ultimately, the three women secured a landmark victory at the Supreme Court of Canada for gender equality in the workplace.

Joanne's Early Life and Career

Ever since she was in grade school, Joanne Fraser had wanted to be a police officer. She was born in 1965 and grew up in Milton, Ontario. From a young age, Joanne was involved in her community: She was a Girl Guide and a volunteer at local non-profit organizations through her teenage years. Joanne saw that, like her, the police officers in Milton were heavily involved in the community, and she viewed them as local heroes.

At the age of twenty-three, Joanne joined the RCMP. She met her future husband while completing basic training in Regina in 1990. She was posted to Fort Saskatchewan, Alberta, while her husband-to-be was posted in neighbouring Sherwood Park. From the moment Joanne started her first posting, she knew she had made the right career choice. The job could be gruelling, the hours were often long and unpredictable, but the work was rewarding. At the same time, Joanne was building a family life. She and her husband married in 1991, when she was twenty-five years old.

Motherhood, Maternity Leave, and Return to Work

Because of their schedules, Joanne and her husband saw each other relatively infrequently; both worked long, rotating shifts. In November 1993, Joanne gave birth to the couple's first child. She took just six months of

RCMP Sergeant Joanne Fraser at RCMP National Headquarters in Ottawa on December 3, 2012.

maternity leave and then returned to work full-time in May 1994. They were able to find a reliable babysitter, which made things a bit easier, but their shift work made it difficult to plan even the simplest family activities ahead of time.

At work, Joanne tried not to let on that she was feeling overwhelmed. She was always striving to prove herself, and she worried that her co-workers might perceive her as weak or as a less valuable member of the team.

Joanne gave birth to her second child in September 1996. She initially planned to take another six-month maternity leave; however, during that period, her babysitter informed her that she would not be able to watch the children when Joanne returned to work full-time. The Frasers searched for other child-care options, but they were posted to a small town where choices were extremely limited. With no other reasonable choices, Joanne and her husband decided that she would take a five-year leave of absence without pay, after which she planned to return to work full-time. Joanne began her unpaid leave in March 1997.

The RCMP Job-Sharing Program

In December 1997, the RCMP introduced a program to help members balance their careers with their personal lives. The new job-sharing program allowed two or three members to share a single full-time position for a fixed period of time. This program was intended to benefit both the RCMP and its members.

Colleen Fox was one of the first RCMP members to take advantage of the job-sharing program. She had joined the force in 1987, when she was twenty-two. Her husband was also in the RCMP, and the two were posted to Grand Falls, Newfoundland, a small town of thirteen thousand people. Colleen gave birth to two children, and she and her husband struggled with child-care and other issues. Colleen had been forced to retire from the RCMP in 1994 due to the inflexibility of the force's policies.

Allison Pilgrim learned about the job-sharing program shortly after she finished her second maternity leave in 1998. She had also joined the RCMP in 1987, at twenty-six years old. The RCMP interviewer told her she was the most qualified candidate he had encountered all year. She now had two daughters and had taken two six-month maternity leaves. Like Joanne and Colleen, Allison struggled to balance her job and caring for her young children.

Joanne, Colleen, and Allison all eagerly signed up for the job-sharing program, which had a positive impact on their careers and their family lives. It reduced their stress and helped them to feel like they were contributing to the workplace at the level they had before they had children. Allison said job sharing enabled her to rediscover her love for police work. For Joanne, it allowed her to feel present in her children's lives. She was able to participate in important moments such as school trips, sporting events, and birthday parties. Overall, she felt much more in control of her life, both at work and at home.

The job-sharing program was great for the three women. But it came with a catch.

The RCMP's Pension Buy-Back Program

One of the benefits of working for the RCMP is that both the member and the force make contributions to the member's pension each paycheque. If a member goes on an unpaid leave, they have the opportunity to "buy back" their pension benefits for that period when they return to full-time service, allowing them to receive credit for that time toward their pension. The way a buy-back works is that the member pays both the employee and the employer contributions for that pay period — the buy-back is thus cost-neutral for the RCMP.

Pension Buy-Back Issues and Internal Grievances

Unlike other RCMP members returning from leave, Joanne, Allison, and Colleen were not permitted to participate in the force's pension buy-back program. They had been under the impression that their time in the job-sharing program would be eligible for pension buy-back but soon discovered this was not the case. Both Colleen and Allison initially assumed that this issue must be an oversight — there was no logical reason for the RCMP to prevent them from buying back their pension contributions, as it didn't cost the force any money.

In the summer of 2000, Colleen, Allison, and the ten other job-sharing participants wrote a memo to the commissioner of the RCMP. They requested that pension buy-back for job-sharing be included in a new pension policy, explaining that they felt the current pension policy was penalizing those who chose to participate in the job-sharing program, despite the fact that the RCMP also benefitted from their participation. They pointed out that all twelve of the current job-sharing members were women, and that the policy of not allowing buy-backs for job-sharing was inconsistent with the RCMP's core values.

The assistant commissioner and chief human resources officer responded to the memo, saying that job-sharing roles were considered part-time work and were therefore not eligible for pension buy-back. The assistant commissioner noted that this was a common feature of many pension plans.

During this time, Colleen returned to full-time service and was in a position to buy back any eligible time. She asked to buy back her job-sharing time, and after her request was denied, she filed a formal grievance on November 14, 2000. Allison and another job-sharing member filed similar grievances. In their grievances, Colleen and Allison argued that the pension policy was discriminatory. They argued that all of the job-sharing participants were women, and that the inability to buy back pension benefits put them at a disadvantage compared to those who did not have to use the job-sharing program or who opted instead for full leave without pay.

Due to a backlog of grievances, it took six and a half years for Colleen to receive a decision from the committee reviewing her grievance. On April 30, 2007, the External Review Committee recommended that the RCMP commissioner undertake a full review of discriminatory pension practices. It took until 2010 for the commissioner to consider this recommendation, and in the end the commissioner decided to dismiss Colleen's grievance.

While Colleen's and Allison's grievances were working their way through the system, Joanne ran into the same issue with the pension buy-back. When she returned to full-time service in 2003, she paid $24,000 to buy back her three years of unpaid leave but learned she could not buy back her time spent job-sharing. This came as a surprise because when she was approached about joining the program in 2000, she had been told she would be allowed to buy back job-sharing time. Joanne was disappointed and expressed her view that the policy sent the message that the RCMP did not want women with children to return to duty.

Off to Federal Court

After the commissioner dismissed Colleen and Allison's grievances in 2010, it took another four years before they, along with Joanne, took the next step in their challenge of the pension policy. The three women began their case against the RCMP on November 14, 2014 — fourteen years to the day from when Colleen filed her initial grievance. They advanced two claims. First, they argued that the proper interpretation of the current pension plan was that it allowed job-sharing participants to buy back pension benefits. Second, if that was not the case, they argued that the policy violated their right to equality under section 15(1) of the Charter by preventing women with children (the vast majority of participants in the program) from contributing to their pensions at the same level as those who work full-time or take leave without pay.

Their claim was an "adverse effects" discrimination claim. This type of discrimination arises where a law or policy appears neutral but has a disproportionate impact on members of groups protected by section 15(1). Here, the policy was not blatantly discriminatory on its face, but the applicants argued that it had a disproportionate negative impact on working mothers, who were the primary participants in the job-sharing program.

Joanne, Allison, and Colleen were unsuccessful at the federal court. In a 2017 decision, Justice Catherine Kane found that the job-sharers were properly considered part-time workers and that the buy-back policy was not discriminatory. Justice Kane said there was insufficient evidence to show that the women experienced disadvantages compared to those on unpaid leave and that any potential disadvantages were due to their own personal choices — that is, their choice to participate in the job-sharing program rather than to go on unpaid leave or work full-time.

They lost again at the Federal Court of Appeal, leaving their last hope with the Supreme Court, which agreed to hear their case.

At the Supreme Court of Canada

The full bench of nine judges heard their case on December 12, 2019. It was an uphill battle because the Supreme Court had not accepted a claim of adverse effects discrimination in more than twenty years. However, bucking history, on October 16, 2020, Joanne, Allison, and Colleen received the news that they had won. By a 6–3 margin, the court found that the RCMP's pension policy violated their equality rights under section 15(1) of the Charter due to its adverse effects on women.

Justice Rosalie Silberman Abella wrote for the majority. Abella was known as a champion of equality. She was the first Jewish woman and the first refugee to sit on the high court, and had coined the term "employment equity" as a one-woman commissioner of the federal Royal Commission on Equality in Employment in 1983–84.

Justice Abella noted that adverse effects discrimination is much more prevalent than direct discrimination, and it can pose a greater threat to disadvantaged groups. Therefore, adverse effects discrimination claims can be a powerful tool for disadvantaged groups in Canadian society to seek equality through the court system.

Justice Abella's analysis was guided by the idea of substantive equality, which she said is the "animating norm" of section 15 case law. Substantive equality requires that courts go beyond rigid templates or definitions of discrimination and instead consider the actual impact on the claimants, as well as the full context of the claim, including systemic disadvantages faced by a given group. With this approach in mind, Justice Abella applied the following framework of analysis: First, does the law impose differential treatment on protected grounds, either directly or through adverse impact? And second, if so, does this reinforce existing disadvantages? Applying this test, Abella found that the pension policy had a disproportionate impact on women and that it reinforced existing disadvantages for women in the workplace. It was therefore a violation of Joanne's, Allison's, and Colleen's section 15(1) equality rights.

A key sticking point between the majority and the dissent was the issue of causation: whether the adverse effects were caused by the job-sharers' protected characteristics (in this case, that they were women) or by their own personal *choice* to participate in the program. Justices Malcolm Rowe and Russell Brown took the view that any negative effects on pension benefits were caused by the job-sharers' choice to participate in the program. Their dissent also offered a general criticism of Justice Abella's approach to equality. They said substantive equality would discourage governments from offering ameliorative programs because they would be open to Charter challenges if they did not eliminate disadvantages completely. Moreover, they wrote, substantive equality allows courts to push their own policy preferences because it is a vague concept with moving "goalposts."

The Aftermath for Joanne, Allison, and Colleen

With the Supreme Court ruling in their favour, Joanne, Allison, and Colleen were allowed to buy back their pension credit for the time they spent job-sharing. In her initial court filings, Allison estimated that her pension benefits would be increased by 5 percent if she were able to do a buy-back. All three women are now enjoying retirement.

Speaking about the Supreme Court's decision, Joanne said, "I'm ecstatic. It paves the way for women of the future, for anyone in any position where they have to look after their children and ... their profession at the same time."

The Aftermath for Women in the RCMP

The year 2024 marked fifty years since the first women were sworn in as regular members of the RCMP. Currently, around 20 percent of regular members are women, and there have been two female commissioners. Still, the RCMP has a long way to go in achieving gender equality in the workplace. In addition to the issues faced by mothers like Joanne, Allison, and Colleen, the force has come under fire in recent years for a culture that tolerates misogyny, homophobia, and sexual violence. Between 2016 and 2020, the federal government set aside $100 million to compensate women in the RCMP who were subject to gender-based discrimination and sexual violence.

21

Educating Their Children in French in Alberta: Jean-Claude Mahé, Angéline Martel, and Paul Dubé

Jean-Claude Mahé, Angéline Martel, and Paul Dubé were raising their kids in Edmonton's small francophone community. They wanted their children to maintain their language and culture, but there was one big problem: There were no French schools in the province. So they created one and then, having shown it could be done, took the province to court and invoked the minority language education rights provision of the new Canadian Charter of Rights all the way to the Supreme Court of Canada. They established the right of francophones outside Quebec not only to be educated in French but also to manage their own schools.

Standing Outside the Playground

It all started outside a playground. When parents wait around to pick up their kids after school, they often engage in small talk. They chat about the weather, about sports, and about their kids' activities. But when Jean-Claude

Mahé, Angéline Martel, and Paul Dubé gathered at the fence outside the playground where their children went to a French immersion school in Edmonton, they discussed serious subjects. The three francophone parents were concerned about the education their children were getting. Paul's son was in grade one, and he was making grammatical errors that a native French speaker would never make.

The parents were worried their children were spending more time helping the anglophone children learn French than learning French themselves. Learning was so boring that Paul's son didn't even want to go to school. The three parents were told point-blank by school officials that the French immersion school wasn't for them; it was for anglophones who wanted to learn French. Jean-Claude, Angéline, and Paul dreamed of sending their kids to a school where they would be educated in French. No such school existed in Alberta, but they were determined to change that.

Minority Language Rights Lost in Alberta

Language has always been a central defining characteristic of Canada. Ignoring the presence and the contribution of Indigenous Peoples, the English and the French were seen as the two "founding nations" of Canada. The Constitution Act of 1867 recognized the right to use English or French in the Parliament of Canada, the Quebec Legislature, any court established by the federal government, and any Quebec court. It required that all federal laws and all Quebec laws be printed and published in both French and English.

Prime Minister Pierre Trudeau championed official bilingualism and official minority language rights — rights for francophones outside Quebec and for anglophones in Quebec. Parliament enacted the Official Languages Act in 1969, but the Charter of Rights and Freedoms was the real game changer. In addition to enshrining language rights in the Constitution, it also recognized minority language education rights: the right of minority francophones (or anglophones in Quebec) to be educated in their language, where numbers warranted.

French was the first European language spoken in what became Alberta, and by 1875, most white inhabitants were French-speaking Roman Catholics.

By the early 1890s, English settlers outnumbered the French, and an 1892 law required that schools teach all mandatory subjects in English. After Alberta became a province, laws continued to restrict the use of French in schools, and the government provided no support for French teaching. Everything was left in the hands of volunteers.

Although there were no French schools, there were bilingual schools, which essentially became French immersion due to their increased popularity among anglophones. Jean-Claude, Angéline, and Paul sent their children to such a school, and they noted the lower quality of French being taught, as well as the English cultural setting of these schools. They worried about a loss of francophone identity and cultural assimilation, as francophone assimilation was upward of 70 percent in Alberta.

Three Determined Parents

Jean-Claude and Paul had become close friends while attending the University of Alberta. Angéline and Jean-Claude were married and had two young children who attended the same primary school as Paul's son. The three francophones had grown up in an environment where French was very much in the minority: Paul was originally from rural Manitoba, while Angéline and Jean-Claude were both from northern Alberta.

Many Franco-Albertan parents were dissatisfied with the school program, which was poorly suited to kids with French as their mother tongue. Paul noticed that his son's French was actually getting worse. However, the majority of French parents settled for immersion schools. After decades of assimilation and feeling invisible in politics, they could not imagine anything better. Many no longer believed in French education and were pessimistic about the possibility of obtaining major change from a government that had done so little for them. Some also feared that placing their children in separate French schools would marginalize them.

Jean-Claude, Angéline, and Paul decided to take action. Jean-Claude first approached the Association canadienne-française de l'Alberta to propose a new French school but received a discouraging response. Undeterred, the parents sought a meeting with the minister of Education. The Alberta government was reluctant to initiate anything, as it was handling the negative economic impacts of federal energy policies and the political fallout from Quebec's restrictive language law, Bill 101, the Charter of the French Language, which was deeply unpopular outside Quebec. The government told the parents to negotiate with the two Edmonton boards of education — public and Catholic. Both boards refused their entreaties.

The parents decided to go it alone. In June 1982, Jean-Claude, Angéline, and Paul, along with six other parents, formed l'Association de l'école Georges et Julia Bugnet, named after the Albertan author Georges Bugnet and his wife. Bugnet had advocated for education in French within school boards, had been an editor for a French journal, and had worked the land. This last endeared him to Jean-Claude, Angéline, and Paul, who were all raised on small farms.

The association opened a small private French elementary school in Edmonton in 1983 to prove that a French school was viable and would respond to the needs of the community. The parents did everything: They hired the teachers, designed the curriculum, bought the supplies, and even cleaned the classroom every night. Two months after the school's opening, the parents were already seeing a change in their children: Now immersed in French education, traditions, and culture, they had started playing in French. Franco-Albertans were moving closer to the French school, something they themselves did not have access to growing up, so that their children could attend. The school had to close after a year due to a lack of funding, but it was seen as a success because it had mobilized the community. In order to succeed, French schools needed public funding and support. The parents now had a legal basis to obtain them.

Jean-Claude, Angéline, and Paul Bring Their Fight to Court

Section 23 of the Charter of Rights and Freedoms protects minority language education rights for francophones outside Quebec and for anglophones in Quebec. It applies only to Canadian citizens and gives parents the right not only to have their children educated in French (or English, in Quebec) if they meet certain criteria but also to have the state pay for that education, as it does other public schooling.

In 1983, Jean-Claude, Angéline, and Paul decided to take the Albertan government to court to seek recognition of their right to educate their children in French, in schools managed by francophones and financed by public funds, as guaranteed in section 23 of the Charter. They had to show that the Alberta School Act did not adequately provide section 23's guarantees, with its restrictions on education in French.

Once the trial began, the parents needed statistics. There were English schools with only fifty students, meaning fifty students would be enough for a French school. The parents searched through the Edmonton phone book and called every French-sounding name. In the end, they had identified 158 francophone children, enough to open two French schools.

In 1985, the Alberta Court of Queen's Bench recognized the right to French-language instruction, as well as a certain degree of management, for French speakers where the number of children warranted it. The parents had won a partial victory, but they were not satisfied. They wanted the right to full management of their schools, so they appealed.

In 1987, the parents won in principle at the Alberta Court of Appeal but lost in application. The court of appeal agreed that section 23 guarantees an equivalent education system fully run by the minority language group where numbers warrant it. However, the judges concluded that the parents had not demonstrated that there were a sufficient number of students in Edmonton to warrant the establishment of a school. Again the parents appealed the decision.

Victory at the Supreme Court

With *Mahé*, as the case became known, Jean-Claude, Angéline, and Paul had brought the first minority language education rights case outside of Quebec to the Supreme Court. They were supported by francophone groups outside Quebec and anglophone groups in Quebec. The court was packed with lawyers representing provincial governments, school boards, and minority language associations. The hearing was on June 16, 1989, one of the last cases before the high court went on its summer break.

In March 1990, a unanimous Supreme Court ruled in favour of the parents on all issues. In a decision written by Chief Justice Brian Dickson, the court embraced a large and generous interpretation of section 23. The ruling stated that section 23's objective was to reverse the progressive erosion of minority official language groups by creating education opportunities and encouraging linguistic and cultural vitality. The court noted that section 23 reflected Canada's commitment to bilingualism and biculturalism. The judges also recognized the strong link between language and culture, stating: "Language is more than a mere means of communication, it is part and parcel of the identity and culture of the people speaking it. It is the means by which individuals understand themselves and the world around them."

The Supreme Court found that Alberta had violated the rights of Franco-Albertans through its inaction. Official language minorities could now claim the right not only to an education in their language, but also to the management of their schools everywhere in Canada.

The decision was front-page news in Edmonton, with a self-explanatory headline — "Franco-Albertans Win" — and below that: "Parents have the right to run all schools." The story was carried across the country.

What *Mahé* Accomplished

Mahé helped define the "sliding scale" approach for minority language education rights, with the lowest level being minority language instruction and the highest being "instruction in minority language educational facilities provided out of public funds." A community's placement on the scale decides which type and level of rights and services is appropriate, and is based on the number of children with eligible parents.

Mahé was a milestone for francophones outside Quebec, as it clarified the right of linguistic minorities to have and manage their own schools. The case recognized the need for provincial and territorial governments to enact legislation to ensure compliance with the constitutional obligations of section 23. That was one of the most innovative aspects of the ruling. In other areas of the Charter, the government does not have positive obligations; they simply cannot act in a manner that deprives individuals of a constitutionally protected right. Such is the case with fundamental rights like freedom of expression or the right to life, liberty, and security of the person (chapters 11 and 13). *Mahé* was the first time a court recognized that the state not only has to ensure that constitutional rights are not violated but also must act positively to ensure that rights can be exercised.

French Education in Alberta and Canada After *Mahé*

After the Supreme Court decision, Alberta's minister of Education established the French Language Working Group. The group submitted a report in May 1991 with its recommendations for French-language education and the governance of francophone schools. In 1993, Alberta amended its laws to give Albertan francophones the right to manage their schools alongside three school boards and three coordinating councils. This advancement gave Alberta the best French school system in Canada outside of Quebec and New Brunswick. In March 1994, francophone school trustees were elected in multiple regions of the province, representing a historic moment in the Franco-Albertan community's 101-year-long struggle for French-language education in the province.

French schools are one of the Franco-Albertan community's most important legacies. As of 2020, thirty years after the decision, Alberta has forty-two K–12 French schools, with 8,800 students, managed by four French school boards. In the rest of French Canada outside Quebec, *Mahé* has a legacy of thirty school boards managing 712 schools and 170,000 students.

Life Afterward for Jean-Claude, Angéline, and Paul

During the seven-year legal battle, Jean-Claude began to work at the National Film Board of Canada. Angéline obtained a master's in lettres françaises and a Ph.D. in secondary education, curriculum, and sociolinguistics from the University of Alberta. In 1988, she became a professor in sociolinguistics and linguistics at Université TÉLUQ, a distance-learning university within the Université du Québec network. Paul also became an academic, working as a professor of French, Quebec, and French Canadian literature at the Institut d'études canadiennes at the Campus Saint-Jean of the University of Alberta.

In 1997, the Association de l'école Georges et Julia Bugnet received the Prix Boréal from the Fédération des communautés francophones et acadienne du Canada. The prize recognizes exceptional contributions to the francophone community in Canada. In 2011, Jean-Claude, Angéline, and Paul won the Prix Maurice-Lavallée from l'Association canadienne-française de l'Alberta for their contribution to the education of Franco-Albertans. In 2015, they received the Meritorious Service Cross from the governor general. The honour celebrates Canadians who have achieved an exceptional deed or activity in any field that brings honour to Canada. The parents were recognized for their contribution in ensuring access to quality education for minority official language communities across Canada.

Of the three, Paul was the only one to remain in Alberta; both Jean-Claude and Angéline moved to Quebec after the Supreme Court's decision. Paul had a long and productive career as a professor at the University of Alberta.

Paul is now a grandfather. His grandson was able to obtain an education in French in Alberta because of the battles that Paul, Jean-Claude, and Angéline waged for their children and for the children of all francophones outside Quebec.

PART III

INDIGENOUS RIGHTS

22

Captaining Change for Indigenous Rights: Ronald Sparrow

Ronald Sparrow was a fisherman who had the vision, the will, and the determination to stand up for his people's sovereign rights as an Indigenous nation. In May 1984, when Sparrow cast his net in the Fraser River outside Vancouver, the winds of change were blowing over Canada with the entrenchment of the Canadian Charter of Rights and Freedoms and "Aboriginal Rights" in the Constitution Act, 1982. Ronald Sparrow helped steer the ship of change for Indigenous Peoples, ushering in a new era of constitutional recognition of Aboriginal rights.

Born to Fish

From the age of two, Ronald Sparrow knew he wanted to be a fisherman. Ronald Edward Sparrow was born in Richmond, British Columbia, in the summer of 1944. He was given the nickname "Bud" by his younger sister. It was fitting because many described Ronald as a generous man who was a true buddy to all those around him.

Ronald was a member of the Musqueam Nation and grew up in the communities that surround the Fraser and Skeena rivers. The Fraser River is the longest in British Columbia, running from the western side of the Rocky Mountains all the way to the Strait of Georgia in Vancouver. The Skeena River flows from the northern part of British Columbia, in the Skeena Mountains, southwestward into the Pacific Ocean near Prince Rupert. Ronald learned his fishing skills from his father, uncles, and grandfather.

At the young age of thirteen, Ronald was able to run his first gillnetter boat along the Fraser River all on his own. A gillnetter is a type of boat that casts a large net known as a gillnet, which hangs vertically into the water to catch fish that swim into it. Ronald's early fishing experiences were formative to his future career as a commercial fisher on the Fraser River, the traditional fishing area of the Musqueam peoples.

The Musqueam

The Musqueam are an Indigenous people descended from the Coast Salish and have lived since time immemorial along the Fraser River and in the surrounding areas of what is now known as Vancouver. The Musqueam Indian Reserve in Vancouver is located on and near some of the most expensive real estate in the province. The band has over thirteen hundred members. As in many other Indigenous communities in Canada, Musqueam cultural practices remain strong despite systemic efforts to erase their culture and existence.

Musqueam have long used their territory and resources for fishing, hunting, trapping, and gathering. Fishing is central to Musqueam practices, and salmon is a staple food source. Musqueam people see salmon as relatives and treat them with the utmost respect. As a fishing and river people, the Musqueam have been fishing in the Fraser River and surrounding areas for centuries, and their traditional fishing practices were formative for Ronald's fishing career.

A Legend on the Water

At twenty-four, Ronald bought his first seine boat — a type of boat with fishing nets that hang vertically from it. He then built two of his own

Ronald Sparrow on the shore of the Fraser River in Vancouver, British Columbia, in 2011.

boats, which he named *Shani Lynne* and *Shani Lynne No 2*, after his first daughter. Ronald opened his own business, Sthakwy Fishing Co. Ltd, which is still in operation today. As an independent fisher, Ronald was highly respected and earned a reputation as a legend on the water. Ronald had an astounding career that spanned sixty-one years, and he was an expert in the migration patterns and cycles of herring and several species of salmon. In addition to his work as a fisher, Ronald had a strong presence in Musqueam through his work in the community and with other First Nations communities in British Columbia. Along with fishing, he was an avid hunter of birds and big game, and often frequented Medicine Hat, Penticton, and Cypress Hill for his hunting expeditions.

Canada's History of Regulating Indigenous Fishing

Ronald's fishing took him across the West Coast of British Columbia to provide for his family. While he was fishing in the ancestral territory of his people, he was required to obtain an Indian food fishing licence from the federal Department of Fisheries. Since 1868, the Fisheries Act has regulated and restricted Indigenous fisheries and Indigenous Peoples' ability to fish by creating a licensing system. A licence issued by the minister of Marine

Fisheries to an individual "Indian" or an Indigenous band allowed them to fish for a specific purpose outlined in the licence.

Initially, the regulations restricted Indigenous fishing solely to what was needed for food and sustenance. Under the licensing system, Indigenous fishers were not allowed to fish for commercial purposes. In other words, they were denied the opportunity to develop their own commercial fishing industry despite having used their lands, waters, and resources for centuries for both cultural and economic purposes.

Regulation of Indigenous fishing increased over the twentieth century and ultimately had a significant impact on Ronald's life and career and on the livelihood of Indigenous fishers across Canada.

Not Just Another Day on the Water

On May 25, 1984, a crisp spring morning, Ronald set out on a fishing expedition in Canoe Passage, also known as Canoe Pass, near Ladner, a suburb of Vancouver. While fishing for chinook salmon, Ronald was arrested under section 61(1) of the Fisheries Act for the offence of fishing with a drift net that was longer than permitted under the terms of his band's food fishing licence. Under the licence, fisheries patrol vessels were responsible for monitoring infractions and reporting violations to authorities. Ronald's licence permitted him to use a drift net that did not exceed 25 fathoms (a fathom is about 6 feet, or 1.8 metres); his drift net was 45 fathoms, nearly twice the length permitted. Ronald argued that the licence was invalid because he had an Aboriginal right to fish that could not be taken from him.

Ronald's arrest occurred in a climate where Indigenous fishers were looking to assert themselves against ongoing government regulations aimed at decreasing their access to traditional waters. While Indigenous communities had always been fighting to assert their rights, Ronald's arrest came at a pivotal time because the Canadian Charter of Rights and Freedoms and section 35 of the Constitution Act, 1982, were only two years old. Although section 35 "recognized and affirmed" existing Aboriginal and treaty rights in Canada, the federal government intended to continue regulating Indigenous fishing, creating a confrontational political climate in the fight to have Indigenous rights recognized.

Ronald Takes On the Queen

Ronald was adamant that he would fight the charges against him, and he pleaded not guilty. He wanted to ensure that Indigenous communities could continue to fish for generations to come. He retained noted Vancouver lawyer Marvin Storrow, who had represented the Musqueam before, acting as counsel in the landmark case of *Guerin v. The Queen*, in which the Supreme Court of Canada established that the Canadian government had a fiduciary duty toward Indigenous Peoples.

Ronald's trial was held in the British Columbia Provincial Court, where he was convicted of violating section 61(1) of the Fisheries Act. The trial judge did not accept his claim of an Aboriginal right. Ronald and his counsel argued that the Musqueam had been fishing in their territory since time immemorial, which established an Aboriginal right to fish that could not be breached. The judge ruled that an Aboriginal right did not exist because it was not "supported by a special treaty, proclamation, contract, or other document" but rather was based on historical practice. Since no treaty articulated the Aboriginal right to fish, the judge held that section 35(1) of the Constitution Act, 1982, had no application in Ronald's case. Ultimately, the trial judge found Ronald guilty.

Ronald appealed the decision to the County Court of Vancouver, which dismissed his appeal and upheld his conviction. Next, Ronald appealed to the British Columbia Court of Appeal, the highest court in that province. Unlike the lower courts, the court of appeal found that an Aboriginal right could continue to exist even if the right was regulated by something like the Fisheries Act. The court of appeal was clear that there was an Aboriginal right to fish but that this right could be limited through regulations because Parliament retained the power to regulate fisheries and Indigenous land under the Constitution Act, 1867. The court of appeal ruled that the lower court's findings were insufficient to result in an acquittal but indicated that Ronald's conviction was based on an incorrect understanding of the law and thus could not stand. It set aside Ronald's conviction and ordered a new trial.

Neither the Crown nor Ronald was satisfied with this decision, and both requested permission from the Supreme Court of Canada to appeal the case.

Taking the Case to the Highest Court

In 1987, the Supreme Court of Canada granted leave to appeal. The case was heard in November 1988, but the court did not render its decision until May 31, 1990. For Ronald, the Musqueam, and Indigenous Peoples across the country, the decision was worth waiting for: It was a monumental victory for them. The court held that Ronald had an existing and constitutionally recognized Aboriginal right to fish for food and social and ceremonial purposes that had not been extinguished.

In a unanimous decision, the Supreme Court found that "existing" Aboriginal rights meant those that had not been extinguished through clear and plain intent via treaty or legislation. Importantly, the court rejected a competing interpretation that "existing" meant only those Aboriginal rights that were being exercised as they had been when the Constitution Act, 1982, came into effect. The court also held that regulating a right — as in the case of the Fisheries Act — does not extinguish it. Thus, the Fisheries Act did not extinguish the Musqueam's Aboriginal right to fish. In this sense, when Ronald was arrested, he was exercising his existing Aboriginal right to fish, and this right could not be taken away by the Fisheries Act.

Moreover, the court articulated that while government policies can regulate Aboriginal rights, any government intervention must respect the Aboriginal rights and title laid out in section 35(1) of the Constitution Act, 1982.

Breakthrough for Aboriginal Rights

As a result of Ronald's case, the Supreme Court of Canada established the "*Sparrow* test," which outlines whether infringement of an Aboriginal right is justifiable. The *Sparrow* test for Aboriginal rights under section 35 can be seen as a complement to the *Oakes* test for the infringement of Charter rights. Once an Aboriginal right has been established, and it has been shown that this right has not been extinguished, the *Sparrow* test requires the claimant to demonstrate that the right has been infringed. A right is infringed if the government activity at play imposes undue hardship, is unreasonable, or denies the right holder "their preferred means of exercising that right." If a right has been infringed, then there is sufficient evidence to suggest that a breach of section 35 has occurred.

The second step of the *Sparrow* test is to determine whether the infringement of the right was justified. An infringement may be justified if the government activity serves a valid legislative objective, such as conservation or managing natural resources. It is up to the Crown to demonstrate that the infringement was as minimal as possible to achieve the results intended. Furthermore, the infringement is justified if the government activity is for the purpose of expropriation and fair compensation is provided. Finally, for an infringement to be justified, the government must prove that it consulted the Indigenous groups that would be impacted by the government action involved.

The Supreme Court of Canada held that Ronald's conviction should be set aside and the case sent back to trial to be analyzed under the *Sparrow* test. The Crown decided to stay the case, meaning it would not pursue charges against Ronald. After six intense years in court, he had finally achieved victory for himself and for Indigenous communities across the country.

The Bigger Picture

Ronald's case was the first to recognize and affirm that Indigenous fishing rights are protected in Canada's Constitution. More generally, the case established strong legal foundations for Indigenous rights, which to that point had rarely been recognized. It was widely celebrated as a victory for Indigenous rights in Canada.

The case opened a legal pathway for Indigenous communities to fight to have their rights recognized and laid the foundation for section 35 Aboriginal rights and title claims. Following *Sparrow*, Fisheries and Oceans Canada launched its Aboriginal Fisheries Strategy in 1992 to amend its fisheries management processes to align with the *Sparrow* decision.

While the case was a major success for Indigenous rights, it also met with criticism because the court had confirmed that those rights were not absolute and could be infringed. Nevertheless, the *Sparrow* case established a foundation for the recognition of Aboriginal rights under section 35 upon which others would build.

Ronald's Legacy

Ronald was heralded as a champion of the Musqueam people, British Columbia First Nations, and Indigenous Peoples across the country. Following his victory in court, he returned to his home in Ladner, British Columbia. Despite winning a precedent-setting case at the highest court in the country, Ronald did not have any big celebrations. He remained humble and continued to live as a fisher. He passed his love of fishing and knowledge of the tides to his son Jarred, who continued to carry on his father's fishing legacy.

In the early 2000s, Ronald became a member of the Musqueam Fisheries Commission. Each year, he negotiated with Fisheries and Oceans Canada for Musqueam fishing rights, ensuring that Musqueam conservation concerns were communicated with government officials.

Ronald was recognized by the Indigenous community for his leadership. In 2011, he received a prestigious National Aboriginal Achievement Award to honour his significant impact on his community and his astounding achievements as a commercial fisher.

Ronald passed away on September 14, 2020, more than thirty years after his monumental victory in court. His story appeared in several obituaries across the country. Tributes flowed in from notable Canadians figures, including British Columbia Premier John Horgan, Minister of Crown-Indigenous Relations Carolyn Bennett, and the president of the University of British Columbia.

The winds of change do not blow by themselves; they need people like Ronald Sparrow to cast their nets upon the water and make change.

23

More Than Just Selling Salmon: Dorothy Van der Peet

Sometimes small transactions set in motion a larger chain of events. When Dorothy Van der Peet sold ten salmon to her neighbour, as she had many times before, she could never have anticipated that she would be launched into a near decade-long struggle leading to one of the most important Aboriginal rights cases in Canadian history.

Dorothy's Early Life

Dorothy Marie ("Dot") Van der Peet was born in the early 1960s in Chilliwack, British Columbia, about two hours east of Vancouver. Her biological mother, Doris James, was an active member of the Stó:lō Nation and a renowned Salish weaver. In common with the experience of too many Indigenous children, Dorothy was separated from her mother and placed into a non-Indigenous adoption. The Van der Peets immigrated to Canada in 1954 from Holland and eventually moved to a small farm plot in Sardis, British Columbia, just outside Chilliwack, in 1960. The family adopted and fostered a number of children in Chilliwack, including Dorothy. Like her five adoptive brothers and sisters and two foster sisters, Dorothy attended Chilliwack Senior Secondary School, from which she graduated in 1980. Dorothy maintained a relationship with her biological mother until she passed away in 2014.

In 1982, Dorothy had her first child. She had a second child with fellow Stó:lō Charles "Chuck" Jimmy and they shared a life together. Chuck helped provide for the growing family. To make money and put food on the table, he and his brother fished in the Fraser River. They were under the impression that, as members of the Stó:lō Nation operating under an Indian food fishing licence, they had a right to eat and sell the fish they caught.

The history of Dorothy Van der Peet's people on the land in and surrounding the Fraser Valley would be central to the decision on whether the fishery regulation was a breach of her Aboriginal right to sell fish, and whether such a right even existed.

The Stó:lō Nation, Fish, and Trade

Archeological evidence shows that humans have inhabited and used the Fraser Valley for over nine thousand years. Stó:lō means "people of the river" in Halq'eméylem, the Stó:lō's dialect of the Coast Salish language. Their ancestral lands span the Fraser Valley and the Fraser Canyon, following the Fraser River, which served as their primary means of transportation. They developed a distinctive culture oriented around family and respect for the land and especially for the Fraser River. Multiple families lived in longhouses along the river, gathering, hunting, and, most importantly, fishing.

The Stó:lō people have a deep spiritual connection to the Fraser River and the fish that inhabit it. Salmon play an important role in the Stó:lō's connection to the land. For thousands of years, the Stó:lō have respected the salmon not only for the food they bring to the community but also because of a deep connectedness to the animal as a major part of Stó:lō spirituality.

Stó:lō oral history and archeological evidence show that the Stó:lō have maintained trading relationships with neighbouring Indigenous groups since before Confederation. Their main item of trade was and continues to be fish caught in the Fraser River. Between 1820 and the assertion of British sovereignty in 1846, and for years afterward, the Stó:lō people played a significant role in a robust commercial salmon fishery in partnership with the Hudson's Bay Company.

Local Indigenous fisheries were one of the main reasons for the establishment of Fort Langley as a trading post. Its proximity to the Stó:lō allowed for bountiful trade of salmon and other fish, which were shipped throughout the British Empire. Though at first they did not trade the fish for money (currency would reach the Fraser Valley only in 1860), oral history and historical evidence show that fish was traded in bulk.

How Dorothy Found Herself in Court

To make a living for themselves and their family, Chuck and Dorothy fished both for food and to trade, selling some of the fish they caught to their neighbours. One might assume that as members of a nation that had practised such trade for generations, they would be permitted to do so. But the federal Fisheries Regulations were unambiguous: The Indian food fishing licence could not be used to sell fish. Thus, even though Chuck held a food fishing licence, Dorothy's sale of salmon to her neighbour was illegal under Canadian law. She was charged on September 11, 1987, with violating the Fisheries Regulations.

There was nothing exceptional about Dorothy's case. It was quite common for Fisheries officers to charge Indigenous individuals with selling fish without a licence or with fishing outside of permitted times. As she was being charged, many similar cases were ongoing in British Columbia courts. Though the law was clear, those charged with these offences believed the regulations were direct violations of their right as Indigenous Peoples to use the land as they had for generations. They, and so many other Indigenous Peoples across Canada, lived in uncertainty. There had never been a ruling by a Canadian court on whether Indigenous Peoples had an Aboriginal right under section 35 to sell the fish they caught, despite a number of assertions to that effect by Indigenous groups.

In 1988, the year after Dorothy was charged, Fisheries officers seized over eight tons of salmon caught by Indigenous Peoples. They raided homes and confiscated fishing equipment, including boats and cars. The federal government held the position that, as a matter of fairness with respect to resource management, Indigenous Peoples should be held to the same rules as any fishers. They should respect licensing rules and should limit their fishing to the permitted times and seasons.

The Stó:lō leadership decided that Dorothy's case was one that could lead to real change and recognition of their constitutional right. It was an important moment in Stó:lō political history when both the Stó:lō Nation Chiefs Council and the Stó:lō Tribal Council came together to support Dorothy. The two organizations lobbied the community, attempting to raise over $100,000 to help with her defence. They secured the services of Mandell Pinder LLP, which had represented Ronald Sparrow the year before. The two councils and the community funded Dorothy's foray through the court system, all the way to the highest court in the country.

Provincial Court

Dorothy's case went to trial in 1991 before the British Columbia Provincial Court in Surrey. The only issue at trial, and all the way to the Supreme Court, was whether the regulation preventing her from selling salmon without a licence violated an existing Aboriginal right for the Stó:lō to sell fish under section 35 of the Constitution Act, 1982. The Supreme Court had decided *Sparrow* only a year before, establishing the test for recognition of Aboriginal rights under section 35 and for limiting such rights.

The defence prepared and brought forward substantial expert evidence and oral testimony describing the history of salmon fishing and trade for the Stó:lō people. The provincial court gave little weight to the oral history provided by Stó:lō witnesses. Despite the extensive sale of salmon by the Stó:lō since before colonization, the court determined that it had not been done in a "regularized or systematic" way. There was no Aboriginal right to sell fish for the Stó:lō, as Dorothy Van der Peet did, because that right had not truly ever existed. The court imposed a $50 fine on Dorothy, which she subsequently appealed to the British Columbia Supreme Court.

Appellate Courts

After a mixed decision at the British Columbia Supreme Court, which ordered a new trial, Dorothy appealed her case to the British Columbia Court of Appeal, the highest court in the province. In 1993, the court of appeal overturned the supreme court's decision for a second trial, reinstating the guilty verdict. The court held that for a practice to be protected as an Aboriginal right under section 35(1) of the Constitution Act, 1982, it must have been exercised at the time that sovereignty was asserted and for such a time that it had become integral to the Indigenous culture, not the result of influence by European contact. Since the Stó:lō's commercial trade of fish was influenced by European trade, the court of appeal ruled that it did not qualify as an Aboriginal right.

The Case at the Supreme Court of Canada

The Supreme Court of Canada heard Dorothy's appeal, along with two companion cases, over three days in November 1995, and released its decision in August 1996. The result was disappointing for Dorothy and for the Stó:lō. With Justice Claire L'Heureux-Dubé and future Chief Justice Beverley McLachlin dissenting, the court ruled 7–2 to dismiss Dorothy's appeal, convicting her of violating the Fisheries Act and the relevant British Columbia regulation. They found that the Stó:lō had no Aboriginal right to sell the fish they caught; thus, the regulations were constitutional and did not infringe any section 35(1) right.

In the process, the court redefined the scope of Aboriginal rights and the protection offered to them by the Constitution. It articulated a "distinctive culture test" for Aboriginal rights, which immediately became known as "the *Van der Peet* test." The court identified section 35(1)'s underlying purpose as "the protection and reconciliation of the interests which arise from the fact that prior to the arrival of Europeans in North America aboriginal peoples lived on the land in distinctive societies, with their own practices, customs and traditions." For that reason, the court said, any test to identify an Aboriginal right "must be directed at identifying the crucial elements of those pre-existing distinctive societies." The aim of the *Van der Peet* test they developed was to identify the distinctive, central or integral practices, traditions, and customs of an Indigenous society. More specifically, Aboriginal rights were defined as protecting only those practices, traditions, and customs that existed prior to contact with Europeans, which were very challenging for an Indigenous group to prove.

The court found that Dorothy's claim did not meet the distinctive culture test, concluding that before contact with Europeans, exchanges of fish were incidental to the Stó:lō's central practice of fishing for food and ceremonial use, rather than being a widespread or defining feature of their society. The judges said that to qualify as an Aboriginal right, a custom must be integral to the community's distinctive culture and not merely incidental to another practice, such as fishing for sustenance.

The majority said the evidence from trial showed that the Stó:lō did not have a "regularized trading system" before contact, which further suggested that fish exchange was not widespread enough to be considered central to their culture. They characterized the trade that developed between the Stó:lō and the Hudson's Bay Company at Fort Langley as a post-contact adaptation and said it did not demonstrate continuity with pre-contact practices. The majority determined that trade, if central to the Stó:lō, was only so because of the European presence and could not be deemed Indigenous in nature.

Wider Criticism and the Dissents

Van der Peet narrowed the scope of what could be deemed an Aboriginal right. Existing Aboriginal rights no longer meant what they did when the Constitution Act, 1982, came into effect; they were to be defined by the Indigenous societies' relationship and contact with European settlers. Critics of the decision pointed out that anchoring the legal protection of Aboriginal rights to a single point of contact with European settlers ignores the evolving and dynamic nature of culture. What makes a culture distinctive may evolve over time as its environment evolves. The majority's decision froze Indigenous rights in time. It also gave the power to non-Indigenous judges to determine what is "integral" to Indigenous Peoples.

Some of these criticisms were reflected in the dissents of Justices L'Heureux-Dubé and McLachlin. As Justice McLachlin put it, "by insisting that Mrs. Van der Peet's modern practice of selling fish be replicated in pre-contact Stó:lō practices, [the majority] effectively condemns the Stó:lō to exercise their right precisely as they exercised it hundreds of years ago and precludes a finding that the sale constitutes the exercise of an aboriginal right." Both McLachlin and L'Heureux-Dubé would have found that the evidence of sale and trade of fish should have been sufficient to trigger an Aboriginal right for Dorothy to sell fish as a means to a moderate livelihood, the fishing and subsequent trade of salmon being integral to and distinctive of Stó:lō society.

Despite criticism from the legal and Indigenous communities, the *Van der Peet* test still applies today, governing when and how an Aboriginal right will be recognized and protected.

Dorothy After *Van der Peet*

For Dorothy, the outcome of her case was undoubtedly anti-climactic and unsatisfactory. Though the fine imposed on her was minor, the fallout of the decision for her community was not. To this day, federal regulations forbid the sale of fish caught by Stó:lō people without an adequate licence, despite evidence showing that the Stó:lō had been trading to sustain their livelihood for thousands of years.

For Dorothy, life went on. She lives on the Ch'íyáqtel First Nation in Chilliwack, British Columbia, where she is self-employed as a cleaner. She is a doting mother and grandmother and boasts about her five dogs. Though she may not feel it as she goes about her everyday life outside the spotlight, Dorothy Van der Peet had a profound impact on the world of Aboriginal law. Her name is cited in courts across the country as Indigenous groups attempt to assert their sovereignty before the courts and ensure that their traditional ways can be maintained.

24

From Wrongful Conviction to Vindicator of Treaty Rights: Donald Marshall Jr.

Donald Marshall Jr. is a member of a select club — a very small group of people involved in three Supreme Court of Canada cases. The first, a Royal Commission into his wrongful conviction, exposed the systemic discrimination against Indigenous Peoples in Nova Scotia. The second and third, called *Marshall I* and *Marshall II*, were important treaty rights cases. Together, they made Donald Marshall Jr. one of the most influential figures in the modern history of Canadian law.

Junior's Early Life

Donald Marshall Jr. — called "Junior" — was born in 1953, in Sydney, Nova Scotia. He and his twelve younger siblings lived on the Membertou reserve with their parents. Their father had been relocated there as an infant from King's Road Reserve, by court order in 1926. The relocation was the source of continued tension and resentment between the citizens of Membertou and the people of Sydney. In the late 1960s and early 1970s, when Junior was a teenager, the police conducted "roundups" on Membertou. They would target individuals with unpaid fines and bring them to county jail. In the city, police would tell Mi'kmaq people to return to their reserves.

Like many reserves, conditions were bad on Membertou. It was accessible only by a single dirt road. Most residents lived in homes made of plywood, with no access to basic amenities. Even by the 1970s, many residents lived without electricity or running water. Despite the difficulties in the community, the Marshall family lived in relative comfort. In 1964, when Junior was eleven years old, his father became Grand Chief of the Mi'kmaq. Donald Sr.'s drywall and plastering business, and his important place in the community, allowed the family to live and thrive in Membertou. Junior was expected to eventually take over the drywall business, and perhaps even take the role of Grand Chief.

As a child, Donald Jr. loved to play baseball and, more than anything, loved to go fishing. He also enjoyed watching hockey and baseball. He was a fan of the Detroit Red Wings and, later in life, the Toronto Blue Jays. He was known to his teachers and to local police as a rebellious and rambunctious child. At fifteen, he was expelled from his high school for hitting one of his teachers. Soon afterward, Junior joined a number of Sydney's Mi'kmaq youth in what they called the Shipyard Gang. Like other youth his age, Junior liked to drink, do drugs, and generally "get up to no good" in the town. The Shipyard Gang vandalized property and stole from the residents of Sydney. By the time Junior was sixteen, he had already been charged with a number of liquor-related offences. The gang was often the target of police surveillance and investigation. A few months before Junior's arrest, for example, he was brought into the Sydney police station to speak with an investigator in connection with extensive property damage to a local graveyard caused by vandalism.

Junior's Wrongful Conviction

Junior's childhood ended on May 28, 1971, when he was seventeen. That night, he was with Sanford Seale, a Black youth whom Junior knew casually. They were hanging out in a park when they were accosted by older white men, one of whom pulled a knife on the boys, stabbing Seale and slashing Junior's arm. Everyone fled, leaving Seale dead.

Junior was wrongfully convicted of Seale's murder and given a life sentence. He would spend eleven years in prison before a Royal Commission exposed the ingrained racism against Indigenous Peoples that polluted the judgment of all the actors in the justice system, from the police to the prosecutors to the judges. The commission made "Donald Marshall Jr." a household name in Nova Scotia and showed the Canadian public that wrongful convictions do occur. As the commission stated, "the evidence is once again persuasive and the conclusion inescapable that Donald Marshall, Jr, was convicted and sent to prison, in part at least, because he was a Native person."

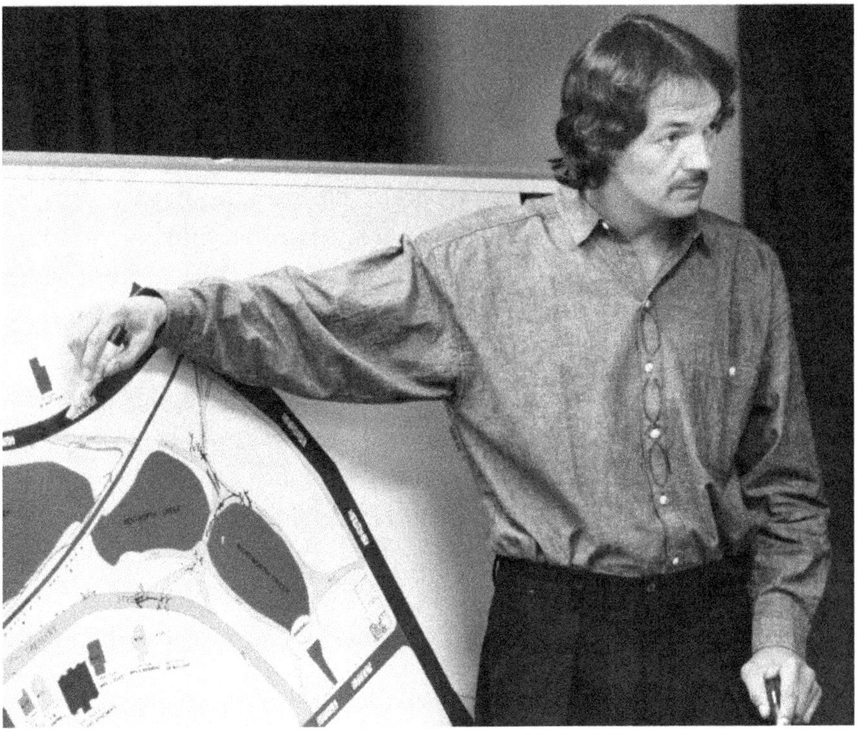

Donald Marshall Jr. providing testimony in 1988 about the 1971 slaying of Sanford Seale, for which he was wrongfully convicted.

Junior's years in prison were traumatic, but he managed to make the best of a horrendous situation. He trained to become a plumber, played sports, advocated for prisoners' rights, ran a canteen, and made and sold Indigenous arts and crafts. He also wrote poetry and letters to friends and family expressing his loneliness and isolation.

Advocating for Prisoners' Rights and At-Risk Youth

In the early years after his acquittal, Donald Jr.'s life was taken over by legal battles regarding the compensation owed to him for his time spent in prison. Although he was now able to assert his innocence, he was never able to return to his "normal" life. Instead of taking up his father's business, as he had intended, he spent the 1990s working to ensure that no one ever lived a nightmare like his ever again.

In 1992, Donald, now married, moved to a farm in Aberdeen, in Cape Breton. He had been involved in advocating for prisoners' rights while in prison, and he continued similar work from his farm. As the first well-known case of a wrongful conviction in Canada, Donald became involved in the Association in Defence of the Wrongly Convicted. The association, now called Innocence Canada, educates legal professionals, spreads awareness about wrongful convictions, and directly assists wrongfully convicted individuals in applying for a review of their convictions. Donald spoke about his experiences at conferences around Canada, helping to spread awareness of the factors that led to his conviction.

He was particularly devoted to Mi'kmaq youth, consulting on projects dealing with Mi'kmaq young offenders. In 1995, he created an Aboriginal youth camp in his father's name for at-risk Mi'kmaq youth and young offenders. Donald found great satisfaction in helping the youth in his community by reconnecting them to their roots.

Finding Meaning in Fishing

Donald's life after prison was not all political activism. He also found time to go fishing, as he had when he was a boy. At first he fished recreationally, but soon he wanted to make a living while working in connection with the land around him. Donald and his wife, Jane McMillan, began a small-scale eel fishing operation in Cape Breton. Grounded in Mi'kmaq customary practices, the fishing operation gave meaning to their lives. In keeping with the Mi'kmaq ethos, Donald would share his harvest with his community at funerals, weddings, and other celebrations.

Throughout his time as an eel fisherman, Donald was operating without a licence, as did many other Mi'kmaq fishers in the area. Their people had been fishing for eels on that water since well before Confederation. They believed their right to fish and sell their harvest was protected by treaties signed between the Mi'kmaq and the Crown in 1760 and 1761. For the first few seasons of Donald's fishing career, he encountered no problems. That all changed in 1993.

That year, officers from Fisheries and Oceans Canada stopped Donald on the water and asked to see his licence. When he could not provide one, the officers confiscated his nets. He was later charged with the offences of selling eels without a licence, fishing without a licence, and fishing out of season with illegal nets. Thus began Donald's second foray into the Canadian justice system.

The Lower Court Decisions

Donald's trial at the Nova Scotia Provincial Court began on October 17, 1994. The hearing focused solely on whether or not the Mi'kmaq had a constitutional treaty right to fish and sell fish under treaties signed in 1760 and 1761. Seeing the importance of this trial as a test case for treaty rights, the Union of Nova Scotia Indians and the Confederacy of Mainland Mi'kmaq got together to amass evidence and to help with Donald's legal defence. A team of young Mi'kmaq lawyers and law students was assembled to help with legal research. The students on the team came from Dalhousie's Indigenous Blacks and Mi'kmaq (IB&M) Initiative, a program that was a direct result of the Marshall Inquiry's recommendations.

Section 35(1) of the Constitution Act, 1982, states: "The existing aboriginal and treaty rights of the aboriginal peoples of Canada are hereby recognized and affirmed." Donald claimed a constitutionally protected treaty right under the 1760 Treaty of Peace and Friendship between the Mi'kmaq and the British.

Throughout the 1750s, the British and Mi'kmaq clashed on multiple occasions. The Mi'kmaq in what is now Nova Scotia had allied with the French to fend off British colonization. The French were eventually defeated, and the Acadians were expelled from the region. This left the Mi'kmaq alone against a stronger British power. The "intermittent hostilities" between the nations were unsustainable. A multitude of similar treaties were signed in 1760 and 1761. On March 10, 1760, the Chief of the LaHave Mi'kmaq signed a Treaty of Peace and Friendship with the Crown, which granted jurisdiction and dominion over Nova Scotia to the Crown and included guarantees that the Mi'kmaq would not violate or harm British settlers or their property. In return, it promised the Mi'kmaq the right to trade commodities with the Crown at "truck houses," which were Crown-appointed trading posts. The relevant clause in the treaty explicitly limited Mi'kmaq trade to truck houses.

In 1996, the Nova Scotia Provincial Court released its decision, convicting Donald. The court interpreted the truck house provision narrowly, ruling that the right to trade commodities was limited to trade at British-operated truck houses. Since no truck houses existed when Donald was fishing, nor any other scheme between the Crown and the Mi'kmaq for trade, no treaty right existed for Donald to fish and sell the fish. He appealed the decision and was released on bail.

In 1997, Donald lost again at the Nova Scotia Court of Appeal. The court decided that the treaty did not even grant a right to trade at truck houses. Donald and his team had known before this trial began that they would most likely be going to the Supreme Court of Canada. They appealed and were granted leave to appear before the highest court in Canada.

In Front of the Supreme Court

The hearings took place in November 1998, and the Supreme Court released its decision nearly a year later. Five of the seven judges ruled in favour of Donald, finding that a treaty right to fish and to sell fish existed under the 1760 Treaty of Peace and Friendship.

The majority tried to identify and enforce the common intentions of the parties to the 1760 treaty. To do so, it examined the full context behind the treaty. It found that the Crown, through this treaty, wanted to establish peaceful relations with the Mi'kmaq, and the Mi'kmaq wanted access to the "necessaries" provided to them through trade with the British. The majority said these goals necessarily implied a right for the Mi'kmaq people of continuing access to harvest wildlife to trade.

Furthermore, the court said "the honour of the Crown" requires courts to examine oral promises made during treaty negotiations and to interpret the treaty in a broad sense. Where ambiguities are found, they should be resolved in favour of the Indigenous group. In the court's interpretation of the treaty, the Mi'kmaq were granted a limited right to trade wildlife with the Crown for necessities. The Crown had made oral promises to the Mi'kmaq that their trade at the truck houses would provide them with the "necessaries" of life. This right was not dependent on the existence of truck houses, as oral promises taken with the written promises of the treaty imply a right going beyond these formal trading posts.

The majority found that the regulations in place infringed Donald's right to fish and trade those fish for the "necessaries" required to establish a "moderate livelihood." Though regulations could be put in place to regulate Indigenous fishing practices in the region, the court said the Mi'kmaq right to support a "moderate livelihood" through trade could never be infringed because of the protection afforded to treaty rights under the Constitution.

The court's decision was confusing and it created uncertainty. The court's ruling did not appear to be limited only to Donald and the Mi'kmaq in Nova Scotia. The *Marshall* decision was interpreted to apply to treaties signed with thirty-four First Nations across the Maritimes and the Gaspé Peninsula. The impact of this decision cannot be understated. Suddenly, thirty-four nations were empowered to fish in Eastern Canada to earn a moderate livelihood.

Clashes on the Water

The impact of the *Marshall* decision quickly reverberated across Atlantic Canada. The bounds of the treaty right that had just been affirmed were blurry. The thirty-four concerned First Nations could fish and trade to earn a moderate livelihood, but the term "a moderate livelihood" was undefined, and it was unclear what the Supreme Court meant by it. Non-Indigenous people in the industry were worried that the courts had granted Indigenous Peoples an unfettered right to fish without the regulations that restricted non-Indigenous fishers. This interpretation of the decision sparked outrage and worry in the Maritime fishing industry.

The *Marshall* decision was released in September 1999, as the fall fishing season began. Indigenous fishers rushed to capitalize on their newfound right. Media at the time exaggerated instances of overfishing by Indigenous fishers. Protests from non-Indigenous fishers erupted. Conflict began to brew and eventually escalated to a breaking point when, on October 3, 1999, a group of non-Indigenous protesters destroyed more than three thousand lobster traps set by Indigenous fishers off the coast of the Burnt Church Reserve in New Brunswick. They destroyed fishing equipment, vandalized a school, burned a structure used in traditional ceremonies, and assaulted multiple individuals. They wanted exclusive access to the fisheries and felt slighted because they were obliged to follow regulations that the Indigenous fishers were excused from.

A lobbying group representing non-Indigenous fishers, the West Nova Fishermen's Coalition, applied to the Supreme Court for a rehearing of the *Marshall* case on the federal government's regulatory authority over Indigenous fishers. This application was rejected, and that would usually have been the end of things. However, in the wake of Burnt Church, and given the mounting unrest, the Supreme Court decided to do something it hardly ever does.

Marshall II

On November 17, 1999, the Supreme Court of Canada released its reasons for denying the application for a rehearing. These reasons became known as *Marshall II*. The court clarified, and arguably limited, the treaty rights it had affirmed in its previous decision, which became known as *Marshall I*. It said treaty rights could be limited by the minister through regulation in the name of conservation, economic, and regional fairness, or recognition of the historical reliance on the fishery by non-Indigenous group. The right, then, was not unfettered. The court was clearly responding to the outcry in Eastern Canada.

Implementing the *Marshall* Decisions

Since the *Marshall* decisions, rights-based regulations have been incorporated into the commercial fishing industry in the Maritimes so that Indigenous fishers are also subject to restrictions on their fishing activity. Negotiations between the government, industry workers, and Indigenous groups led to a boom in Indigenous commercial activity. Despite this integration, tensions remain. Indigenous fishers feel limited by government regulations and believe they cannot fully benefit from their right in the absence of a proper definition for "a moderate livelihood." Non-Indigenous fishers protest any perceived further intrusion on their industry by Indigenous fishers. In October 2020, these tensions once again reached a breaking point when, in a series of separate incidents, non-Indigenous fishers destroyed a Mi'kmaq lobster boat and a lobster facility in Nova Scotia and targeted businesses selling Indigenous-caught lobster.

Life After the Supreme Court Decisions

Donald's life was deeply affected by the *Marshall* decisions. In his home community of Sydney, non-Indigenous fishers would stop him and hurl insults his way, mirroring the harassment he had received as a child. They blamed him for what they perceived as an Indigenous intrusion into their territory.

At the same time, Donald was struggling with serious illness. Years of smoking and exposure to chemicals as a plumber had led to considerable respiratory damage. Despite his health issues, Donald was able to continue fishing throughout the 1990s and early 2000s. In 2002, he suffered respiratory failure, an incident that almost cost him his life and required substantial surgical intervention. In May 2003, Donald underwent a double lung transplant in a Toronto hospital. The surgery was a success, but the ensuing years were difficult for Donald. Doctors had prescribed medication to prevent the organs from being rejected. Donald experienced negative side effects from this medication, which impacted his mood and his social ties.

Despite these challenges, Donald maintained ties with his community, moving to Membertou and building a house there. In the summer of 2008, complications from the lung transplant led to him being hospitalized. Donald passed away on August 6, 2009. He was fifty-five years old.

25

Establishing Aboriginal Title: Chief Roger William and the Tŝilhqot'in Nation

Roger William was the Chief of the Xeni Gwet'in First Nation, one of the six First Nations comprising the Tŝilhqot'in Nation. The Tŝilhqot'in had a long and conflicted relationship with colonial officials, European settlers, and then the Canadian government. This includes the Chilcotin War in 1864, when colonial authorities hanged six Tŝilhqot'in Chiefs who were on a peace mission. The Tŝilhqot'in were naturally defensive about intrusions into their territory. In 1990, after the Crown granted logging licences on their land, Roger William and the Tŝilhqot'in Nation launched a twenty-four-year legal battle that culminated in the first-ever judicial declaration of Aboriginal title in Canada.

Roger William Becomes Chief

Roger William was born on a farm in Konni Lake, British Columbia, where he was raised by his mother. He grew up raising cattle and playing hockey.

He was a championship bull rider, and in 1993 he took home the first-place prize at the Cariboo-Chilcotin Rodeo. Roger's adventurous personality led him to participate in horseback mountain races, which are like downhill mountain bike races but with horses instead of bikes. He mountain-raced for nearly thirty-two years and was crowned the king of the Mountain Race Championship two years in a row. William grew up speaking Tŝilhqot'in and did not learn English until the age of six, when he was forced to attend residential schools in Williams Lake and Kamloops.

Ever since he was a child, William had wanted to work to protect the traditional territory he'd grown up on and to preserve its pristine beauty from logging. Reflecting on his teenage years, he recalled the Ministry of Forests coming through the Nemiah Valley to conduct logging operations, and BC Hydro announcing plans to build roads and dams in Tŝilhqot'in territory. The lack of community engagement and consent prior to the start of the projects left the Tŝilhqot'in community disappointed and angry.

Seeing the injustice in his community, William ran for band council fresh out of high school. His first attempt was unsuccessful, but on his second run, at the age of twenty-two, William was elected. Three short years later, William became Chief of the Xeni Gwet'in First Nation. His youth and fluency in Tŝilhqot'in tradition and language allowed William to act as a bridge between generations, which guided him in cultivating meaningful relationships with all members of his community.

A Legacy of Distrust

The Tŝilhqot'in Nation is composed of six First Nations of the Chilcotin Plateau with a population of roughly four thousand members. "Tŝilhqot'in" roughly translates to "people of the river" or "people of the blue water." The Chilcotin Plateau and Chilcotin region in British Columbia were named after the Tŝilhqot'in people. Their territory is roughly a half-hour's drive west of the city of Williams Lake, in the Cariboo region. Tŝilhqot'in language and culture remains strong despite repeated efforts to erase and eliminate their existence. Tŝilhqot'in culture is entrenched in the relationship to the land. Conservation, protection of the environment, and nurturing natural resources are central to Tŝilhqot'in practices.

In the early 1860s, during the Cariboo Gold Rush, there were violent clashes between the Tŝilhqot'in and settlers who were accused of infringing on their territory. The Tŝilhqot'in were struggling to deal with starvation, illness, and the death of a significant portion of their population due to the deadly spread of diseases brought by European settlers.

In July 1864, colonial officials recognized that they would face defeat and invited members of the Tŝilhqot'in to their camp in Quesnel to conduct peace talks. When Tŝilhqot'in warriors and Chiefs arrived in Quesnel, they were arrested. Colonial officials hanged six Tŝilhqot'in Chiefs for murder. These events would become known as the Chilcotin War.

One hundred and fifty years after the Chilcotin War, the BC government acknowledged the injustice of the hangings. In 2018, Prime Minister Justin Trudeau recognized that the Canadian government had betrayed the trust of the Tŝilhqot'in Nation and exonerated the six Chiefs who had been unjustly hanged.

The Chilcotin War and colonial intrusions on Tŝilhqot'in territory led to a long history of tension and distrust between the Tŝilhqot'in Nation and Canadian governments. The contentious relationship again came to a head when the province continued to issue logging licences to lumber companies in Xeni Gwet'in and Tŝilhqot'in territory without receiving permission from either nation. To protect Tŝilhqot'in language, culture, tradition, and way of life, Chief William was determined to put an end to the government's track record of denying Aboriginal title.

The Trigger for a Long Legal Battle

In 1983, six years before William was elected to band council for the first time, British Columbia's provincial government issued a commercial licence to Carrier Lumber to conduct logging operations on Xeni Gwet'in territory. The licence allowed Carrier to cut down trees in an area known as the Trapline Territory, which ran through the Xeni Gwet'in's traditional territory. The Tŝilhqot'in Nation wanted to prohibit logging and tree harvesting on their land and fought to deny access to Carrier.

In 1989, the Nemiah Declaration was created by the Xeni Gwet'in to prohibit commercial mining, logging, hydro dams, and other projects on their traditional territory unless their consent was obtained first. They said the declaration was a necessary response to address the threat that clear-cutting posed on the traditional landscape of the Xeni Gwet'in. However, the declaration had no legal force because title over the land had not been proven in the eye of the law. The Xeni Gwet'in and Tŝilhqot'in Nation set up roadblocks to keep commercial loggers off their land.

Then, in 1990, Chief William commenced legal action against the regional manager of the Cariboo Forest Region, British Columbia, Carrier Lumber, and other forest companies. Although Chief William brought the case to the court, its official name was *Tŝilhqot'in Nation v. British Columbia* because the claim area involved all of Tŝilhqot'in territory. Chief William sought an injunction to prevent the defendants from continuing to clear-cut on traditional territory in the Trapline Territory.

In 1998, Chief William amended his initial lawsuit to seek a declaration of Aboriginal title and to prevent the defendants from conducting

Chief Roger William of the Tŝilhqot'in Nation.

logging operations in an area known as the Brittany Triangle, which was also located on Xeni Gwet'in territory. Chief William wanted the court to award the Tŝilhqot'in Nation damages for the government's infringement of Aboriginal rights and title, provide compensation for the government breaching their fiduciary duty, and issue a ruling that clarified the issuance and use of forestry licences.

A Five-Year Trial

The trial at the British Columbia Supreme Court began in November 2002. It lasted 339 trial days over the course of five years. The length of the trial was due in part to the complexity behind the legal questions presented in the claim for Aboriginal title, but also because Justice David Vickers conducted trips to the contested area — a highly unusual practice, as judges rarely leave the courtroom to examine evidence in the field. Justice Vickers also heard oral history and traditional evidence from Elders and studied extensive historical documents.

In April 2007, Justice Vickers issued his four-hundred-page decision declaring that the Tŝilhqot'in Nation was entitled to a declaration of Aboriginal title over part of the claim area that included village sites and areas used regularly and exclusively by Tŝilhqot'in ancestors for hunting, fishing, and other activities. He affirmed that a territorial use–based approach to Aboriginal title should be used, as opposed to a site-specific approach. The territorial use–based approach focuses on the territory used by the Tŝilhqot'in, whereas a site-specific approach would focus only on the sites where they live or build structures.

Justice Vickers criticized the governments of Canada and British Columbia for advancing an "impoverished view of Aboriginal title" by considering the Tŝilhqot'in Nation's claim through a "postage stamp" approach to title. He saw this approach as preventing genuine negotiations and hindering the process of reconciliation. Ultimately, for procedural reasons, Justice Vickers was unable to make the declaration of Aboriginal title, but his judgment laid out important principles that would later be picked up at the Supreme Court of Canada.

In 2012, the BC government appealed to the British Columbia Court of Appeal, which disagreed with Justice Vickers and held that Aboriginal title had not been established. The Tŝilhqot'in Nation was disappointed with the outcome and applied for leave to appeal to the Supreme Court of Canada, which granted permission in January 2013. The Tŝilhqot'in would now bring their case from the interior of British Columbia to the nation's capital, where they would continue their battle to have their Aboriginal title recognized at Canada's high court.

Chief William Meets Chief Justice McLachlin

On November 7, 2013, *Tŝilhqot'in Nation v. British Columbia* was heard at the Supreme Court of Canada before all eight judges who were on the court at the time. Seven months later, Chief Justice Beverley McLachlin issued a unanimous decision, which declared that the Xeni Gwet'in had proven title over 1,750 square kilometres of land in their traditional territory. Chief Justice McLachlin was an advocate of "conscious objectivity," which meant putting herself in the position of the parties before her to understand their perspective and lived experience while also balancing the importance of fairness, accountability, and justice. This approach was evident in her analysis of the case, as she considered the perspectives of both the BC government and the Tŝilhqot'in Nation, whose perspective was informed by their tradition, culture, and practices.

In articulating the test for Aboriginal title, the Supreme Court rejected the court of appeal's argument that to be granted title, the Tŝilhqot'in were required to demonstrate intensive occupation of site-specific areas of land. Rather, Chief Justice McLachlin agreed with the British Columbia Supreme Court that Aboriginal title could be declared because the Tŝilhqot'in were able to prove that their ancestors had had regular use, control, and presence in the claim area, and that a territorial use–based approach was the proper method for establishing title. In arriving at this decision, the court ensured that a culturally sensitive approach was used to define sufficiency, continuity, and exclusivity to balance the perspectives between the common law and Indigenous tradition, law, culture, and customs.

The court recognized that the Tŝilhqot'in and Xeni Gwet'in had a pre-existing right to Aboriginal title. Aboriginal title as an inherent right of Indigenous Peoples was first recognized in 1763 in the Royal Proclamation issued by King George III in England but was ignored by the Canadian government, which was more concerned with land and resource development than respecting Indigenous rights.

Aboriginal title concedes that a nation has a *sui generis* (unique) interest in the contested land because of their occupation of their traditional territory prior to European settlement. Granting Aboriginal title allows the nation to use its land in modern ways, so long as that use is reconcilable with their relationship to the land that formed the basis for their original claim to Aboriginal title, and the land is not deprived so that future generations are unable to use it. The declaration of Aboriginal title gave the Tŝilhqot'in and Xeni Gwet'in the right to use, control, and enjoy the benefits of their land.

The Supreme Court was clear that the rights associated with Aboriginal title mean that governments and other parties that want to use the land covered by title must obtain the consent of the Indigenous group first. If the Indigenous group does not consent, and the government wishes to infringe upon Aboriginal title, it must demonstrate that it has a compelling and substantial governmental objective, that it took steps to consult and accommodate the Indigenous group, and that its actions align with Canada's fiduciary obligation to Indigenous Peoples.

After more than thirty years, the Tŝilhqot'in Nation had won a long and complex battle. Chief William and other Indigenous leaders were in a boardroom in Vancouver early that Thursday morning in June 2014 when they received the news. They were ecstatic; the whole room erupted in cheers and tears.

Tŝilhqot'in's Significance and Legacy

Jody Wilson-Raybould, who went on to become the first Indigenous federal justice minister, was the Regional Chief of the Assembly of First Nations at the time of *Tŝilhqot'in*. She called the decision "a game changer in terms of the landscape in British Columbia and throughout the rest of the country." The case clarified and provided a framework that outlines what is required in order to establish Aboriginal title, what the Crown must prove if they want to override this title, and how semi-nomadic groups, like the Tŝilhqot'in, can prove Aboriginal title.

The decision was particularly important for Indigenous communities in British Columbia who live on land that was never covered by a treaty, thus leaving Aboriginal title outstanding. Once Aboriginal title was applied to part of Tŝilhqot'in territory, it allowed other Indigenous groups in the province to demand more in-depth consultation processes and more flexible accommodation practices.

Although the legal ability to get a declaration of Aboriginal title was widely celebrated, the practical application remains a work in progress. Aboriginal title has not easily translated on the ground because such cases are extremely expensive and lengthy, which increases barriers for Indigenous groups trying to obtain a declaration of title over their territory. Critics of Canadian governments say they have failed to honourably reach agreements or engage in proper consultation and consent processes with Indigenous communities looking to exercise their Aboriginal title.

Life After *Tŝilhqot'in* for Chief William

Chief William viewed the decision as monumental and described it as the most important decision that he had ever been part of. He became the director of the Cariboo Regional District and has been a member of the Cariboo Chilcotin Aboriginal Training Employment Centre since 1990. He also acted as a councillor for the Xeni Gwet'in First Nation Government. From 1990 to 2003, he served on the RCMP E Division's Commanding Officer's Aboriginal Advisory Committee. In 2015, he was awarded an honorary doctorate of law from the University of Northern British Columbia to commemorate his hard work and dedication to advancing Indigenous rights and title in Canada.

After a brief break from being Chief, he was once again elected as Chief of the Xeni Gwet'in First Nation in February 2023. He articulated his desire to involve his people more in consultation processes. As of 2025, Chief William was working on creating a Tŝilhqot'in Charter that would involve all six First Nations groups that fall under the Tŝilhqot'in National Government. He hoped to cultivate and develop stronger public education tools and programs aimed at promoting Tŝilhqot'in language, culture and tradition. He also co-authored a book, *Lha yudit'ih (We Always Find a*

Way): Bringing the Tŝilhqot'in Title Case Home, published in 2023, chronicling the oral history of the Tŝilhqot'in community in connection with the *Tŝilhqot'in Nation* case.

26

Constitutionalizing Métis Rights: Harry Daniels

Harry "the Hat" Daniels was one of Canada's most charismatic and influential Indigenous leaders. He led successful political and legal battles for the constitutional recognition of Métis and Non-Status Indians. He combined his intelligence and his deep knowledge of history with his sartorial elegance, quick wit, and charisma to charm both his political allies and adversaries and achieve constitutional recognition for his Métis community.

Harry's Early Life

Harry Daniels was born in 1940 in Regina Beach, Saskatchewan, into an old Métis family with strong ties to the Red River Métis community. When he was nine, his father left the family, leaving his mother to care for Harry and his three siblings on her own. When Harry turned seventeen, he dropped out of high school to join the navy. He returned home a few years later and enrolled at the University of Saskatchewan, studying political science. His interest in Indigenous politics was piqued by a course in Native law. While completing his undergraduate degree, Harry travelled to the United States and met with leaders of the American Indian Movement and the Black Panther Party. This experience inspired him to fight for the rights of Indigenous Peoples in Canada. After that, it is fair to say, Harry never looked back.

Political Activism

In 1971, Harry began his career in Indigenous politics when he was elected as vice-president of the Métis Association of Alberta. A year later, he served as the representative for Indigenous Peoples at the United Nations Conference on the Human Environment in Stockholm, Sweden. Harry moved to the national stage in 1974, when he was elected secretary-treasurer of the Native Council of Canada. He went on to serve as its president from 1976 to 1981.

Those years were ones of near constant constitutional negotiations between Ottawa and the provinces. Prime Minister Pierre Trudeau was focused on patriation of the Constitution, an amending formula, and a Charter of Rights of Freedoms. The provincial premiers had other concerns and priorities. Indigenous rights — known as "Aboriginal rights" at the time — were not on the agenda. Indigenous groups were not invited to the table, but they stormed onto the scene. During the heat of the negotiations in 1980, a movement that became known as the Constitution Express brought pressure to bear on the governments to include Aboriginal rights in the new Constitution. Harry Daniels was very much a part of this effort.

Métis History in Canada

Harry was concerned that the Métis would be left out of the Constitution — and he had reason to be, given the history of governments' broken promises and neglect when it came to the Métis.

The history of the Métis Nation is rooted in the Red River Valley in Manitoba and the creation of that province. The Métis Nation is a post-contact Indigenous community of people who are descendants of eighteenth-century European fur traders and First Nations women. The Métis have a common culture, ancestral language, history, and political tradition. They developed along fur trade routes that expand across the Prairies and into parts of British Columbia, Ontario, and the northern United States.

The Métis contributed to the development of transportation routes which linked the North and West to the rest of Canada to allow goods and people to travel across Canada. The Métis acted as guides, interpreters, clerks, canoe men, fur packers, and trade negotiators during the fur trade. They played an essential role in Canada's westward expansion and increasing wealth. However, colonial and then Canadian governmental authorities not only failed to recognize the Métis contribution but also took advantage of the Métis, if not outright swindling them. Most notably, the federal government imposed a "scrip" system upon the Métis — a substitute for legal tender — providing it with an inexpensive way to access Métis land. Subject to government restrictions, these scrips allowed colonists to clear land, establish white settlements, and allocate land for commercial development.

During the 1930s, local Métis communities began a nationalist revival. Between the late 1960s and the early 1970s, the Métis banded together with Non-Status Indians — Indigenous people who had been denied or had revoked their legal status as "Indian" in the eyes of the government. Both had an estranged relationship with the federal government.

Harry lived and breathed Métis history. In 1979, he published three books on the subject: *We Are the New Nation: The Métis and National Native Policy*; *The Forgotten People: Métis and Non-Status Indian Land Claims*; and *A Declaration of Métis and Indian Rights*. In the 1980 federal election, Harry ran unsuccessfully as the New Democratic Party candidate for the Athabasca riding in Alberta. It is interesting to speculate on what would have happened if he had been elected and had been appointed to the Special Committee on the Constitution, which heard from witnesses representing nearly a hundred groups between the fall of 1980 and March 1981. Instead, Harry was one of those witnesses, lecturing the parliamentarians about Métis and Indigenous history and rights.

The Inclusion of the Métis in Section 35

Harry convinced the Canadian government to explicitly recognize the Métis in the new Constitution. Section 35(1) of the Constitution Act, 1982, states: "The existing aboriginal and treaty rights of the aboriginal peoples of Canada are hereby recognized and affirmed." But who were these "aboriginal peoples of Canada"? This was precisely the question that Harry put to Minister of Justice Jean Chrétien during the discussions at the special parliamentary committee devoted to the constitution. According to Harry, Chrétien pointed to the Indigenous representatives in the room: First Nations, Métis, and Inuit. Fine, said Harry, but put that in the Constitution. This led to the enactment of section 35(2), which specifically defines the term "aboriginal peoples of Canada" as including "the Indian, Inuit and Métis peoples of Canada."

Continued Constitutional Ambiguity for the Métis

Although the Métis were recognized in the new Constitution of 1982, their status under the old Constitution of 1867 continued to be a point of contention. The 1867 Constitution Act gave Ottawa the power to make laws for "Indians and lands reserved for Indians," but did this include the Métis? The federal government said no and the provinces often said yes, meaning they eschewed responsibility for the Métis. Consequently, Métis communities often found themselves in a "jurisdictional wasteland," treated as the unwanted orphans of Confederation. At times, both governments denied constitutional responsibility for Métis people.

This void had real consequences for Métis people. Métis and Non-Status communities were denied access to federally funded programs such as the Aboriginal Justice Strategy, the Aboriginal Representative Organization Program, and the Department of Indian Affairs and Northern Development's annual economic development programs. Moreover, they did not receive the same benefits as Status Indians. For example, Métis and Non-Status Indians were not able to hunt, trap, fish, and gather on public land or negotiate and enter treaties with the federal government under the Indian Act. Harry Daniels sought to redress this inequity.

Starting *Daniels v. Canada*

In 1999, Harry began an action for a declaration that Métis and Non-Status Indians be considered "Indians" under section 91(24) of the Constitution Act, 1867. Harry was represented by noted constitutional law expert Professor Joseph Magnet of the University of Ottawa's Faculty of Law. Magnet had advised and represented the Métis and Non-Status Indians for decades, including before the Special Joint Committee on the Constitution, 1980–81, which resulted in the constitutional entrenchment of Indigenous rights in section 35. Magnet and Harry quickly discovered that the Government of Canada was going to fight them at every stage on every issue. The minister of Indian Affairs and Northern Development tried twice to have Harry's claim "struck out," or dismissed. The government failed both times.

Meanwhile, Harry was battling cancer. In the early stages of the case, Harry died in Regina Beach on September 6, 2004, succumbing to cancer. He was just ten days shy of his sixty-fourth birthday. His death was a huge loss to the Métis people and to Canada. But the lawsuit that bore his name continued after his death. Although Harry died before the case went to trial, his name remained on the lawsuit, and his son, Gabriel, joined the case. Unlike his father, Gabriel was not a politician. He worked as a carpenter in Winnipeg. However, Gabriel's participation ensured that a Daniels would see the lawsuit through to its end.

The Trial and the Appeal

At trial, Justice Michael Phelan of the Federal Court granted the declaration that the term "Indian" in section 91(24) of the Constitution Act, 1867, included Non-Status Indians and Métis. Justice Phelan analyzed the historical, philosophical, and linguistic context of the use of the term to conclude that it was a broad term referring to all Indigenous Peoples in Canada. He found that the declaration would alleviate constitutional uncertainty and end the categorial denial of benefits to the Métis and Non-Status Indians.

The Federal Court of Appeal largely accepted Justice Phelan's findings, but excluded Non-Status Indians from the definition of "Indian" under the Constitution Act, 1867. The government appealed to the Supreme Court.

Daniels at the Supreme Court

The *Daniels* case finally reached the Supreme Court of Canada on October 15, 2015, nearly sixteen years after it began and more than a decade after Harry's passing. Six months later, the court delivered a unanimous decision in favour of all Métis and Non-Status Indians. Writing for the court,

Justice Rosalie Abella held that section 35 of the Constitution Act, 1982, and section 91(24) of the Constitution Act, 1867, should be read together and consistently.

Justice Abella recognized that declaring Métis and Non-Status Indians as "Indians" under the Constitution had the positive benefit of "ending a jurisdictional tug-of-war" and would guarantee certainty and accountability. Disagreeing with the Federal Court of Appeal, Justice Abella stated that there was no need for consensus on who is considered Métis or a Non-Status Indian. She suggested that cultural and ethnic labels cannot be categorized.

In analyzing whether the Métis should be considered "Indians," the court turned to the history of the Métis people and their relationship with the federal government. The court noted that "Indian" had been used as a general term referring to Indigenous Peoples, including communities of mixed

A Canada Post stamp commemorating Indigenous leader Harry Daniels.

ancestry. The court also examined treaties, federal laws, and actions by the federal government that suggested the Métis were under federal jurisdiction.

Remembering Harry

Harry was more than just a politician. He had movie star good looks, the sartorial style to grace the red carpet, and charisma and wit to match. He was the rare politician who makes a successful crossover into film and television. In 1986, Harry starred in *Mistress Madeleine*, a Canadian production that won several Gemini Awards for chronicling the Métis relationship with the Hudson's Bay Company in the 1850s. He also played Gabriel Dumont in *Big Bear*, an award-winning miniseries about the Cree leader. In his last year of life, Harry appeared in an episode of the CBC series *Renegadepress.com*.

Harry was known for his warmth, his wit, and his compassion. His goodwill was demonstrated in an incident on September 18, 1984, when Pope John Paul II was visiting the Northwest Territories. After the Pope's flight to Fort Simpson was delayed, Harry noticed that the Pope was cold. In a gesture of welcome, Harry took off his buckskin jacket and wrapped it around the Pope's shoulders as a gift, leaving himself to shiver in short sleeves.

Harry's long-time friend Tony Belcourt recalls that he "had a personality that commanded attention" and "was very fast on his feet." His Métis pride was demonstrated by his ability to speak Michif, and he loved doing so. Métis author, playwright, and Elder Maria Campbell remembers Harry as "such a crazy, beautiful man, who loved conferences that were full of laughter, passion and politics." Harry twice contributed to the recognition of the Métis under the Canadian Constitution. Few leaders can boast of such accomplishments.

Acknowledgements

This project had its genesis in my earlier book *The Canadian Constitution*, published by Dundurn and now in its third edition. In that book, I tried to explain — very briefly — key Supreme Court of Canada decisions in a way that would be accessible to ordinary Canadians.

In this book, I set out to profile the people involved in some of the most important Canadian constitutional law cases. I enlisted nine University of Ottawa law students from my small group Introduction to Public and Constitutional Law in their first year of law school, 2022–23, who researched and wrote profiles of prospective protagonists. Yasmeen Atassi, Jamie Bell, Dominique Charland, Bionca Chu, Sean Cousins, Sébastien Cyr, Judson Nickerson, Asha Sahota, and Marna Swart all graduated in 2025 and are beginning their professional careers. Not all of their work made it into the book, but they all made important contributions to the success of this project.

Susan Lightstone and Ellen Zweibel helped me frame the book. Many people had opinions on what cases to include, but Rosalie Abella, Constance Backhouse, Alison Crawford, and Daphne Gilbert provided invaluable advice that helped guide my decisions. Stephen Bindman, Signa Daum

Shanks, François Larocque, Carissima Mathen, Marion Sandilands, and Ellen Zweibel read drafts of chapters and provided very helpful feedback. Sue Sumeraj proofread and edited the entire manuscript. Nicole Goldstone and Ben Dodek were enthusiastic supporters.

Geoff Cowper, Pascale Fournier, Yves Le Bouthillier, Joanne Lysyk, Roy Millen, Leslie Pal, Shelagh Scarth, and Lynn Smith provided important insights on various cases. My colleague Constance Backhouse emphasized the importance of pictures in telling legal history, and Elia Anoia at Canada Post, Andrea Gordon at CP Images, Elena Novikova at Postmedia, and Bronwyn Smith at the Vancouver Archives enabled me to find and use the photos in this book.

This is my fifth project with Dundurn. I have had the privilege of working with this great Canadian company for almost fifteen years. It has always been a pleasure working with Dundurn's dedicated and professional staff. Chief Publishing Officer Meghan Macdonald, Managing Editor Elena Radic, and Senior Editor Kathryn Lane embraced this project from its inception. Janna Green has steadily steered the project along. Carrie Gleason did a great job editing the manuscript, and Laura Boyle designed the wonderful cover.

Sources

1 Janey Canuck, Personhood, and the Famous Five: Emily Murphy

CASE LAW

Edwards v. Canada (Attorney General), 1929 CanLII 438 (UK JCPC).

Reference re meaning of the word "Persons" in s.24 of British North America Act, 1928 CanLII 55 (SCC), [1928] SCR 276.

SECONDARY SOURCES

Amazing Women in History. "The Canadian Persons Case: Are Women People?" Accessed March 1, 2025. amazingwomeninhistory.com/the-canadian-persons-case-are-women-people/.

Canadian Press. "Privy Council Rules Women Are 'Persons.'" *Montreal Gazette*, October 19, 1929, 1.

Cavanaugh, Catherine. "Famous Five." *Canadian Encyclopedia*, June 1, 2006; last edited November 20, 2020, by Andrew McIntosh. thecanadianencyclopedia.ca/en/article/famous-5.

Cavanaugh, Catherine, and Susanna McLeod. "Irene Parlby." *Canadian Encyclopedia*, October 27, 2009; last edited November 20, 2020, by Andrew McIntosh. thecanadianencyclopedia.ca/en/article/mary-irene-parlby.

de Bruin, Tabitha, and David A. Cruickshank. "Persons Case." *Canadian Encyclopedia*, February 7, 2006; last edited November 6, 2020, by Andrew McIntosh. thecanadianencyclopedia.ca/en/article/persons-case.

Emily Murphy Centre. "Emily Murphy." Accessed March 1, 2025. emilymurphycentre.com/history/.

Famous 5 Foundation. "The Famous Five: The Women." Accessed March 1, 2025. famous5.ca/the-famous-five-women.

Government of Canada. "Women Are Persons!" Last modified October 15, 2024. canada.ca/en/canadian-heritage/services/art-monuments/monuments/women-are-persons.html.

Manitoba Historical Society Archives. "Memorable Manitobans: Emily Gowan Ferguson Murphy (1868–1933)." Last revised March 31, 2008. mhs.mb.ca/docs/people/murphy_egf.shtml.

Nellie McClung Foundation. "Nellie McClung: Canada's Most Famous Suffragist." Accessed March 1, 2025. nelliemcclungfoundation.com/about-nellie.

New World Encyclopedia. "Emily Murphy." Last revised January 21, 2023. newworldencyclopedia.org/entry/Emily_Murphy.

Pettinger, Tejvan. "Emily Murphy." Biography Online, February 1, 2010; last edited February 12, 2018. biographyonline.net/women/emily-murphy.html.

Sharpe, Robert J., and Patricia I. McMahon. *The Persons Case: The Origins and Legacy of the Fight for Legal Personhood*. Osgoode Society for Canadian Legal History. University of Toronto Press, 2008.

Silverman, Eliane Leslau, and Susanna McLeod. "Henrietta Muir Edwards." *Canadian Encyclopedia*, March 25, 2008; last edited November 20, 2020, by Andrew McIntosh. thecanadianencyclopedia.ca/en/article/henrietta-louise-edwards.

Silverman, Eliane Leslau, and Susanna McLeod. "Louise McKinney." *Canadian Encyclopedia*, April 1, 2008; last edited November 20, 2020, by Andrew McIntosh. thecanadianencyclopedia.ca/en/article/louise-mckinney.

2 Fighting Racism in Western Canada: Quong Wing

CASE LAW

Quong Wing v. The King (1914), 49 SCR 440, 1914 CanLII 608.

Rex v. Quong Sing, 1913 CanLII 117 (SK CA), 12 DLR 656.

LEGISLATION

An Act to Prevent the Employment of Female Labour in Certain Capacities, SS 1912, c. 17.

SECONDARY SOURCES

Backhouse, Constance. "The White Women's Labor Laws: Anti-Chinese Racism in Early Twentieth-Century Canada." *Law and History Review* 14, no. 2 (Fall 1996): 315–68. doi.org/10.2307/743786.

City of Moosejaw, Saskatchewan. "Old CPR Station." Accessed March 1, 2025. moosejaw.ca/heritage_properties/old-cpr-station/.

Government of Canada. "History of Citizenship Legislation." Accessed March 1, 2025. canada.ca/en/immigration-refugees-citizenship/corporate/publications-manuals/operational-bulletins-manuals/canadian-citizenship/overview.html#s5.

Lu, Yixi, and Li Zong. "The Development of the Chinese Community in Saskatoon." *Canadian Ethnic Studies* 49, no. 3 (2017): 71–91.

Meister, Daniel, Emily Burton, Erica Gagnon, et al. "Chinese Immigration Act, 1923." Canadian Museum of Immigration at Pier 21. Accessed March 1, 2025. pier21.ca/research/immigration-history/chinese-immigration-act-1923.

Walker, James W. St. G. *"Race," Rights and the Law in the Supreme Court of Canada: Historical Case Studies*. Osgoode Society for Canadian Legal History. Wilfrid Laurier University Press, 1997.

3 Unlikely Champion of the Rule of Law: Frank Roncarelli

CASE LAW

Boucher v. The King, 1950 CanLII 2 (SCC), [1951] SCR 26.

Chaput v. Romain, 1955 CanLII 74 (SCC), [1955] SCR 83.

Roncarelli v. Duplessis, 1959 CanLII 50 (SCC), [1959] SCR 121.
Saumur v. The City of Quebec, 1953 CanLII 3 (SCC), [1953] 2 SCR 299.

SECONDARY SOURCES

Adams, Eric M. "Building a Law of Human Rights: *Roncarelli v. Duplessis* in Canadian Constitutional Culture." *McGill Law Journal* 55, no. 3 (September 2010): 437–60. doi.org/10.7202/1000619ar.
CBC Archives. "Revisiting the Roncarelli Affair in Quebec, 1965." cbc.ca/player/play/video/1.3594300.
Fish, Morris J. "The Effect of Alcohol on the Canadian Constitution ... Seriously." *McGill Law Journal* 57, no. 1 (November 2011): 189. doi.org/10.7202/1006421ar.
International Hockey Wiki. "Frank Roncarelli." Accessed March 1, 2025. internationalhockey.fandom.com/wiki/Frank_Roncarelli.
Kaplan, William. *State and Salvation: The Jehovah's Witnesses and Their Fight for Civil Rights*. University of Toronto Press, 1989.
Montreal Gazette. "Group Urges Roncarelli Case Appeal." March 20, 1959, 39.
Montreal Gazette. "Mrs. E. Roncarelli Dies Aged 55 Years." December 28, 1940, 7.
Montreal Gazette. "No Appeal: Public Opinion to Decide Roncarelli Case: Premier." March 12, 1959, 1.

4 Ahead of Her Time: Stella Bliss

CASE LAW

Bliss v. Attorney General of Canada, 1978 CanLII 25 (SCC), [1979] 1 SCR 183.
Brooks v. Canada Safeway, 1989 CanLII 96 (SCC), [1989] 1 SCR 1219.
Re Attorney-General of Canada and Bliss, 1977 CanLII 3202 (FCA), [1978] 1 FC 208.

SECONDARY SOURCES

Dodek, Adam. *The Charter Debates: The Special Joint Committee on the Constitution, 1980–81, and the Making of the Canadian Charter of Rights and Freedoms*. University of Toronto Press, 2018.
Pal, Leslie A., and F.L. Morton. "Bliss v. Attorney General of Canada: From Legal Defeat to Political Victory." *Osgoode Hall Law Journal* 24, no. 1 (1986): 141–60. doi.org/10.60082/2817-5069.1881.

5 The Most Famous Name in Canadian Constitutional Law: David Oakes

CASE LAW

R v. Oakes, [1986] 1 SCR 103, 1986 CanLII 46.

LEGISLATION

Narcotic Control Act, RSC 1970, c. N1, s. 8.

SECONDARY SOURCES

Bowal, Peter, and Mark Kelndorfer. "Whatever Happened to ... *R. v. Oakes.*" LawNow, November 1, 2016. lawnow.org/whatever-happened-to-r-v-oakes/.

Calamai, Peter. "Court Must Decide if Drug Case Suspects Must Prove Innocence." *Ottawa Citizen*, March 13, 1985, 3.

Ellwand, Geoff. "From Minor Drug Case to a Charter Landmark." *Lawyers Weekly* 31, no. 46 (April 13, 2012).

Ellwand, Geoff. "Routine Drug Arrest Becomes Oakes Test." *Lawyers Weekly* 31, no. 3 (May 20, 2011).

Martin, Chip. "Judge Upholds Drug Traffic Law." *Toronto Star*, September 18, 1982, A4.

Martin, Chip. "'Reverse-Onus' Laws Ruled Unconstitutional." *London Free Press*, March 1, 1986.

Taber, Jane. "Ruling on Narcotics Laws 'Won't Hamper Drug Enforcement.'" *Ottawa Citizen*, February 4, 1983, 40.

TheCourt.ca. "Top 10 Charter Cases: As Revealed at the Symposium on the 25th Anniversary of the Charter, a Tribute to Chief Justice Roy McMurtry." April 12, 2007. thecourt.ca/top-10-charter-cases-as-revealed-at-the-symposium-on-the-25th-anniversary-of-the-charter-a-tribute-to-chief-justice-roy-mcmurtry/.

Toronto Star. "Court Rules Drug Law Violates Rights Charter." February 3, 1981, 2.

6 A Boy with a Kirpan: Gurbaj Singh Multani

CASE LAW

Commission scolaire Marguerite-Bourgeoys v. Singh Multani, 2004 CanLII 31405 (QC CA).

Multani v. Commission scolaire Marguerite-Bourgeoys, 2006 SCC 6 (CanLII), [2006] 1 SCR 256.

Singh Multani c. Commission scolaire Marguerite-Bourgeois, 2002 CanLII 473 (QC CS).

SECONDARY SOURCES

Emara, Merna. "Where Are They Now?" Supreme Advocacy, March 19, 2020. supremeadvocacy.ca/2020/03/19/where-are-they-now/.

Fine, Sean. "Sikh Student Who Won Kirpan Case Now Considers Leaving Quebec." *Globe and Mail*, October 22, 2013.

Ha, Tu Tanh. "Sikh Student Wins Case, but He Must Carry Kirpan in Scabbard." *Globe and Mail*, May 18, 2002.

Hanes, Allison. "Quebec to Appeal Kirpan Ruling." *Montreal Gazette*, May 28, 2002.

Jamal, Mahmud. "Freedom of Religion in the Supreme Court: Some Lessons from Multani." *National Journal of Constitutional Law* 21 (2006): 291.

Johnston, David. "'Kirpan Kid' Didn't Hang on Hearings: As a 13-Year-Old, Multani Spent a Year out of School as His Family Waged a Legal Battle." *Montreal Gazette*, May 23, 2008.

Loten, Angus. "Boy Going to Class with New Kirpan: Gurbaj Singh Is Off to His School in LaSalle Today Wearing a Ceremonial Dagger in a Wooden Sheath. His Family Hopes It's the End to a Long Dispute." *Montreal Gazette*, May 22, 2002.

Peritz, Ingrid. "Police on Guard as Boy Wearing Kirpan Returns to Face Insults." *Globe and Mail*, April 18, 2002.

Peritz, Ingrid. "Sikh Student Gives Up Fight over Kirpan in Classroom." *Globe and Mail*, August 1, 2002.

Quebec Consultation Commission on Accommodation Practices Related to Cultural Differences. *Report: Building the Future: A Time for Reconciliation*. Quebec, 2008.

7 Teaching Hate in High School: Jim Keegstra

CASE LAW

R v. Keegstra, 1988 ABCA 234 (CanLII), 5 WWR 211.

R v. Keegstra, 1990 CanLII 24 (SCC), [1990] 3 SCR 697.

R v. Keegstra, 1994 ABCA 293 (CanLII), 77 WAC 1.

R v. Keegstra, 1996 ABCA 308 (CanLII), 187 AR 216.

R v. Keegstra, 1996 CanLII 221 (SCC), [1996] 1 SCR 458.

SECONDARY SOURCES

Advocate Staff. "Holocaust Denier Keegstra Dead at Age 80." *Red Deer Advocate*, June 13, 2014. reddeeradvocate.com/news/holocaust-denier-keegstra-dead-at-age-80-7096171.

Bercuson, David, and Douglas Wertheimer. *A Trust Betrayed: The Keegstra Affair*. Doubleday Canada, 1985.

B'nai Brith Canada. "Annual Audit of Antisemitic Incidents 2023." Accessed March 1, 2025. bnaibrith.ca/antisemitic-incidents/.

Boyko, John. "Keegstra Case." *Canadian Encyclopedia*, February 7, 2006; last edited August 25, 2021. thecanadianencyclopedia.ca/en/article/keegstra-case.

Elman, Bruce P. "Combatting Racist Speech: The Canadian Experience." *Alberta Law Review* 32, no. 4 (August 1, 1994): 623–66. doi.org/10.29173/alr1155.

Mertl, Steve, and John Ward. *Keegstra: The Issues, The Trial, The Consequences*. Western Producer Prairie Books, 1985.

Weinrib, Lorraine Eisenstat. "Hate Promotion in a Free and Democratic Society: R. v. Keegstra." *McGill Law Journal* 36, no. 4 (September 1991): 1416–49.

8 Canada's Most Notorious Child Pornographer: Robin Sharpe

CASE LAW

R v. Sharpe, 1999 BCCA 416 (CanLII).

R v. Sharpe, 1999 CanLII 6380 (BC SC).

R v. Sharpe, 2001 SCC 2, [2001] 1 SCR 45 (CanLII).

R v. Sharpe, 2002 BCSC 423 (CanLII).

R v. Sharpe, 2007 BCCA 191 (CanLII).

LEGISLATION

Bill C-2, An Act to Amend the Criminal Code (Protection of Children and Other Vulnerable Persons) and the Canada Evidence Act, 1st Sess, 38th Parl, 2004 (Royal Assent: 20 July 2005).

Bill C-12, An Act to Amend the Criminal Code (Protection of Children and Other Vulnerable Persons) and the Canada Evidence Act, 2nd Sess, 37th Parl, 2003 (First Reading: 5 December 2002).

Criminal Code, RSC 1985, c. C-46, s. 163.

SECONDARY SOURCES

Associated Press. "Canada Judge Threatened." *New York Times*, January 23, 1999. nytimes.com/1999/01/23/world/canada-judge-threatened.html.

Bell, Shannon. *Fast Feminism*. Brooklyn: Autonomedia, 2010.

"Can Child Pornography Have Artistic Merit?" *Maclean's*, April 8, 2002, 18.

Canadian Press. "Shielding Kids More Important than Protecting Pedophiles, Feds Say." April 15, 1999.

CBC News. "B.C. Court Delivers Split Decision on Child Porn Activist." March 12, 2004. cbc.ca/news/canada/b-c-court-delivers-split-decision-on-child-porn-activist-1.469528.

CBC News. "Sex Offender Sharpe Wanted on Canada-Wide Warrant." November 17, 2006. cbc.ca/news/canada/sex-offender-sharpe-wanted-on-canada-wide-warrant-1.624233.

CBC News. "Sharpe Not Guilty of Possessing Written Child Pornography." March 26, 2002. cbc.ca/news/canada/sharpe-not-guilty-of-possessing-written-child-pornography-1.339142.

CBC News. "Sharpe Sentenced in B.C. Child Pornography Case." May 3, 2002. cbc.ca/news/canada/sharpe-sentenced-in-b-c-child-pornography-case-1.315991.

Cohen, Lynn. "John Robin Sharpe as Exemplary Citizen." *Report Newsmagazine*, May 27, 2002.

Globe and Mail. "Sharpe Sentenced to Two Years." July 19, 2004.

Ordóñez, Maria-Belén, and Robert Teixeira. "John Robin Sharpe: Sexual Outlaw." *Now*, November 8, 2015. nowtoronto.com/news/john-robin-sharpe-sexual-outlaw/.

Persky, Stan, and John Dixon. *On Kiddie Porn: Sexual Representation, Free Speech and the Robin Sharpe Case*. Vancouver: New Star Books, 2001.

Scott, Alec. "On Kiddie Porn: Sexual Representation, Free Speech and the Robin Sharpe Case." Book review. *Quill & Quire*, February 2, 2004. quillandquire.com/review/on-kiddie-porn-sexual-representation-free-speech-and-the-robin-sharpe-case/.

Sharpe, Robin. "Abandon Your Rectitudes and Tune In ..." Accessed March 1, 2025. robinsharpe.ca/.

Shaw, Duncan W. "Child Pornography and the Media: *R v. Sharpe*." *Dialogues About Justice* (September 2002): 99–106.

Theodore, Terri. "John Robin Sharpe Hopes His Case Means Part of Child-Porn Law Is Dead." Canadian Press, April 25, 2002.

9 Championing LGBTQ Expression: Jim Deva, Bruce Smyth, and the Little Sister's Bookstore

CASE LAW

Little Sisters Book and Art Emporium v. Canada (Minister of Justice), 2000 SCC 69 (CanLII), [2000] 2 SCR 1120.

LEGISLATION

Criminal Code, RSC 1985, c. C-46.

SECONDARY SOURCES

Babineau, Guy. "Little Sister's: 25 Years of Determination." *Xtra*, April 22, 2008. xtramagazine.com/power/little-sisters-25-years-of-determination-38322.

Barker, Harvie. "Seeing Others as Equal." *Penticton Herald*, November 3, 2014. pentictonherald.ca/opinion/article_13c041fe-63c0-11e4-a365-001a4bcf6878.html.

Canadian Press. "Feisty Vancouver Gay Bookshop up for Sale." *CTV News*, April 20, 2008. bc.ctvnews.ca/feisty-vancouver-gay-bookshop-up-for-sale-1.290513.

CBC News. "Vancouver LGBTQ Bookstore at Centre of Landmark Legal Case Celebrates 40th Anniversary." April 29, 2023. cbc.ca/news/canada

/british-columbia/little-sisters-book-art-emporium-vancouver-40th-anniversary-1.6826874.

Deva, Jim. "How Little Sister's Got to Court." *Xtra*, February 13, 2007. xtramagazine.com/power/how-little-sisters-got-to-court-19605.

Dunphy, Martin. "Little Sister's Cofounder Bruce Smyth Dies." *Georgia Straight*, December 23, 2019. straight.com/news/1340651/little-sisters-cofounder-bruce-smyth-dies.

Hainsworth, Jeremy, and Robin Perelle. "'We're Not Going to Live in Shame': The Legacy of Jim Deva." *Xtra*, October 10, 2014. tinyurl.com/vr5yrfha.

Lawton, Valerie. "Fight over Gay Books Arrives at Top Court." *Toronto Star*, March 15, 2000, 7.

Little Sister's. "About." Accessed March 1, 2025. littlesisters.ca/pages/about.

Mackie, John. "Obituary: Little Sister's Owner Dies After Fall from Ladder." *Vancouver Sun*, September 21, 2014; last updated September 23, 2014. vancouversun.com/news/metro/obituary-little-sisters-owner-dies-after-fall-from-ladder.

Montreal Gazette. "Top Court to Rule on Book Seizures." February 19, 1999.

Rau, Krishna. "2SLGBTQ+ Rights in Canada." *Canadian Encyclopedia*, June 16, 2014; last edited December 12, 2024, by Clayton Ma. thecanadianencyclopedia.ca/en/article/lesbian-gay-bisexual-and-transgender-rights-in-canada.

Thomas, Sandra. "'A Wonderful Man and a Wonderful Friend.'" Vancouver Is Awesome. September 23, 2014. vancouverisawesome.com/courier-archive/living/a-wonderful-man-and-a-wonderful-friend-2985706.

10 Even Prisoners Have the Right to Vote: Rick Sauvé

CASE LAW

Sauvé v. Canada (AG), (1988), 66 OR (2d) 234, 1988 CanLII 4571 (ON SC).

Sauvé v. Canada (AG), (1992), 7 OR (3d) 481, 1992 CanLII 2786 (ON CA).

Sauvé v. Canada (AG), 1993 CanLII 92 (SCC), [1993] 2 SCR 438 (*Sauvé I*).

Sauvé v. Canada (Chief Electoral Officer), 1995 CanLII 3565 (FC), [1996] 1 FC 857.

Sauvé v. Canada (Chief Electoral Officer), 1999 CanLII 9382 (FCA), [2000] 2 FC 117.

Sauvé v. Canada (Chief Electoral Officer), 2002 SCC 68 (CanLII), [2002] 3 SCR 519 (*Sauvé II*).

LEGISLATION

Canada Elections Act, RSC 1970, c. 14 (1st supp).

SECONDARY SOURCES

Christie, Erin. "Prisoner's Rights Activist Tells Tales of Injustice." *Vernon Morning Star*, February 8, 2018. vernonmorningstar.com/news/prisoners-rights-activist-tells-tales-of-injustice-3274288.

Edwards, Peter. *Unrepentant: The Strange and (Sometimes) Terrible Life of Lorne Campbell, Satan's Choice and Hells Angels Biker*. Random House Canada, 2013.

Emara, Merna. "Where Are They Now." Supreme Advocacy. March 2020. supremeadvocacy.ca/wp-content/uploads/2020/03/SCC-Famous-Litigants.pdf.

Jackson, Michael. "Analysis and Highlights of *Sauvé v. Canada*." Justice Behind the Walls. December 2002. justicebehindthewalls.net/resources/news/sauve.pdf.

Lowe, Mick. *Conspiracy of Brothers: A True Story of Bikers, Murder, and the Law*. Vintage Canada, 2013.

Ontario Justice Education Network. "The Top Five — 2003: Richard Sauvé v. The Attorney General of Canada, the Chief Electoral Officer of Canada and the Solicitor General of Canada." November 2016. ojen.ca/wp-content/uploads/2016/10/Richard-Sauv%C3%A9-v-Attorney-General-of-Canada-Aug-2009.pdf.

White, Patrick. "Rick Sauvé's Prisoner-Coaching Program Life Line Faces Potential Cancellation." *Globe and Mail*, December 14, 2017.

Young, Jim. "Sauvé v. Canada (2002) — Limits on Voting Rights for Prisoners." Centre for Constitutional Studies. May 27, 2010. constitutionalstudies.ca/2010/05/sauve-v-canada-2002-limits-on-voting-rights-for-prisoners/.

11 Abortion Crusader: Dr. Henry Morgentaler

CASE LAW

PEI (Minister of Health and Social Services) v. Morgentaler, 1996 CanLII 3713 (PE SCAD), 144 Nfld & PEIR 263.

R v. Morgentaler (No. 4), 1973 CanLII 1540 (QC CQ), 42 DLR (3d) 444.

R v. Morgentaler, 1976 CanLII 1255 (QC CA), 64 DLR (3d) 718.
R v. Morgentaler, 1988 CanLII 90 (SCC), [1988] 1 SCR 30.
R v. Morgentaler, [1993] 3 SCR 463, 1993 CanLII 74 (SCC).

SECONDARY SOURCES

CBC News. "Abortion Rights Activist Dr. Henry Morgentaler Dies at 90." May 29, 2013. cbc.ca/news/canada/abortion-rights-activist-dr-henry-morgentaler-dies-at-90-1.1321542.

de Bruin, Tabitha, and Angus McLaren. "Henry Morgentaler." *Canadian Encyclopedia*, July 11, 2013; last edited May 19, 2023, by Jessica Poulin. thecanadianencyclopedia.ca/en/article/henry-morgentaler.

Dunphy, Catherine. *Morgentaler: A Difficult Hero*. Random House Canada, 1996.

Hunter, Paul. "Henry Morgentaler: Driven by Tragedy, Abortion Doctor Made History." *Toronto Star*, May 30, 2013. thestar.com/news/canada/henry-morgentaler-driven-by-tragedy-abortion-doctor-made-history/article_f151b1bb-e66a-57a7-96e2-ef78f8961c7d.html.

Martin, Sandra. "Abortion Rights Crusader Henry Morgentaler, Revered and Hated, Dead at 90." *Globe and Mail*, May 29, 2013. theglobeandmail.com/news/national/abortion-rights-crusader-henry-morgentaler-revered-and-hated-dead-at-90/article12221564/.

McFadden, Robert D. "Henry Morgentaler, 90, Dies; Abortion Defender in Canada." *New York Times*, May 29, 2013. nytimes.com/2013/05/30/world/americas/henry-morgentaler-abortion-doctor-in-canada-dies-at-90.html.

The Morgentaler Decision. "About Henry Morgentaler." Last revised July 15, 2016. morgentaler25years.ca/about-henry-morgentaler/.

Pelrine, Eleanor Wright. *Morgentaler: The Doctor Who Couldn't Turn Away*. Gage Publishing, 1975.

12 A Woman Who Would Not Submit: Chantale Daigle

CASE LAW

Borowski v. Canada (AG), [1990] 1 SCR 342, 1989 CanLII 123 (SCC).
Daigle c. Tremblay (1989), 59 DLR (4th) 609, 1989 CanLII 894 (QC CA).

R v. Morgentaler, [1988] 1 SCR 30, 1988 CanLII 90 (SCC).
Tremblay v. Daigle, [1989] 2 SCR 530, 1989 CanLII 33 (SCC).

SECONDARY SOURCES

Barron, James. "Canada's Supreme Court Rejects Ex-Lover's Effort to Halt Abortion." *New York Times*, August 9, 1989, A1.

Bilodeau, Johanne. "Chantal Daigle, une heroine." *La Tribune*, August 10, 2009. latribune.ca/2009/08/10/chantal-daigle-une-heroine-babc6cbe3495fd9262561804624a5c99/.

Boston Globe. "Canadian Woman's Lawyer Said She Got Boston Abortion." August 11, 1989.

Daigle, Chantale. *Le seul choix, le mien*. Montreal: Magazine Sérénité, 1990.

Durand-Brault, Alexis, dir. *Désobéir: le choix de Chantale Daigle*. Crave, 2023. crave.ca/fr/tv-shows/disobey.

Maclean's. "Abortion Agony: Contentious Issues Remain to Be Resolved After the Top Court's Decision." August 21, 1989.

Sharpe, Robert J., and Kent Roach. *Brian Dickson: A Judge's Journey*. University of Toronto Press, 2003.

Van Dusen, Lisa. "A Unanimous View: The Supreme Court Finds No Fetal Rights." *Maclean's*, November 27, 1989, 16.

13 The Right to the Basic Necessities of Life: Louise Gosselin

CASE LAW

Gosselin c. Québec (Procureur général), 1986 CarswellQue 598, J.E. 87–239.
Gosselin c. Québec (Procureur général), 1992 CarswellQue 1685, [1992] RJQ 1647.
Gosselin c. Québec (Procureur général), 1999 CanLII 13818 (QC CA).
Gosselin v. Québec (Attorney General), 2002 SCC 84 (CanLII), [2002] 4 SCR 429.

COURT RECORDS

Appellant's record, volume 1, *Gosselin v. Québec* (SCC File No. 27418).

SECONDARY SOURCES

Amanat, Hayatullah. "1 in 5 Single Adults in Canada Live in Poverty, Many of Whom

Are Food Insecure: Report." *CTV News*, June 15, 2023. ctvnews.ca/canada/article/1-in-5-single-adults-in-canada-live-in-poverty-many-of-whom-are-food-insecure-report/.

Brodsky, Gwen, Rachel Cox, Shelagh Day, and M. Kate Stephenson. "Gosselin v. Québec (Attorney General)." *Canadian Journal of Women and the Law* 18, no. 1 (2006): 189–249. muse.jhu.edu/article/230231.

Cameron, Jamie. "Positive Obligations Under Sections 15 and 7 of the Charter: A Comment on Gosselin v. Quebec." *Supreme Court Law Review* 20 (2003): 66–91.

Chwialkowska, Luiza. "Court to Hear Quebec Case on Welfare for Young Adults." *National Post*, June 2, 2000.

Edmonton Journal. "Social Assistance Isn't a Right (Editorial)." October 30, 2001.

Fortin, Pierre. "Le chômage des jeunes au Québec: Aggravation et concentration, 1966–1982." *Relations industrielles* 39, no. 3 (1984): 419–48.

Jackman, Martha. "One Step Forward and Two Steps Back: Poverty, the Charter and the Legacy of *Gosselin*." *National Journal of Constitutional Law* 39, no. 1 (January 2019): 85–121.

Laurent, Rene. "Young Welfare Recipient Gets OK for Class Action." *Montreal Gazette*, December 16, 1986.

Martin, Don. "Sadly, a Legal Case Rooted in Laziness." *Edmonton Journal*, October 30, 2001.

Thompson, Elizabeth. "Welfare Cuts Ruled OK." *Montreal Gazette*, December 20, 2002.

Tibbetts, Janice. "The Charter Debate." *Ottawa Citizen*, April 13, 2002.

Tyler, Tracey. "Equality Revolution Marches On, 20 Years Later." *Toronto Star*, April 16, 2005.

14 Canada's Dominatrix: Terri-Jean Bedford

CASE LAW

Bedford v. Canada, 2010 ONSC 4264 (CanLII).

Canada (AG) v. Bedford, 2012 ONCA 186 (CanLII).

Canada (AG) v. Bedford, 2013 SCC 72 (CanLII), [2013] 3 SCR 1101.

Reference re ss. 193 and 195.1(1)(C) of the criminal code (Man), 1990 CanLII 105 (SCC), [1990] 1 SCR 1123 ("*Prostitution Reference*").

LEGISLATION

Bill C-36, Protection of Communities and Exploited Persons Act, 2nd Sess., 41st Parl., 2014.

Bill C-36, Protection of Communities and Exploited Persons Act, Standing Committee on Justice and Human Rights, Evidence, 41–2, No. 38 (July 9, 2014).

Criminal Code, RSC 1985, c. C-46, as repealed by An Act to amend the Criminal Code, the Youth Criminal Justice Act and other Acts and to make consequential amendments to other Acts, SC 2019, c. 25.

Criminal Code, RSC 1985, c. C-46, as repealed by Protection of Communities and Exploited Persons Act, SC 2014, c. 25.

SECONDARY SOURCES

Allen, Mary, and Cristine Rotenberg, Canadian Centre for Justice and Community Safety Statistics. "Crimes Related to the Sex Trade: Before and After Legislative Changes in Canada." Statistics Canada. June 21, 2021. 150. statcan.gc.ca/n1/pub/85-002-x/2021001/article/00010-eng.htm.

Bedford, Terri-Jean. *Dominatrix on Trial: How a Canadian Dominatrix Fought the Law and Won*, 2nd ed. Riverdale Avenue Books, 2022.

House of Commons, Standing Committee on Justice and Human Rights. *The Challenge of Change: A Study of Canada's Criminal Prostitution Laws*. Chair: John Maloney. December 2006.

Nanda, Avnish. "Oral Arguments: Professor Alan Young on Bedford." theCourt.ca. January 29, 2014. thecourt.ca/oral-arguments-professor-alan-young-on-bedford/.

Shutt, Sandra. "Bad Law." *Canadian Lawyer*, May 5, 2014. canadianlawyermag.com/news/general/bad-law/269396.

Stewart, Hamish. "The Constitutionality of the New Sex Work Law." *Alberta Law Review* 54, no. 1 (October 31, 2016): 69–88. doi.org/10.29173/alr461.

15 The Right to Die with Dignity: Sue Rodriguez

CASE LAW

Carter v. Canada (Attorney General), 2015 SCC 5 (CanLII), [2015] 1 SCR 331.

Rodriguez v. British Columbia (Attorney General), 1993 CanLII 75 (SCC), [1993] 3 SCR 519.

Rodriguez v. British Columbia (Attorney General), 1993 CanLII 1191 (BC CA), 3 WWR 553.

LEGISLATION

Criminal Code, SC 1985, c. C-46, s. 241.

SECONDARY SOURCES

ALS Association. "ALS Symptoms and Diagnosis." Accessed March 1, 2025. als.org/understanding-als/symptoms-diagnosis.

Bartlett, Sharon, dir. *Who Owns My Life? The Sue Rodriguez Story*. Canadian Broadcasting Corporation, 1994.

Bereza, Eugene. "The Private and Public Deaths of Sue Rodriguez." *McGill Law Journal* 39, no. 2 (September 1994): 719–24.

Birnie, Lisa, and Sue Rodriguez. *Uncommon Will: The Death and Life of Sue Rodriguez*. MacMillan Canada, 2015.

Choices in Dying Victoria. "Chris Considine and the Memory of Sue Rodriguez." YouTube. March 29, 2015. youtube.com/watch?v=ApONbz0s1LU.

de Bruin, Tabitha. "Assisted Suicide in Canada." *Canadian Encyclopedia*, November 14, 2016; last edited December 3, 2021. thecanadianencyclopedia.ca/en/article/assisted-suicide-in-canada.

Somerville, Margaret A. "'Death Talk' in Canada: The *Rodriguez* Case." *McGill Law Journal* 39, no. 2 (September 1994): 602–17.

16 Trial Within a Reasonable Time: Elijah Askov

CASE LAW

R v. Askov, 1987 CanLII 6787 (ON CA).

R v. Askov, 1987 CanLII 9462 (ON SC).

R v. Askov, [1990] 2 SCR 1199, 1990 CanLII 45 (SCC).

R v. Askov, 2003 CarswellOnt 6664 (ONCJ) [WL].

R v. Jordan, 2016 SCC 27 (CanLII), [2016] 1 SCR 631.

R v. Morin, [1992] 1 SCR 771, 1992 CanLII 89 (SCC).
R v. Popovic and Askov, 1975 CanLII 30 (SCC).

COURT RECORDS

Appeal court record, *R v. Askov* (SCC File No. 20560).
Appeal court record, *R v. Popovic and Askov* (SCC File No. 13418).

SECONDARY SOURCES

Baar, Carl. "Criminal Delay and the Charter: The Use and Misuse of Social Facts in Judicial Policy Making." *Canadian Bar Review* 72, no. 3 (September 1993): 305–36.
Bindman, Stephen. "Judges Says Case Dismissals 'a Shock' to High Court." *Ottawa Citizen*, July 16, 1991, A1.
Cleland, Dave. "Pittsburgh Institution Inmates to Host Weekend Party for Children." *Kingston Whig-Standard*, February 27, 1992.
Coughlan, Steve. "Making Trial Within a Reasonable Time a Right Once More." *The Supreme Court Law Review: Osgoode's Annual Constitutional Cases Conference* 81, no. 2 (2017): 213. doi.org/10.60082/2563-8505.1354.
Crawford, Michael. "Wheels of Justice in Fast-Forward." *National Post*, November 29, 1990.
Crook, Farrell. "Man Who Won Case on Delays Is Jailed." *Toronto Star*, June 1, 1991.
Forestell, Michelle Dorey. "Summer of Fear: The 1972 Millhaven Prison Break 50 Years Later." *Kingstonist*, July 8, 2022. kingstonist.com/news/summer-of-fear-the-1972-millhaven-prison-break-50-years-later/.
Forsyth, Paul. "Elijah Askov Tangles with Law Again." *St. Catharines Standard*, September 22, 1993.
Payne, Elizabeth. "Askov Fallout: New Test Cases Won't Solve Basic Problem in Local Courts." *Ottawa Citizen*, July 27, 1991.
Powell, Betsy. "Ontario Most Affected by Askov Court Ruling." *Owen Sound Sun Times*, April 15, 1991, 5.
Toronto Star. "2 Lifers Escape Prison One Flees to Yugoslavia." December 4, 1974.
Wells, Paul. "The Askov Ruling Brought More Grief for a Dead Man's Parents." *Montreal Gazette*, April 18, 1992.

17 Equality in Substance: Mark Andrews

CASE LAW

Andrews v. Law Society of British Columbia (1985), 66 BCLR 363, 1985 CanLII 604 (BC SC).

Andrews v. Law Society of British Columbia (1986), 2 BCLR (2d) 305, 1986 CanLII 1287 (BC CA).

Andrews v. Law Society of British Columbia, 1989 CanLII 2 (SCC), [1989] 1 SCR 143.

SECONDARY SOURCES

Fasken. "In Memoriam — Mark Andrews, QC." March 21, 2020. fasken.com/en/news/2020/03/inmemoriammarkandrews.

Fine, Sean. "Lawyer Mark Andrews Won a Landmark Victory for Equality in Canada." *Globe and Mail*, April 23, 2020.

Globe and Mail. "Mark Andrews Obituary." April 4–8, 2020. legacy.com/ca/obituaries/theglobeandmail/name/mark-andrews-obituary?id=40611192.

Supreme Court of Canada. *Wastech Services Ltd. v. Greater Vancouver Sewerage and Drainage District*. Webcast of the hearing on December 6, 2019. scc-csc.ca/cases-dossiers/search-recherche/38601/#webcasts.

Women's Legal Education & Action Fund. "Case Summary: Andrews v. Law Society of British Columbia (1989)." Accessed March 1, 2025. leaf.ca/case_summary/andrews-v-law-society-of-british-columbia-1989/.

18 Making Equality Real for LGBTQ People: Delwin Vriend

CASE LAW

Vriend v. Alberta, 1994 AR 1, 1994 CanLII 8949 (AB QB).

Vriend v. Alberta, 1996 ABCA 87 (CanLII).

Vriend v. Alberta, [1998] 1 SCR 493, 1998 CanLII 816 (SCC).

LEGISLATION

Human Rights, Citizenship and Multiculturalism Amendment Act, 2009, SA 2009, c. 26.

The Individual's Rights Protection Act, 1990, SA 1990, c. 23.

The Individual's Rights Protection Act, SA 1972, c. 2.

SECONDARY SOURCES

City of Edmonton Archives. "Series 2 — Gay and Lesbian Awareness (GALA)." February 10, 2023. cityarchives.edmonton.ca/gay-and-lesbian-awareness-gala-2.

Edmonton Community Foundation and the Edmonton Queer History Project. *Vriend Versus Alberta*. edmontonqueerhistoryproject.ca/vriend-versus-alberta.

Kinsman, Gary, and Patrizia Gentile. *The Canadian War on Queers: National Security as Sexual Regulation*. UBC Press, 2010.

Simons, Paula. "Gay Rights Pioneer Delwin Vriend Did Not Set Out to Be a Hero. He Became One Anyway." *Edmonton Journal*, last updated March 22, 2018. edmontonjournal.com/news/insight/paula-simons-gay-rights-pioneer-delwin-vriend-didnt-set-out-to-be-hero-he-became-one-anyway.

19 Seeking Same-Sex Marriage: The Michaels

CASE LAW

Halpern v. Canada (AG) (2002), 60 OR (3d) 321, CanLII 42749 (ONSC).

Halpern v. Canada (AG) (2003), 65 OR (3d) 161, CanLII 26403 (ONCA).

Reference re Same-Sex Marriage, 2004 SCC 79 (CanLII), [2004] 3 SCR 698.

SECONDARY SOURCES

Abbate, Gay. "Lovers Now at Liberty to Pop Big Question." *Globe and Mail*, July 13, 2002. theglobeandmail.com/news/national/lovers-now-at-liberty-to-pop-big-question/article4137658/.

Anderssen, Erin. "Doing Canada Justice." *Globe and Mail*, December 13, 2003.

Brown, Eleanor. "The Odd Couple: The Diva & the Quiet One Find Common Ground." *Xtra*, May 20, 2001. xtramagazine.com/power/the-odd-couple-46204.

Bunch, Adam. "The Michaels' Extraordinary Love Story." Toronto Time Traveller. June 11, 2023. torontohistory.substack.com/p/the-michaels-extraordinary-love-story.

CBC News. "Gay Couple Time's Canadian Newsmaker for 2003." December 21, 2003. cbc.ca/news/canada/gay-couple-time-s-canadian-newsmaker-for-2003-1.369894.

de Montigny, Philippe. "Still Fighting." *CBC News*, June 10, 2023. cbc.ca/newsinteractives/features/same-sex-marriage-canada-lgbtq.

Gadd, Jane. "Same-Sex Marriage Challenge Begins." *Globe and Mail*, November 6, 2001.

Gordon, Raven. "June 17, 2003: Federal Government Announces Plans to Legalize Same-Sex Marriage." *CTV News*, June 17, 2016. ctvnews.ca/lifestyle/article/june-17-2003-federal-government-announces-plans-to-legalize-same-sex-marriage/.

Mastroianni, Julia. "How They Met: Canada's First Legal Same-Sex Marriage 20 Years Later." *Streets of Toronto*, June 9, 2023. streetsoftoronto.com/how-they-met-the-michaels-first-legal-same-sex-marriage-canada-anniversary/.

Robinson, B.A. "Same-Sex Marriage: Canadian Public Opinion Polls 2005-Jan-01 to the Present." Religious Tolerance.org. Last updated March 25, 2006. web.archive.org/web/20150905141207/religioustolerance.org/homssmpoll05.htm.

Stark, Michael. "Mike's Page." The Michaels. Accessed March 1, 2025. themichaels1.com/themichaels1.com/Welcome.html.

20 Unlikely Equality Militants: Joanne Fraser, Colleen Fox, and Allison Pilgrim

CASE LAW

Fraser v. Canada (Attorney General), 2017 FC 557 (CanLII).

Fraser v. Canada (Attorney General), 2018 FCA 223 (CanLII).

Fraser v. Canada (Attorney General), 2020 SCC 28, [2020] 3 SCR 113 (CanLII).

COURT RECORDS

Appeal court record, *Fraser v. Canada* (SCC File # 38505).

SECONDARY SOURCES

Civilian Review and Complaints Commission for the RCMP. *Report into Workplace Harassment in the RCMP*. April 2017. crcc-ccetp.gc.ca/pdf/harassmentFinR-eng.pdf.

Fine, Sean. "RCMP Discriminated Against Female Staff in Job-Sharing Program: Supreme Court." *Globe and Mail,* October 17, 2020. theglobeandmail.com/canada/article-rcmp-discriminated-against-female-staff-in-job-sharing-program/.

Harris, Kathleen. "Mounties Offer Apology and $100M Compensation for Harassment, Sexual Abuse Against Female Members." *CBC News,* October 6, 2016. cbc.ca/news/politics/rcmp-paulson-compensation-harassment-1.3793785.

Kirschner, Wendy. "RCMP Troop 17." *Canadian Encyclopedia,* July 7, 2023. thecanadianencyclopedia.ca/en/article/rcmp-troop-17.

Royal Canadian Mounted Police. "50th Anniversary of Women Police Officers in the RCMP: Celebrating Women in the RCMP." Last modified May 30, 2024. rcmp.ca/en/campaigns-and-promotions/50th-anniversary-women-police-officers-rcmp-celebrating-women.

Royal Canadian Mounted Police. "Four Members of Troop 17 Reflect on Earning Credibility and Sticking Together." *RCMP Gazette,* January 23, 2024. rcmp.ca/en/gazette/four-members-troop-17-reflect-earning-credibility-and-sticking-together.

21 Educating Their Children in French in Alberta: Jean-Claude Mahé, Angéline Martel, and Paul Dubé

CASE LAW

Mahé v. Alberta, [1985] 64 AR 35, 1985 CanLII 1199 (AB QB).

Mahé v. Alberta, [1987] 80 AR 161, 1987 ABCA 158 (CanLII).

Mahé v. Alberta, 1990 CanLII 133 (SCC), [1990] 1 SCR 342.

LEGISLATION

School Act, SA 1988, c. S-3.1, ss. 5–6.

SECONDARY SOURCES

Alberta Online Encyclopedia. "Francophone Education in Alberta: A Brief Outline." Accessed March 1, 2025. wayback.archive-it.org/2217/20101208165840/abheritage.ca/francoedmonton/modern/franco-education_e.html.

Alberta Online Encyclopedia. "The Laws Governing Francophone Education in Alberta." Accessed March 1, 2025. wayback.archive-it.org/2217/20101208165841/abheritage.ca/francoedmonton/modern/rights_e.html.

Bastarache, Michel, and Antoine Trépanier. *What I Wish I Had Told My Children*. Trans. Julie da Silva. University of Ottawa Press, 2023.

Centre de recherche en civilisation canadienne-française. "Droit Comme un F: l'affaire Mahé." October 5, 2017.

Dubé, Paul. "Une ré-écriture de l'histoire d'hier et d'aujourd'hui: 'L'affaire Mahé.'" *Cahiers franco-canadiens de l'Ouest* 27, no. 2 (2015): 211–40.

Dupuis, Serge. "L'Histoire de l'école de langue française en milieu minoritaire au Canada: Résistances et développement — Synthèse historique." Fédération nationale des conseils scolaires francophones. March 13, 2023. fncsf.ca/wp-content/uploads/2023/05/ELF_synthese_historique_13mars2023.pdf.

Fédération des communautés francophones et acadienne du Canada. "La FCFA lance l'appel de candidatures pour les prix Boréal 2022." April 20, 2022. fcfa.ca/la-fcfa-lance-lappel-de-candidatures-pour-les-prix-boreal-2022-2/.

Foucher, Pierre. "L'affaire Mahé: Le jugement de la décennie en droits linguistiques." *Constitutional Forum constitutionnel* 1, no. 3 (1990): 10–12. doi.org/10.21991/C9PH23.

Government of Canada. "Section 23 — Minority Language Educational Rights." Last modified August 13, 2024. justice.gc.ca/eng/csj-sjc/rfc-dlc/ccrf-ccdl/check/art23.html.

Hamilton, Ian. "Franco-Albertans Win." *Edmonton Journal*, March 16, 1990, 1.

Levasseur-Ouimet, France, and François McMahon. "French-Language Education in Alberta." Encyclopedia of French Cultural Heritage in North America. Accessed March 1, 2025. ameriquefrancaise.org/en/article-603/French-language_Education_in_Alberta.html.

Poirier, Marc. "30 ans plus tard, l'héritage incroyable de l'arrêt Mahé." Francopresse. March 14, 2020. francopresse.ca/education/2020/03/14/en-rappel-education-pour-les-francophones-en-situation-minoritaire-30-ans-plus-tard-lheritage-incroyable-de-larret-mahe/.

Provincial Archives of Alberta. *Documenter L'Alberta francophone: Recueil des ressources francophones aux Archives provinciales, 1965 à 2010*. Government of Alberta, 2012.

Riddell, Troy. "The Impact of Section 23 of the 'Charter' of Rights on Official Minority-Language Education Policy Outside Quebec Since 1982." *The Windsor Yearbook of Access to Justice* 21 (2002): 255–76.

Rocher, Anne-Marie, dir. *The Fight for Francophone Rights—Part One—Winning the Case.* National Film Board, 2015.

22 Captaining Change for Indigenous Rights: Ronald Sparrow

CASE LAW

R v. Sparrow, 1990 CanLII 104 (SCC), [1990] 1 SCR 1075.

R v. Sparrow, 9 BCLR (2d) 300, 1986 CanLII 172 (BC CA).

SECONDARY SOURCES

CBC News. "Ronald Sparrow, Defendant in Major Indigenous Rights Case, Has Died." Last updated September 16, 2020. cbc.ca/news/canada/british-columbia/bud-sparrow-obituary-1.5725029.

Harris, Douglas C. "Legal Capture." In *Fish, Law, and Colonialism: The Legal Capture of Salmon in British Columbia*, 14–78. University of Toronto Press, 2017.

Hellinga, Evaleen. "The Legacy of *R v Sparrow*." TheCourt.ca. February 6, 2020. thecourt.ca/the-legacy-of-r-v-sparrow/.

IMPAC5. "xʷməθkʷəy’əm (MUSQUEAM)." Accessed March 1, 2025. impac5.ca/partners-and-organizers/host-governments/host-first-nations/musqueam/.

Indspire. "Ronald Edward Sparrow." Accessed March 1, 2025. indspire.ca/laureate/ronald-edward-sparrow-2/.

Musqueam: A Living Culture. "Musqueam's Story." Accessed March 1, 2025. musqueam.bc.ca/our-story/.

Robinson, Matt. "Obituary: Ronald Sparrow Won a National Precedent Protecting Aboriginal Fishing Rights." *Vancouver Sun*, September 17, 2020. vancouversun.com/news/local-news/obituary-ronald-sparrow-won-a-national-precedent-protecting-aboriginal-fishing-rights.

Salomons, Tanisha, and Erin Hanson. "Sparrow Case." First Nations Study Program. Accessed March 1, 2025. indigenousfoundations.arts.ubc.ca/sparrow_case/.

Vancouver Sun. "Ronald 'Bud' Sparrow." September 17, 2020. vancouversunandprovince.remembering.ca/obituary/ronald-bud-sparrow-1080081397.

Wilson, Odette. "Statement on the Passing of Ronald 'Bud' Sparrow." Musqueam: A Living Culture. September 15, 2020. musqueam.bc.ca/statement-passing-ron-bud-sparrow/.

Xu, Xiao. "B.C. Fisherman Ronald (Bud) Sparrow Was at the Centre of a Key Ruling for Aboriginal Rights." *Globe and Mail*, September 22, 2020. theglobeandmail.com/canada/article-bc-fisherman-ronald-bud-sparrow-was-at-the-centre-of-a-key-ruling/?login=true.

23 More Than Just Selling Salmon: Dorothy Van der Peet

CASE LAW

R v. Gladstone, 1996 CanLII 160 (SCC), [1996] 2 SCR 723.

R v. NTC Smokehouse, 1996 CanLII 159 (SCC), [1996] 2 SCR 672.

R v. Van der Peet (1991), 59 BCLR (2d) 392, 1991 CanLII 1936 (BC SC).

R v. Van der Peet (1993) 80 BCLR (2d) 75, 1993 CanLII 4519 (BC CA).

R v. Van der Peet, 1996 CanLII 216 (SCC), [1996] 2 SCR 507.

COURT RECORDS

R v. Van der Peet, Supreme Court File No. 23803.

LEGISLATION

British Columbia Fishery (General) Regulations, SOR/84-248, s. 27(5), as read on September 11, 1984.

Fisheries Act, RSC 1970, c. F-14, s. 61(1), as read on September 11, 1984.

Fisheries Act, RSC 1985, c. F-14, s. 33.

Fishery (General) Regulations, SOR/93-53, s. 35.

SECONDARY SOURCES

Carlson, Keith Thor. "Stó:lō Exchange Dynamics." *Native Studies Review* 11, no. 1 (1996): 5–48.

Chilliwack Progress. "A 'Right' to Sell Fish." August 16, 1991.

Chilliwack Progress. "CSSS Grads." June 25, 1980.

Chilliwack Progress. "Defence Lawyers Eye Constitution." September 28, 1988.

Chilliwack Progress. "Fishing Laws Challenged." May 10, 1989.

Chilliwack Progress. "Johanna Van der Peet." February 9, 2019. theprogress.com/obituaries/johanna-van-der-peet-1889047.

Chilliwack Progress. "Native Fishing Rights on Trial." June 21, 1989.

Chilliwack Progress. "Nicolaas (Nick) Van der Peet." October 20, 1993.

Chilliwack Progress. "Tons of Seizures." November 2, 1988.

Chilliwack Progress. "Weaving a World Reputation." March 26, 1975.

Mission Museum. "The Stó:lō 'People of the River.'" Accessed March 1, 2025. missionmuseum.com/local-history/stolo/.

Rotman, Leonard I. "Hunting for Answers in a Strange Kettle of Fish: Unilateralism, Paternalism and Fiduciary Rhetoric in *Badger* and *Van der Peet*." *Constitutional Forum constitutionnel* 8, no. 2 (1997): 40–45. doi.org/10.21991/C98Q12.

Stó:lō Service Agency. "'Sxwōxwiyám and Sqwélqwel': Our Stories of Tomorrow and Today." Accessed March 1, 2025. stolonation.bc.ca/about#history.

Tokawa, Kenji. "Van der Peet Turns 20: Revisiting the Rights Equation and Building a New Test for Aboriginal Rights." *UBC Law Review* 49, no. 2 (2016): 817–33.

24 From Wrongful Conviction to Vindicator of Treaty Rights: Donald Marshall Jr.

CASE LAW

R v. Marshall, [1972] 4 NSR (2d) 517.

R v. Marshall, [1983] 57 NSR (2d) 86, 1983 CanLII 5140 (NS CA).

R v. Marshall, [1996] NSJ No 246.

R v. Marshall, 1997 NSCA 89 (CanLII).

R v. Marshall, 1999 CanLII 665 (SCC), [1999] 3 SCR 456, ("*Marshall I*").

R v. Marshall, 1999 CanLII 666 (SCC), [1999] 3 SCR 533 ("*Marshall II*").

SECONDARY SOURCES

Butts, Edward. "Donald Marshall Jr." *Canadian Encyclopedia*, August 6, 2009; last edited June 4, 2024. thecanadianencyclopedia.ca/en/article/donald-marshall-jr.

Coates, Ken. "Canada's Courts and Governments Have Themselves to Blame for the Lobster-Fishery Dispute." *Globe and Mail*, last updated October 16, 2020. theglobeandmail.com/opinion/article-canadas-courts-and-governments-have-themselves-to-blame-for-the/.

Coates, Ken. "The Marshall Decision and the Impact of Two Decades of Commercial Re-Empowerment: New MLI Report." Macdonald-Laurier Institute. October 24, 2019. macdonaldlaurier.ca/marshall-decision-impact-two-decades-commercial-re-empowerment-new-mli-report/.

Coates, Ken. "Nova Scotia Fisheries Conflict Decades in the Making: Ken Coates in the Epoch Times." Macdonald-Laurier Institute. October 26, 2020. macdonaldlaurier.ca/nova-scotia-fisheries-conflict-decades-making-ken-coates-epoch-times/.

Conn, Heather. "Marshall Inquiry." *Canadian Encyclopedia*, April 11, 2020; last edited September 2, 2020. thecanadianencyclopedia.ca/en/article/marshall-inquiry.

Crown-Indigenous Relations and Northern Affairs Canada. "Treaty Texts: 1760–61 Treaty of Peace and Friendship." Government of Canada. Last modified March 7, 2016. rcaanc-cirnac.gc.ca/eng/1100100029046/1581293947580.

Evans, Gregory T., commissioner. *Commission of Inquiry Concerning the Adequacy of Compensation Paid to Donald Marshall Jr. (N.S.): Report of the Commissioner*. Province of Nova Scotia, June 1990.

Johnson, Nicole. "Impact of the Marshall Decision on the Development of a Mi'kmaw Commercial Fishery." Purdy Crawford Chair in Aboriginal Business Studies, Cape Breton University, August 2009.

McMillan, L. Jane. *Truth and Conviction: Donald Marshall Jr. and the Mi'kmaw Quest for Justice*. UBC Press, 2018.

Nova Scotia Department of Education. *Mi'kmaq Past and Present: A Resource Guide*. Mi'kmaq Studies 10 Curriculum. Accessed March 1, 2025. web.archive.org/web/20160304063651/hrsbstaff.ednet.ns.ca/ltemplin/mikmaq10/governance/grandchiefs.pdf.

Province of Nova Scotia. *Royal Commission on the Donald Marshall, Jr., Prosecution: Digest of Findings and Recommendations*. Royal Commission on the Donald Marshall, Jr., Prosecution, December 1989.

25 Establishing Aboriginal Title: Chief Roger William and the Tŝilhqot'in Nation

CASE LAW

Tsilhqot'in Nation v. British Columbia, 2007 BCSC 1700 (CanLII).
Tsilhqot'in Nation v. British Columbia, 2014 SCC 44 (CanLII), [2014] 2 SCR 257.
William v. British Columbia, 2012 BCCA 285 (CanLII).

SECONDARY SOURCES

Bennett, Nelson. "Profile of Roger William, Chief, Xeni Gwet'in First Nation." Wilderness Committee. May 19, 2015. tinyurl.com/ywj3bde6.

Bradley, Andrea, and Senwung Luk. "In a First for a Canadian Court, SCC Recognizes Aboriginal Title for Tsilhqot'in Nation." Olthuis Kleer Townshend LLP. June 26, 2014. oktlaw.com/first-canadian-court-scc-recognizes-aboriginal-title-tsilhqotin-nation/.

Brean, Joseph. "'Conscious Objectivity': That's How the Chief Justice Defines the Top Court's Role. Harper Might Beg to Differ." *National Post*, May 23, 2015. nationalpost.com/news/conscious-objectivity-thats-how-the-chief-justice-defines-the-top-courts-role-harper-might-beg-to-differ/.

Cundari, Laura. "The Tsilhqot'in Decision." *Bar Talk*, April 1, 2016. bartalk.org/article/features/2016-04/the-tsilhqot-in-decision.

Derosa, Katie. "B.C. Clears 6 Chiefs Who Were Hanged in 1864." *Times Colonist*, October 23, 2014. timescolonist.com/local-news/bc-clears-six-chiefs-who-were-hanged-in-1864-4615078.

Flegg, Erin. "Tsilhqot'in First Nation Wins First Canadian Land Claim in History." *Narwhal*, June 30, 2014. thenarwhal.ca/tsilhqot-first-nation-wins-first-canadian-land-claim-history/.

Friends of the Nemiah Valley. "The Tsilhqot'in and Xeni Gwet'in Court Case for Rights and Title." Accessed March 1, 2025. fonv.ca/nemaiahvalley/thecourtcase/.

Irwin, Robert. "Aboriginal Title." *Canadian Encyclopedia*, September 25, 2018. thecanadianencyclopedia.ca/en/article/aboriginal-title.

Kung, Eugene, and Gavin Smith. "Canada's 'Prove It' Approach to Aboriginal Title." *Policy Options*, February 1, 2019. policyoptions.irpp.org/magazines/february-2019/canadas-prove-it-approach-to-aboriginal-title/.

Lane, Robert B. "Tsilhqot'in (Chilcotin)." *Canadian Encyclopedia*, November 30, 2010; last edited August 20, 2024, by Zach Parrott. thecanadianencyclopedia.ca/en/article/chilcotin-tsilhqotin.

Siegel, Leah. "The Tsilhqot'in War: A Nation Defends Its Land from an Encroaching Colony." Knowledge Network: British Columbia An Untold History. Accessed March 1, 2025. bcanuntoldhistory.knowledge.ca/1860/the-tsilhqotin-war.

Talonbooks. "Profile: Chief Roger William." Accessed March 1, 2025. talonbooks.com/authors/chief-roger-william/.

Tatla Communities. "Tsilhqot'in First Nations." Accessed March 1, 2025. tatlacommunities.ca/tsilhqotin.

Tŝilhqot'in National Government. Accessed March 1, 2025. tsilhqotin.ca/about/.

Walker, Connie. "First Nations 'Ecstatic' over Historic Supreme Court Ruling." *CBC News*, last updated June 27, 2014. cbc.ca/news/indigenous/first-nations-ecstatic-over-historic-supreme-court-ruling-1.2688509.

Weir, Lorraine, with Chief Roger William. *Lha yudit'ih We Always Find a Way: Bringing the Tsilhqot'in Title Case Home*. Vancouver: Talonbooks, 2023.

Xeni Gwet'in First Nations Government. "Who We Are." Accessed March 1, 2025. xeni-gwetin.ca/.

26 Constitutionalizing Métis Rights: Harry Daniels

CASE LAW

Daniels v. Canada, 2011 FC 230 (CanLII).

Daniels v. Canada (Indian Affairs and Northern Development), 2014 FCA 101 (CanLII), [2014] 4 FCR 97.

Daniels v. Canada (Indian Affairs and Northern Development), 2016 SCC 12 (CanLII), [2016] 1 SCR 99.

Daniels v. Canada (Minister of Indian Affairs and Northern Development) (T.D.), 2002 FCT 295 (CanLII), [2002] 4 FC 550.

SECONDARY SOURCES

Anderson, Chris. *"Métis": Race, Recognition, and the Struggle for Indigenous Peoplehood*. UBC Press, 2015.

Barkwell, Lawrence. "Harry Daniels." Louis Riel Institute. Prepared for Congress of Aboriginal Peoples. August 15, 2012. metismuseum.ca/media/document .php/11902.Harry%20Daniels%20final.pdf.

Canadian Press. "Federal Court Grants Rights to Métis, Non-Status Indians." *CBC News*, last updated January 9, 2013. cbc.ca/news/politics/federal -court-grants-rights-to-m%C3%A9tis-non-status-indians-1.1319951.

Chaubun, William. "A Métis Idealist Wins the Day — Posthumously." *Regina Leader-Post*, April 15, 2016.

Cheadle, Bruce. "Non-Status Indians, Métis Receive Rights." *Ottawa Citizen*, April 15, 2016, 45.

Cram, Stephanie. "Harry Daniels." *Canadian Encyclopedia*, January 19, 2018; last updated July 6, 2022. thecanadianencyclopedia.ca/en/article/harry-daniels.

Daum Shanks, Signa A. "The Wastelander Life: Living Before and After the Release of *Daniels v. Canada*." *Osgoode Hall Law Journal* 54, no. 4 (2017): 1341–58. doi.org/10.60082/2817-5069.3192.

Dodek, Adam M. *The Charter Debates: The Special Joint Committee on the Constitution, 1980–81, and the Making of the Canadian Charter of Rights and Freedoms*. University of Toronto Press, 2018.

Gaudry, Adam. "Métis." *Canadian Encyclopedia*, January 7, 2009; last edited November 28, 2023, by Mary Agnes Welch and David Gallant. thecanadianencyclopedia.ca/en/article/metis.

Indigenous Corporate Training Inc. "Harry Daniels: The Man Who Put Métis in the Constitution." September 23, 2016. ictinc.ca/blog/harry -daniels-the-man-who-put-metis-in-the-constitution.

MacCharles, Tonda. "Pride and Practicality Behind Gabriel Daniels' Challenge for Legal Recognition." *Toronto Star*, April 13, 2016. thestar.com/news /canada/2016/04/13/pride-and-practicality-behind-gabriel-daniels-challenge -for-legal-recognition.html.

McIvor, Bruce. "What Does the Daniels Decision Mean?" CanLII Connects. August 30, 2016. canliiconnects.org/en/commentaries/43032.

Métis Nation of Alberta. "History." Accessed March 1, 2025. tinyurl.com /3ebthc6u.

Petten, Cheryl. "Friends Say Goodbye to Harry Daniels." *Alberta Sweetgrass* 11, no. 10 (2004): 2.

Regina Leader-Post. "Memorial for Métis Leader." September 9, 2004, 18.

Samborski, Irina. "Daniels v Canada: Out of the Wasteland, Into the Fray." CanLII Connects. October 4, 2016. canliiconnects.org/en/commentaries/43261.

Saskatoon StarPhoenix. "Harry 'the Dog' Fought for Métis Rights." September 10, 2004, 11.

Saskatoon StarPhoenix. "Métis Threaten to Reject Constitutional Package" April 21, 1981, 30.

Image Credits

8 © Canada Post Corporation, 1985. Reproduced with permission.
12 Moose Jaw Public Library Archives Department.
22 Geraldine Carpenter Palmer. McGill University Archives/PR026131.
28 Deni Eagland/*Vancouver Sun*. City of Vancouver Archives/AM1616-S1-F085083. Material republished with the express permission of the Vancouver Sun, a division of Postmedia Network Inc.
48 CP Photo/Fred Chartrand.
58 The Canadian Press.
66 CP Photo/Chuck Stoody.
75 John Lehmann/*The Globe and Mail*.
84 Blair Gable. Reproduced by permission.
91 The Canadian Press/Andrew Vaughan.
98 The Canadian Press Historical Archive/Canadian Press.
115 The Canadian Press/Adrian Wyld.
123 The Canadian Press/Ward Perrin.
141 Used with permission of the family.
147 The Canadian Press/Kevin Frayer.
154 CP Photo/Frank Gunn.

160 David Kawai/*Ottawa Citizen*. Material republished with the express permission of Ottawa Citizen, a division of Postmedia Network Inc.

179 Nick Procaylo/*Vancouver Sun*. Material republished with the express permission of the Vancouver Sun, a division of Postmedia Network Inc.

195 The Canadian Press/Doug Ives.

206 John Lehmann/*The Globe and Mail*.

218 © Canada Post Corporation, 2022. Reproduced with permission.

Index

Note: Any case beginning with "R v." or "Rex v." has been indexed based on the second half, usually the name of the challenger or group involved in the case (Oakes, Tŝilhqot'in Nation). Within the subentries, cases are referred to by their recognizable part (Morgentaler, Daigle).